The Noble Character

Franciso Bojorquez

PRESENTED TO

Steven A. Dence (Daddy)

BY

1 - 01 - 2016

DATE

Published by
Remnant Publications
649 East Chicago Road
Coldwater MI 49036
800-423-1319
www.remnantpublications.com

Unless otherwise noted, Scripture quotations are taken
from The Holy Bible, King James Version.

Contributing Writers: Dwight Hall, Rudy Hall, and Jeff Wehr
Editors: Karine Sanchez, Alena Wehr, and Dana Williams
Cover Designer: David Berthiaume
Text Designer: Greg Solie • Altamont Graphics

ISBN: 978-1-629130-09-5

THE NOBLE CHARACTER

Remnant
Publications

$\mathscr{I}$NTRODUCTION

Be filled with the knowledge of His will in all wisdom and spiritual understanding;
that you may walk worthy of the Lord, fully pleasing Him, being fruitful
in every good work and increasing in the knowledge of God.
Colossians 1:9, 10

Author John Gardiner writes, "Most of us plateau when we lose the tension between where we are and where we ought to be." Any athlete training to compete in the Olympics understands this proverb well—to win the gold and the glory means to train to be the best.

Yet while this is an insight that could be applied to just about every area of our lives, from our work ethic to our family relationships, it seems especially meaningful and revealing when it comes to our spiritual growth.

The apostle Paul suggests that for people who have accepted Christ, their baptism marks the beginning of their journey, not the end. He writes, "He who has begun a good work in you will complete it until the day of Jesus Christ" (Philippians 1:6).

Sometimes we see the blessings in our lives and the positive changes in our characters after we come to Christ and, perhaps feeling secure in our own abilities, mistakenly take our eyes off Jesus. It is in that moment that we lose that vital tension between where we really are and where God ultimately wants us to be.

And for many of us, we don't just plateau, we actually backslide.

While many see King Saul as a bad guy and King David as a good guy, both essentially travelled the same path as kings. Both were anointed by God, both were tremendously blessed in their administrations ... and both eventually took their eyes off God. The difference between the two, of course, was manifested when God reintroduced, through His prophet, that spiritual tension into their lives. For King Saul, his response was to seek the counsel of a witch and to defy God at the altar. For King David, his response was to fall down in utter shame and repentance, because, unlike Saul, he understood that this spiritual tension, even when it hurts, is an incredible blessing that will keep us focused on the Lord's will.

For the Christian author Ellen White, this tension between who we are and what God wants us to become was the great focus of life. She writes, "The world does not so much need men of great intellect as of noble character. It needs men in whom ability is controlled by steadfast principle." More than being supremely intelligent or capable, the development of a Christ-like character is the most important thing in the world.

And the only way to ensure its completion in our lives is to focus on Jesus. "As we meditate upon the perfections of the divine Model, we shall desire to become wholly transformed, and renewed in the image of His purity. It is by faith in the Son of God that ... the child of wrath becomes the child of God."

She understood that God's goal for us isn't just redemption, but total moral goodness in our hearts and in our actions—just like the noble character we find in Jesus.

That's why this day-by-day devotional is dedicated to helping you keep your eyes focused on Jesus, the Word of God, each and every day; to keep that tension alive of where you are now in your Christian walk and where God is still leading you—toward Jesus' noble character revealed in you.

And it's a wonderful, worthy, and exciting Olympic-sized race to run, isn't it? Instead of a gold medal waiting for us at the finish line, we'll be celebrating with crowns of gold decorated by the souls who saw Christ in us and decided to run the race themselves. So "let us run with endurance the race that is set before us, looking unto Jesus, the author and finisher of our faith" (Hebrews 12:1, 2).

—Your friends at Remnant Publications

JANUARY

CREATED TO REFLECT GOD'S CHARACTER

*And God said, Let us make man in our image, after our likeness.
... So God created man in his own image, in the image of
God created he him; male and female created he them.*
Genesis 1:26, 27

When Adam came from the Creator's hand, he bore, in his physical, mental, and spiritual nature, a likeness to his Maker. "God created man in His own image" (Genesis 1:27), and it was His purpose that the longer man lived the more fully he should reveal this image — the more fully reflect the glory of the Creator.... Face-to-face, heart-to-heart communion with his Maker was his high privilege. Had he remained loyal to God, all this would have been his forever. Throughout eternal ages he would have continued to gain new treasures of knowledge, to discover fresh springs of happiness, and to obtain clearer and yet clearer conceptions of the wisdom, the power, and the love of God. More and more fully would he have fulfilled the object of his creation, more and more fully have reflected the Creator's glory. (*Education*, 15)

REFLECTION: *My highest privilege is communion with my Maker. By communing with Him I will become like Him. Therefore, let us find a time and place to commune with God each day. Let our hearts reach out to God with deep affection. May we learn to enjoy the company of God above the fellowship of men.*

JANUARY 2

THE FIRST SABBATH REST

*Thus the heavens and the earth were finished, and all the host of them.
And on the seventh day God ended his work which he had made; and
he rested on the seventh day from all his work which he had made.
And God blessed the seventh day, and sanctified it: because that in
it he had rested from all his work which God created and made.*
Genesis 2:1–3

In Eden, God set up the memorial of His work of creation,
in placing His blessing upon the seventh day. The Sabbath
was committed to Adam, the father and representative
of the whole human family. Its observance was to be an act of
grateful acknowledgment, on the part of all who should dwell
upon the earth, that God was their Creator and their rightful
Sovereign; that they were the work of His hands and the subjects
of His authority. Thus the institution was wholly commemorative, and given to all mankind. There was nothing in it shadowy
or of restricted application to any people.

God saw that a Sabbath was essential for man, even in
Paradise. He needed to lay aside his own interests and pursuits
for one day of the seven, that he might more fully contemplate
the works of God and meditate upon His power and goodness.
He needed a Sabbath to remind him more vividly of God and
to awaken gratitude, because all he enjoyed and possessed
came from the beneficent hand of the Creator. (*Patriarchs and
Prophets*, 48)

REFLECTION: *This act of love was one of the most important things God
did for us. The Day of Rest allows us to reflect on what we have done
or left undone to build our characters in His likeness. Every Sabbath
we may rest in Him who has given us life and surrounded us with the
beauties of nature. Let us worship Him with grateful hearts.*

JANUARY 3

The First Marriage

*And Adam said, This is now bone of my bones, and flesh of my
flesh: she shall be called Woman, because she was taken out of
Man. Therefore shall a man leave his father and his mother, and
shall cleave unto his wife: and they shall be one flesh.*
Genesis 2:23, 24

God Himself gave Adam a companion. He provided "an help meet for him"—a helper corresponding to him— one who was fitted to be his companion, and who could be one with him in love and sympathy. Eve was created from a rib taken from the side of Adam, signifying that she was not to control him as the head, nor to be trampled under his feet as an inferior, but to stand by his side as an equal, to be loved and protected by him. A part of man, bone of his bone, and flesh of his flesh, she was his second self, showing the close union and the affectionate attachment that should exist in this relation. "For no man ever yet hated his own flesh; but nourisheth and cherisheth it" (Ephesians 5:29). "Therefore shall a man leave his father and his mother, and shall cleave unto his wife; and they shall be one." (*Patriarchs and Prophets*, 46)

REFLECTION: *God Himself performed the first marriage. Adam and Eve, no different than you and me, were created and united to compliment and help one another with their characters. Few things benefit character development like man and woman allied. What a wonderful thing God has done in giving us marriage and family as the backbone of society!*

JANUARY 4

THE TEST OF LOYALTY

And the LORD God commanded the man, saying, Of every tree of the garden thou mayest freely eat: But of the tree of the knowledge of good and evil, thou shalt not eat of it: for in the day that thou eatest thereof thou shalt surely die.
Genesis 2:16, 17

Like the angels, the dwellers in Eden had been placed upon probation; their happy estate could be retained only on condition of fidelity to the Creator's law. They could obey and live, or disobey and perish. God had made them the recipients of rich blessings; but should they disregard His will, He who spared not the angels that sinned, could not spare them; transgression would forfeit His gifts and bring upon them misery and ruin. ...

The tree of knowledge had been made a test of their obedience and their love to God. The Lord had seen fit to lay upon them but one prohibition as to the use of all that was in the garden; but if they should disregard His will in this particular, they would incur the guilt of transgression. Satan was not to follow them with continual temptations; he could have access to them only at the forbidden tree. Should they attempt to investigate its nature, they would be exposed to his wiles. They were admonished to give careful heed to the warning which God had sent them and to be content with the instruction which He had seen fit to impart. (*Patriarchs and Prophets*, 53)

REFLECTION: *God, in His infinite love gave the smallest test of love and loyalty He could. God never planned for Adam and Eve to fail, but deeply wanted them to overcome. He has not changed. God wants you and me to triumph just as much as He did Adam and Eve. As we learn to love Him more we will be successful.*

JANUARY 5

The Enemy of God and Man

Now the serpent was more subtil than any beast of the field which the LORD God had made. And he said unto the woman, Yea, hath God said, Ye shall not eat of every tree of the garden?
Genesis 3:1

No longer free to stir up rebellion in heaven, Satan's enmity against God found a new field in plotting the ruin of the human race. In the happiness and peace of the holy pair in Eden he beheld a vision of the bliss that to him was forever lost. Moved by envy, he determined to incite them to disobedience, and bring upon them the guilt and penalty of sin. He would change their love to distrust and their songs of praise to reproaches against their Maker. Thus he would not only plunge these innocent beings into the same misery which he was himself enduring, but would cast dishonor upon God, and cause grief in heaven.

Our first parents were not left without a warning of the danger that threatened them. Heavenly messengers opened to them the history of Satan's fall and his plots for their destruction, unfolding more fully the nature of the divine government, which the prince of evil was trying to overthrow. It was by disobedience to the just commands of God that Satan and his host had fallen. How important, then, that Adam and Eve should honor that law by which alone it was possible for order and equity to be maintained. (*Patriarchs and Prophets*, 52)

REFLECTION: *God created us for fellowship, but Satan wants to divide us. God wants us to enjoy the fruits of obedience, while Satan wants us to experience the misery of his own rebellion.*

JANUARY 6

The First Shot

And the serpent said unto the woman, Ye shall not surely die.
Genesis 3:4

*H*ad Satan revealed himself in his real character, he would have been repulsed at once, for Adam and Eve had been warned against this dangerous foe; but he worked in the dark, concealing his purpose, that he might more effectually accomplish his object. Employing as his medium the serpent, then a creature of fascinating appearance, he addressed himself to Eve: "Hath God said, Ye shall not eat of every tree of the garden?" (Genesis 3:1)....

The woman said unto the serpent, "We may eat of the fruit of the trees of the garden: but of the fruit of the tree which is in the midst of the garden, God hath said, Ye shall not eat of it, neither shall ye touch it, lest ye die." And the serpent said unto the woman, "ye shall not surely die: for God doth know that in the day ye eat thereof, then your eyes shall be opened, and ye shall be as gods, knowing good and evil" (Verses 2–5). He declared that they would become like God, possessing greater wisdom than before and being capable of a higher state of existence. Eve yielded to temptation; and through her influence, Adam was led into sin. (*The Great Controversy*, 531, 532)

REFLECTION: *In every war, there is always a first shot. Satan took that first shot with the lie that man cannot die. From that first lie, millions have been deceived through the works of spiritualism. Let us never forget that deceit is one of the devil's greatest tools.*

JANUARY 7

Shifting Blame

*And the man said, The woman whom thou gavest to be
with me, she gave me of the tree, and I did eat.*
Genesis 3:12

"The Lord God called unto Adam, and said unto him, Where art thou? And he said, I heard Thy voice in the garden, and I was afraid, because I was naked; and I hid myself. And He said, Who told thee that thou wast naked? Hast thou eaten of the tree, whereof I commanded thee that thou shouldest not eat?"

Adam could neither deny nor excuse his sin; but instead of manifesting penitence, he endeavored to cast the blame upon his wife, and thus upon God Himself: "The woman whom Thou gavest to be with me, she gave me of the tree, and I did eat." He who, from love to Eve, had deliberately chosen to forfeit the approval of God, his home in Paradise, and an eternal life of joy, could now, after his fall, endeavor to make his companion, and even the Creator Himself, responsible for the transgression. So terrible is the power of sin.

When the woman was asked, "What is this that thou hast done?" she answered, "The serpent beguiled me, and I did eat." "Why didst Thou create the serpent? Why didst Thou suffer him to enter Eden?"—these were the questions implied in her excuse for her sin. Thus, like Adam, she charged God with the responsibility of their fall. (*Patriarchs and Prophets*, 57, 58)

REFLECTION: *Another true test of character is our willingness to admit our mistakes. It is so much easier to blame someone else for our deep-rooted problems. Self-justification makes a man unfit for the presence of a holy God and unfallen angels.*

THE HOPE OF REDEMPTION

And I will put enmity between thee and the woman, and between thy seed and her seed; it shall bruise thy head, and thou shalt bruise his heel.

Genesis 3:15

ut man was not abandoned to the results of the evil he had chosen. In the sentence pronounced upon Satan was given an intimation of redemption. "I will put enmity between thee and the woman," God said, "and between thy seed and her seed; it shall bruise thy head, and thou shalt bruise his heel" (Genesis 3:15). This sentence, spoken in the hearing of our first parents, was to them a promise. Before they heard of the thorn and the thistle, of the toil and sorrow that must be their portion, or of the dust to which they must return, they listened to words that could not fail of giving them hope. All that had been lost by yielding to Satan could be regained through Christ.

This intimation also nature repeats to us. Though marred by sin, it speaks not only of creation but of redemption. Though the earth bears testimony to the curse in the evident signs of decay, it is still rich and beautiful in the tokens of life-giving power. The trees cast off their leaves, only to be robed with fresher verdure; the flowers die, to spring forth in new beauty; and in every manifestation of creative power is held out the assurance that we may be created anew in "righteousness and holiness of truth." (*Education*, 27)

REFLECTION: *It doesn't matter what we have done or not done, God still loves us and has the power to redeem us. Like Adam and Eve, He has the backup plan for our cure. All we have to do is make the decision to repent and forsake those things which keep us from the Life-Giver.*

January 9

CAIN AND ABEL

And Abel, he also brought of the firstlings of his flock and of the fat thereof. And the LORD had respect unto Abel and to his offering: But unto Cain and to his offering he had not respect. And Cain was very wroth, and his countenance fell.
Genesis 4:4, 5

The two brothers erected their altars alike, and each brought an offering. Abel presented a sacrifice from the flock, in accordance with the Lord's directions. "And the Lord had respect unto Abel and to his offering." Fire flashed from heaven and consumed the sacrifice. But Cain, disregarding the Lord's direct and explicit command, presented only an offering of fruit. There was no token from heaven to show that it was accepted. ...

Abel grasped the great principles of redemption. He saw himself a sinner, and he saw sin and its penalty, death, standing between his soul and communion with God. He brought the slain victim, the sacrificed life, thus acknowledging the claims of the law that had been transgressed. ...

Cain and Abel represent two classes that will exist in the world till the close of time. One class avail themselves of the appointed sacrifice for sin; the other venture to depend upon their own merits. ... Those who feel no need of the blood of Christ, who feel that without divine grace they can by their own works secure the approval of God, are making the same mistake as did Cain. (*Patriarchs and Prophets,* 71, 72)

REFLECTION: *It doesn't matter what we think of our way of doing things, in the end it's all about trust in God, the Author and Finisher of our faith. If I see myself as reasonably good, I will never exercise great faith in God's power to save.*

JANUARY 10

Enoch Walks With God

And Enoch walked with God: and he was not; for God took him.
Genesis 5:24

Enoch's walk with God was not in a trance or vision, but in all the duties of his daily life. He did not become a hermit, shutting himself entirely from the world; for he had a work to do for God in the world. In the family and in his intercourse with men, as a husband and father, a friend, a citizen, he was the steadfast, unwavering servant of the Lord. ...

Enoch was a man of strong and highly cultivated mind and extensive knowledge; he was honored with special revelations from God; yet being in constant communion with Heaven, with a sense of the divine greatness and perfection ever before him, he was one of the humblest of men. The closer the connection with God, the deeper was the sense of his own weakness and imperfection.

Distressed by the increasing wickedness of the ungodly, and fearing that their infidelity might lessen his reverence for God, Enoch avoided constant association with them, and spent much time in solitude, giving himself to meditation and prayer. Thus he waited before the Lord, seeking a clearer knowledge of His will, that he might perform it. To him prayer was as the breath of the soul; he lived in the very atmosphere of heaven. (*Patriarchs and Prophets*, 85)

REFLECTION: *We have the same opportunity as Enoch — to walk with God. Many times we think it is something great that wins favor with God, but it's simply being faithful in the little things. Let's do first things first. Our first duty is in every day affairs — how we talk, act, and follow through. This, above anything else, will form our characters for heaven.*

JANUARY 11

The Wicked World

And God saw that the wickedness of man was great in the earth, and that every imagination of the thoughts of his heart was only evil continually.
Genesis 6:5

How was it in Noah's day? "God saw that the wickedness of man was great in the earth, and that every imagination of the thoughts of his heart was only evil continually" (Genesis 6:5). The inhabitants of the antediluvian world turned from Jehovah, refusing to do His holy will. They followed their own unholy imagination and perverted ideas. It was because of their wickedness that they were destroyed; and today the world is following the same way. It presents no flattering signs of millennial glory. The transgressors of God's law are filling the earth with wickedness. Their betting, their horse racing, their gambling, their dissipation, their lustful practices, their untamable passions, are fast filling the world with violence. (*The Desire of Ages*, 633)

But Noah stood like a rock amid the tempest. Surrounded by popular contempt and ridicule, he distinguished himself by his holy integrity and unwavering faithfulness. A power attended his words, for it was the voice of God to man through His servant. Connection with God made him strong in the strength of infinite power, while for one hundred and twenty years his solemn voice fell upon the ears of that generation in regard to events, which, so far as human wisdom could judge, were impossible. (*Patriarchs and Prophets*, 96)

REFLECTION: *A man can, by God's grace, stand firm in truth amid popular contempt and ridicule. This is only accomplished by having a constant connection with God.*

BUILDING THE ARK

*Make thee an ark of gopher wood; rooms shalt thou make in the
ark, and shalt pitch it within and without with pitch.*
Genesis 6:14

God gave Noah the exact dimensions of the ark and explicit directions in regard to its construction in every particular. Human wisdom could not have devised a structure of so great strength and durability. God was the designer, and Noah the master builder. ... It was three stories high, with but one door, which was in the side. The light was admitted at the top, and the different apartments were so arranged that all were lighted.

"By faith Noah, being warned of God of things not seen as yet, moved with fear, prepared an ark to the saving of his house; by the which he condemned the world, and became heir of the righteousness which is by faith" (Hebrews 11:7). While Noah was giving his warning message to the world, his works testified of his sincerity. It was thus that his faith was perfected and made evident. He gave the world an example of believing just what God says. All that he possessed, he invested in the ark. As he began to construct that immense boat on dry ground, multitudes came from every direction to see the strange sight and to hear the earnest, fervent words of the singular preacher. Every blow struck upon the ark was a witness to the people. (*Patriarchs and Prophets*, 92)

REFLECTION: *As we decide to follow God more closely, it will not always
be popular. Let us remember that in the end it is God we should please
and not men or women. Men and women are best known by what they
do, not by what they say. Noah demonstrated his faith in God with
every swing of the hammer.*

JANUARY 13

Scoffing at the Warning

And God looked upon the earth, and, behold, it was corrupt;
for all flesh had corrupted his way upon the earth.
Genesis 6:12

Many at first appeared to receive the warning; yet they did not turn to God with true repentance. They were unwilling to renounce their sins…Overcome by the prevailing unbelief, they finally joined their former associates in rejecting the solemn message. Some were deeply convicted, and would have heeded the words of warning; but there were so many to jest and ridicule, that they partook of the same spirit, resisted the invitations of mercy, and were soon among the boldest and most defiant scoffers; for none are so reckless and go to such lengths in sin as do those who have once had light, but have resisted the convicting Spirit of God.

The men of that generation were not all, in the fullest acceptation of the term, idolaters. Many professed to be worshipers of God. They claimed that their idols were representations of the Deity, and that through them the people could obtain a clearer conception of the divine Being. This class were foremost in rejecting the preaching of Noah. …

The world before the Flood reasoned that for centuries the laws of nature had been fixed. The recurring seasons had come in their order. Heretofore rain had never fallen; the earth had been watered by a mist or dew. The rivers had never yet passed their boundaries, but had borne their waters safely to the sea. (*Patriarchs and Prophets*, 95–97)

REFLECTION: *Just because we go to church or believe in God does not mean we are holy. Holiness doesn't come from professing but from trusting and being faithful to God's Word. Let us find and accept the Word — the Bible — today, no matter what man or any church professes.*

January 14

Entering the Ark

And Noah went in, and his sons, and his wife, and his sons' wives with him, into the ark, because of the waters of the flood. Of clean beasts, and of beasts that are not clean, and of fowls, and of every thing that creepeth upon the earth, There went in two and two unto Noah into the ark, the male and the female, as God had commanded Noah.

Genesis 7:7–9

And now the servant of God made his last solemn appeal to the people. With an agony of desire that words cannot express, he entreated them to seek a refuge while it might be found. Again they rejected his words, and raised their voices in jest and scoffing. Suddenly a silence fell upon the mocking throng. Beasts of every description, the fiercest as well as the most gentle, were seen coming from mountain and forest and quietly making their way toward the ark. A noise as of a rushing wind was heard, and lo, birds were flocking from all directions, their numbers darkening the heavens, and in perfect order they passed to the ark. Animals obeyed the command of God, while men were disobedient. Guided by holy angels, they "went in two and two unto Noah into the ark," and the clean beasts by sevens.... But men had become so hardened by their persistent rejection of light that even this scene produced but a momentary impression. (*Patriarchs and Prophets*, 97)

REFLECTION: *Often, when the life-changing message comes to us in such a powerful way, we make all kinds of excuses or mock the one bringing the message. God uses imperfect people to call us. Let us not become so hardened we can't see the simple truth before our eyes.*

THE FLOOD

And the flood was forty days upon the earth; and the waters increased, and bare up the ark, and it was lift up above the earth.
Genesis 7:17

For seven days after Noah and his family entered the ark, there appeared no sign of the coming storm. During this period their faith was tested. It was a time of triumph to the world without. … But upon the eighth day dark clouds overspread the heavens. There followed the muttering of thunder and the flash of lightning. Soon large drops of rain began to fall. The world had never witnessed anything like this, and the hearts of men were struck with fear. All were secretly inquiring, "Can it be that Noah was in the right, and that the world is doomed to destruction?" Darker and darker grew the heavens, and faster came the falling rain. The beasts were roaming about in the wildest terror, and their discordant cries seemed to moan out their own destiny and the fate of man. Then "the fountains of the great deep" were "broken up, and the windows of heaven were opened." Water appeared to come from the clouds in mighty cataracts. Rivers broke away from their boundaries, and overflowed the valleys. Jets of water burst from the earth with indescribable force, throwing massive rocks hundreds of feet into the air, and these, in falling, buried themselves deep in the ground." (*Patriarchs and Prophets*, 98–99)

REFLECTION: *In a time of crisis many turn to God, but when the crisis is over they soon forget Him. It is important to maintain communion with Christ so that our love for Him may grow with each passing day.*

Noah's First Act

*And Noah builded an altar unto the L*ORD*; and took of every clean beast,
and of every clean fowl, and offered burnt offerings on the altar.*
Genesis 8:20

The waters rose fifteen cubits above the highest mountains. It often seemed to the family within the ark that they must perish, as for five long months their boat was tossed about, apparently at the mercy of wind and wave. It was a trying ordeal; but Noah's faith did not waver, for he had the assurance that the divine hand was upon the helm.

As the waters began to subside, the Lord caused the ark to drift into a spot protected by a group of mountains that had been preserved by His power. These mountains were but a little distance apart, and the ark moved about in this quiet haven, and was no longer driven upon the boundless ocean. This gave great relief to the weary, tempest-tossed voyagers....

At last an angel descended from heaven, opened the massive door, and bade the patriarch and his household go forth upon the earth and take with them every living thing. In the joy of their release Noah did not forget Him by whose gracious care they had been preserved. His first act after leaving the ark was to build an altar and offer from every kind of clean beast and fowl a sacrifice, thus manifesting his gratitude to God for deliverance and his faith in Christ, the great sacrifice. (*Patriarchs and Prophets*, 105)

REFLECTION: *When things go well, we tend to forget God. Our first duty is to God who has given us life. It is He who sustains us in this life and promises us eternal life through His Son, Jesus Christ. Let us always remember to begin each day with God.*

The Bow of Promise

*I do set my bow in the cloud, and it shall be for a token of a covenant
between me and the earth... And I will remember my covenant,
which is between me and you and every living creature of all flesh;
and the waters shall no more become a flood to destroy all flesh.*
Genesis 9:13, 15

How great the condescension of God and His compassion for His erring creatures in thus placing the beautiful rainbow in the clouds as a token of His covenant with men! The Lord declares that when He looks upon the bow, He will remember His covenant. This does not imply that He would ever forget; but He speaks to us in our own language, that we may better understand Him. It was God's purpose that as the children of after generations should ask the meaning of the glorious arch which spans the heavens, their parents should repeat the story of the Flood, and tell them that the Most High had bended the bow and placed it in the clouds as an assurance that the waters should never again overflow the earth. Thus from generation to generation it would testify of divine love to man and would strengthen his confidence in God. ...

When man by his great wickedness invites the divine judgments, the Saviour, interceding with the Father in his behalf, points to the bow in the clouds, to the rainbow around the throne and above His own head, as a token of the mercy of God toward the repentant sinner. (*Patriarchs and Prophets*, 106, 107)

REFLECTION: *While man keeps increasing in wickedness, God continues to exercise His great mercy and longsuffering toward us. As we look to the bow in the sky, we are ever reminded that He is a God of perfect love and justice.*

*A*POSTASY *A*FTER THE *F*LOOD

And it came to pass, as they journeyed from the east, that they
found a plain in the land of Shinar; and they dwelt there.
Genesis 11:2

or a time the descendants of Noah continued to dwell among the mountains where the ark had rested. As their numbers increased, apostasy soon led to division. Those who desired to forget their Creator and to cast off the restraint of His law felt a constant annoyance from the teaching and example of their God-fearing associates, and after a time they decided to separate from the worshipers of God. Accordingly they journeyed to the plain of Shinar, on the banks of the river Euphrates. …

Here they decided to build a city, and in it a tower of such stupendous height as should render it the wonder of the world. These enterprises were designed to prevent the people from scattering abroad in colonies. God had directed men to disperse throughout the earth, to replenish and subdue it; but these Babel builders determined to keep their community united in one body, and to found a monarchy that should eventually embrace the whole earth. Thus their city would become the metropolis of a universal empire; its glory would command the admiration and homage of the world and render the founders illustrious. The magnificent tower, reaching to the heavens, was intended to stand as a monument of the power and wisdom of its builders, perpetuating their fame to the latest generations. (*Patriarchs and Prophets*, 118, 119)

REFLECTION: *Men love power and praise. We love to be worshipped in so many ways. God wants to restore His humble image in us. Let us look to God and the things He has created for us. As we do this, the things of this world will grow strangely dim.*

JANUARY 19

THE TOWER OF REBELLION

And they said, Go to, let us build us a city and a tower, whose
top may reach unto heaven; and let us make us a name, lest
we be scattered abroad upon the face of the whole earth.
Genesis 11:4

One object before them in the erection of the tower was to secure their own safety in case of another deluge. By carrying the structure to a much greater height than was reached by the waters of the Flood, they thought to place themselves beyond all possibility of danger. And as they would be able to ascend to the region of the clouds, they hoped to ascertain the cause of the Flood. The whole undertaking was designed to exalt still further the pride of its projectors and to turn the minds of future generations away from God and lead them into idolatry. . . .

Suddenly the work that had been advancing so prosperously was checked. Angels were sent to bring to naught the purpose of the builders. . . . As messages were thus passing from one to another the language was confounded, so that material was called for which was not needed, and the directions delivered were often the reverse of those that had been given. Confusion and dismay followed. All work came to a standstill. There could be no further harmony or co-operation. The builders were wholly unable to account for the strange misunderstandings among them, and in their rage and disappointment they reproached one another. Their confederacy ended in strife and bloodshed. (*Patriarchs and Prophets*, 119)

REFLECTION: *A work that started in unity against God, ended in strife and bloodshed amongst themselves. Such are the fruits of the unconverted heart.*

GOD CALLS ABRAHAM

And I will make of thee a great nation, and I will bless thee,
and make thy name great; and thou shalt be a blessing.
Genesis 12:2

Abraham had grown up in the midst of superstition and heathenism. Even his father's household, by whom the knowledge of God had been preserved, were yielding to the seductive influences surrounding them, and they "served other gods" than Jehovah. But the true faith was not to become extinct. God has ever preserved a remnant to serve Him. Adam, Seth, Enoch, Methuselah, Noah, Shem, in unbroken line, had preserved from age to age the precious revealings of His will. The son of Terah became the inheritor of this holy trust. Idolatry invited him on every side, but in vain. Faithful among the faithless, uncorrupted by the prevailing apostasy, he steadfastly adhered to the worship of the one true God. ...

There was given to Abraham the promise, especially dear to the people of that age, of a numerous posterity and of national greatness: "I will make of thee a great nation, and I will bless thee, and make thy name great; and thou shalt be a blessing." And to this was added the assurance, precious above every other to the inheritor of faith, that of his line the Redeemer of the world should come: "In thee shall all families of the earth be blessed." (*Patriarchs and Prophets*, 125)

REFLECTION: *Though surrounded by apostasy, Abraham remained faithful to the one true God. He would become the father of the faithful. The same is promised for you and me today, if we, like Abraham, stay faithful to Him.*

ABRAHAM'S FIRST TEST

Now the LORD had said unto Abram, Get thee out of thy country, and from thy kindred, and from thy father's house, unto a land that I will show thee.
Genesis 12:1

Yet, as the first condition of fulfillment, there was to be a test of faith; a sacrifice was demanded. The message of God came to Abraham, "Get thee out of thy country, and from thy kindred, and from thy father's house, unto a land that I will show thee." In order that God might qualify him for his great work as the keeper of the sacred oracles, Abraham must be separated from the associations of his early life. The influence of kindred and friends would interfere with the training which the Lord purposed to give His servant.…

It was no light test that was thus brought upon Abraham, no small sacrifice that was required of him. There were strong ties to bind him to his country, his kindred, and his home. But he did not hesitate to obey the call. He had no question to ask concerning the land of promise — whether the soil was fertile and the climate healthful; whether the country afforded agreeable surroundings and would afford opportunities for amassing wealth. God has spoken, and His servant must obey; the happiest place on earth for him was the place where God would have him to be. (*Patriarchs and Prophets*, 126)

REFLECTION: *We all desire to be happy. Like Abraham, we too will be the happiest where God would have us to be. In most cases it is not where we think we should be. Let us continue to trust in Him.*

JANUARY 22

*A*BRAHAM *F*ALTERS

Say, I pray thee, thou art my sister: that it may be well with
me for thy sake; and my soul shall live because of thee.
Genesis 12:13

*D*uring his stay in Egypt, Abraham gave evidence that he was not free from human weakness and imperfection. In concealing the fact that Sarah was his wife, he betrayed a distrust of the divine care, a lack of that lofty faith and courage so often and nobly exemplified in his life. ... He reasoned that he was not guilty of falsehood in representing Sarah as his sister, for she was the daughter of his father, though not of his mother. But this concealment of the real relation between them was deception. No deviation from strict integrity can meet God's approval. Through Abraham's lack of faith, Sarah was placed in great peril. The king of Egypt, being informed of her beauty, caused her to be taken to his palace, intending to make her his wife. But the Lord, in His great mercy, protected Sarah by sending judgments upon the royal household. By this means the monarch learned the truth in the matter, and, indignant at the deception practiced upon him, he reproved Abraham and restored to him his wife, saying, "What is this that thou hast done unto me? ... Why saidst thou, She is my sister? So I might have taken her to me to wife. Now therefore behold thy wife, take her, and go thy way." (*Patriarchs and Prophets*, 130)

REFLECTION: *Many times, in our everyday lives, we think we have to help God out. God allows trials to come to us that our faith may grow. It grows through the exercise of trusting and obeying. Let us not come up with our own plans, but allow God to work His salvation for us.*

JANUARY 23

THE UNSELFISH ABRAHAM

Is not the whole land before thee? Separate thyself, I pray thee,
from me: if thou wilt take the left hand, then I will go to the right;
or if thou depart to the right hand, then I will go to the left.
Genesis 13:9

A braham returned to Canaan "very rich in cattle, in silver, and in gold." ... They soon found that increased possessions brought increased trouble ... The pasturage was not sufficient for the flocks and herds of both, and the frequent disputes among the herdsmen were brought for settlement to their masters. It was evident that they must separate. Abraham was Lot's senior in years, and his superior in relation, in wealth, and in position; yet he was the first to propose plans for preserving peace. ...

"Let there be no strife," he said, "between me and thee, and between my herdmen and thy herdmen; for we be brethren. Is not the whole land before thee? Separate thyself, I pray thee, from me: if thou wilt take the left hand, then I will go to the right; or if thou depart to the right hand, then I will go to the left."

Here the noble, unselfish spirit of Abraham was displayed. How many under similar circumstances would, at all hazards, cling to their individual rights and preferences! How many households have thus been rent asunder! (*Patriarchs and Prophets*, 132)

REFLECTION: *Selfishness is of Satan, but the children of God must possess true courtesy and thus fulfill the command to do unto others as we would have them do unto us. If God cares for the sparrow each day, He will care for us even more. He doesn't need our money. He needs our hearts.*

DOUBT NOT GOD'S WORD

*And Sarai said unto Abram, Behold now, the LORD hath restrained me
from bearing: I pray thee, go in unto my maid; it may be that I may
obtain children by her. And Abram hearkened to the voice of Sarai.*
Genesis 16:2

Abraham had accepted without question the promise of a son, but he did not wait for God to fulfill His word in His own time and way. A delay was permitted, to test his faith in the power of God; but he failed to endure the trial. Thinking it impossible that a child should be given her in her old age, Sarah suggested, as a plan by which the divine purpose might be fulfilled, that one of her handmaidens should be taken by Abraham as a secondary wife. ...

Flattered with the honor of her new position as Abraham's wife, and hoping to be the mother of the great nation to descend from him, Hagar became proud and boastful, and treated her mistress with contempt. Mutual jealousies disturbed the peace of the once happy home. Forced to listen to the complaints of both, Abraham vainly endeavored to restore harmony. Though it was at Sarah's earnest entreaty that he had married Hagar, she now reproached him as the one at fault. (*Patriarchs and Prophets*, 145)

REFLECTION: *When we do not wait upon the Lord to do what He has promised, we begin to take things into our own hands. We begin to trust ourselves more than God. Then, when things don't go like we thought, we blame God. Patience is a fruit of the Spirit. God wants us to bear His fruit.*

THE PROMISE REPEATED

And God said, Sarah thy wife shall bear thee a son indeed; and thou
shalt call his name Isaac: and I will establish my covenant with
him for an everlasting covenant, and with his seed after him.
Genesis 17:19

When Abraham was nearly one hundred years old, the promise of a son was repeated to him, with the assurance that the future heir should be the child of Sarah. But Abraham did not yet understand the promise. His mind at once turned to Ishmael, clinging to the belief that through him God's gracious purposes were to be accomplished. In his affection for his son he exclaimed, "O that Ishmael might live before Thee!" Again the promise was given, in words that could not be mistaken: "Sarah thy wife shall bear thee a son indeed; and thou shalt call his name Isaac: and I will establish My covenant with him." …

The birth of Isaac, bringing, after a lifelong waiting, the fulfillment of their dearest hopes, filled the tents of Abraham and Sarah with gladness. But to Hagar this event was the overthrow of her fondly cherished ambitions. Ishmael, now a youth, had been regarded by all in the encampment as the heir of Abraham's wealth and the inheritor of the blessings promised to his descendants. Now he was suddenly set aside; and in their disappointment, mother and son hated the child of Sarah. (*Patriarchs and Prophets*, 146, 147)

REFLECTION: *The promises of God are sure. If Plan A fails because of us, He has Plan B and Plan C, if needed. Let us work more often on God's "A" plan.*

ABRAHAM AS HUSBAND AND FATHER

For I know him, that he will command his children and his household after him, and they shall keep the way of the LORD, to do justice and judgment; that the LORD may bring upon Abraham that which he hath spoken of him.
Genesis 18:19

The husband and father is the head of the household. The wife looks to him for love and sympathy, and for aid in the training of the children; and this is right. The children are his as well as hers, and he is equally interested in their welfare. The children look to their father for support and guidance; he needs to have a right conception of life and of the influences and associations that should surround his family; above all, he should be controlled by the love and fear of God and by the teaching of His word, that he may guide the feet of his children in the right way.

The father is the lawmaker of the household; and, like Abraham, he should make the law of God the rule of his home. God said of Abraham, "I know him, that he will command his children and his household" (Genesis 18:19). ... Abraham would not only give right instruction, but he would maintain the authority of just and righteous laws. ... Kindly, but firmly, with persevering, prayerful effort, their wrong desires should be restrained, their inclinations denied. (*Ministry of Healing*, 390, 391)

REFLECTION: *What a responsibility fathers have! By precept and example the father is to help his family to become more beautiful in Christ each and every day.*

The Crisis in Sodom

For we will destroy this place, because the cry of them is waxen great before the face of the Lord; and the Lord hath sent us to destroy it.
Genesis 19:13

The strangers whom Lot had endeavored to protect, now promised to protect him, and to save also all the members of his family who would flee with him from the wicked city. The mob had wearied themselves out and departed, and Lot went out to warn his children. He repeated the words of the angels, "Up, get you out of this place; for the Lord will destroy this city." But he seemed to them as one that mocked.... They had great possessions, and they could not believe it possible that beautiful Sodom would be destroyed.

Lot returned sorrowfully to his home and told the story of his failure. Then the angels bade him arise and take his wife and the two daughters who were yet in his house and leave the city. But Lot delayed.... The thought of leaving those whom he held dearest on earth seemed more than he could bear. It was hard to forsake his luxurious home and all the wealth acquired by the labors of his whole life, to go forth a destitute wanderer. Stupefied with sorrow, he lingered, loath to depart. But for the angels of God, they would all have perished in the ruin of Sodom. The heavenly messengers took him and his wife and daughters by the hand and led them out of the city. (*Patriarchs and Prophets*, 159, 160)

REFLECTION: *Lot's daily contact with Sodom made him loose spiritual discernment and become numb to the increasing evil. A very important principle to remember is that by beholding we become changed. What you listen to and who you associate with will slowly, but surely, permeate your whole being. To be like Christ we must behold Him. We will then begin to see how terrible sin really is.*

Sacrifice Your Only Son

*And he said, Take now thy son, thine only son Isaac, whom thou
lovest, and get thee into the land of Moriah; and offer him there for a
burnt offering upon one of the mountains which I will tell thee of.*

Genesis 22:2

God had called Abraham to be the father of the faithful, and his life was to stand as an example of faith to succeeding generations. But his faith had not been perfect. He had shown distrust of God in concealing the fact that Sarah was his wife, and again in his marriage with Hagar. That he might reach the highest standard, God subjected him to another test, the closest which man was ever called to endure. In a vision of the night he was directed to repair to the land of Moriah, and there offer up his son as a burnt offering upon a mountain that should be shown him. ...

Returning to his tent, he went to the place where Isaac lay sleeping the deep, untroubled sleep of youth and innocence. For a moment the father looked upon the dear face of his son, then turned tremblingly away. He went to the side of Sarah, who was also sleeping. Should he awaken her, that she might once more embrace her child? ... He longed to unburden his heart to her, and share with her this terrible responsibility; but he was restrained by the fear that she might hinder him. Isaac was her joy and pride; her life was bound up in him, and the mother's love might refuse the sacrifice. (*Patriarchs and Prophets*, 147, 148)

REFLECTION: *This test was for the perfecting of Abraham's faith. God will take us through tests and trials to perfect our faith as well. Often, when these trials come, we long to share with someone close but can't for risk of failure. In these times of trial let us put our faith wholly in the Lord Almighty.*

*A*BRAHAM AND *I*SAAC

And Abraham rose up early in the morning, and saddled his ass, and took two
of his young men with him, and Isaac his son, and clave the wood for the burnt
offering, and rose up, and went unto the place of which God had told him.
Genesis 22:3

*A*braham at last summoned his son, telling him of the
command to offer sacrifice upon a distant mountain.
Isaac had often gone with his father to worship at
some one of the various altars that marked his wanderings, and
this summons excited no surprise. The preparations for the journey were quickly completed. The wood was made ready and put
upon the ass, and with two menservants they set forth.

Side by side the father and the son journeyed in silence. The
patriarch, pondering his heavy secret, had no heart for words.
His thoughts were of the proud, fond mother, and the day when
he should return to her alone. Well he knew that the knife would
pierce her heart when it took the life of her son.

Even now he did not murmur against God, but strengthened
his soul by dwelling upon the evidences of the Lord's goodness
and faithfulness. This son had been unexpectedly given; and
had not He who bestowed the precious gift a right to recall His
own? Then faith repeated the promise, "In Isaac shall thy seed be
called"—a seed numberless as the grains of sand upon the shore.
(*Patriarchs and Prophets*, 151)

REFLECTION: *Abraham finally got it! He put his whole trust in God. He*
knew, by faith, not by sight, that God's plans are always best. We too,
can have that same faith and trust.

ABRAHAM PASSES THE TEST

*And he said, Lay not thine hand upon the lad, neither do thou
any thing unto him: for now I know that thou fearest God, seeing
thou hast not withheld thy son, thine only son from me.*
Genesis 22:12

At the appointed place they built the altar and laid the wood upon it. Then, with trembling voice, Abraham unfolded to his son the divine message. It was with terror and amazement that Isaac learned his fate, but he offered no resistance. ... Isaac had been trained from childhood to ready, trusting obedience, and as the purpose of God was opened before him, he yielded a willing submission. He was a sharer in Abraham's faith, and he felt that he was honored in being called to give his life as an offering to God. He tenderly seeks to lighten the father's grief, and encourages his nerveless hands to bind the cords that confine him to the altar.

And now the last words of love are spoken, the last tears are shed, the last embrace is given. The father lifts the knife to slay his son, when suddenly his arm is stayed. An angel of God calls to the patriarch out of heaven, "Abraham, Abraham!" He quickly answers, "Here am I," And again the voice is heard, "Lay not thine hand upon the lad, neither do thou any thing unto him: for now I know that thou fearest God, seeing thou hast not withheld thy son, thine only son, from Me." (*Patriarchs and Prophets*, 152)

REFLECTION: *This ultimate test was not for God's sake. He knew what Abraham would do. This was for Abraham's sake. Abraham's fear of God was his acknowledgment of God's authority and honor. He knew God and believed in what He had promised concerning Isaac. What faith!*

JANUARY 31

THE SONS OF ISAAC

And the boys grew: and Esau was a cunning hunter, a man of the field; and Jacob was a plain man, dwelling in tents. And Isaac loved Esau, because he did eat of his venison: but Rebekah loved Jacob.
Genesis 25:27, 28

Jacob and Esau, the twin sons of Isaac, present a striking contrast, both in character and in life. This unlikeness was foretold by the angel of God before their birth. When in answer to Rebekah's troubled prayer he declared that two sons would be given her, he opened to her their future history, that each would become the head of a mighty nation, but that one would be greater than the other, and that the younger would have the pre-eminence. ...

The promises made to Abraham and confirmed to his son were held by Isaac and Rebekah as the great object of their desires and hopes. With these promises Esau and Jacob were familiar. They were taught to regard the birthright as a matter of great importance, for it included not only an inheritance of worldly wealth but spiritual pre-eminence. He who received it was to be the priest of his family, and in the line of his posterity the Redeemer of the world would come. On the other hand, there were obligations resting upon the possessor of the birthright. He who should inherit its blessings must devote his life to the service of God. Like Abraham, he must be obedient to the divine requirements. In marriage, in his family relations, in public life, he must consult the will of God. (*Patriarchs and Prophets*, 177)

REFLECTION: *Blessings and responsibilities work together. He who is called to higher service must choose to honor God in all things.*

FEBRUARY

FEBRUARY 1

A Fateful Trade

And Jacob said, Sell me this day thy birthright. And Esau said, Behold, I
am at the point to die: and what profit shall this birthright do to me?
Genesis 25:31, 32

*J*acob had learned from his mother of the divine intimation that the birthright should fall to him, and he
was filled with an unspeakable desire for the privileges
which it would confer. It was not the possession of his father's
wealth that he craved; the spiritual birthright was the object of
his longing. To commune with God as did righteous Abraham,
to offer the sacrifice of atonement for his family, to be the pro-
genitor of the chosen people and of the promised Messiah, and
to inherit the immortal possessions embraced in the blessings of
the covenant—here were the privileges and honors that kindled
his most ardent desires. ...

When Esau, coming home one day faint and weary from
the chase, asked for the food that Jacob was preparing, the latter, with whom one thought was ever uppermost, seized upon
his advantage, and offered to satisfy his brother's hunger at the
price of the birthright. "Behold, I am at the point to die," cried
the reckless, self-indulgent hunter, "and what profit shall this
birthright do to me?" And for a dish of red pottage he parted
with his birthright, and confirmed the transaction by an oath.
(*Patriarchs and Prophets*, 178, 179)

REFLECTION: *For a short time, Esau was relieved to rid himself of his*
birthright. Today, millions are exchanging eternal life for things that
pass away. May we never sell our character for a bowl of pottage. Make
a commitment to stand firm for the truth, as it is in Jesus.

FEBRUARY 2

DECEIT AND DISASTER

And he said, Art thou my very son Esau? And he said, I am.
Genesis 27:24

*Y*ears passed on, until Isaac, old and blind, and expecting soon to die, determined no longer to delay the bestowal of the blessing upon his elder son. But knowing the opposition of Rebekah and Jacob, he decided to perform the solemn ceremony in secret. In accordance with the custom of making a feast upon such occasions, the patriarch bade Esau, "Go out to the field, and take me some venison; and make me savory meat, … that my soul may bless thee before I die." …

No sooner had Esau departed on his errand than Rebekah set about the accomplishment of her purpose. She told Jacob what had taken place, urging the necessity of immediate action to prevent the bestowal of the blessing, finally and irrevocably, upon Esau. And she assured her son that if he would follow her directions, he might obtain it as God had promised. Jacob did not readily consent to the plan that she proposed. The thought of deceiving his father caused him great distress. He felt that such a sin would bring a curse rather than a blessing. But his scruples were overborne, and he proceeded to carry out his mother's suggestions. It was not his intention to utter a direct falsehood, but once in the presence of his father he seemed to have gone too far to retreat, and he obtained by fraud the coveted blessing." (*Patriarchs and Prophets*, 180)

REFLECTION: *So many are unwilling to leave matters in God's hand. Let's learn from these powerful lessons given to us by God Himself, that the only right way is God's way. If we could only learn from these lessons from history and learn to trust God.*

THE FRUIT OF DECEPTION

And Esau hated Jacob because of the blessing wherewith his father blessed him: and Esau said in his heart, The days of mourning for my father are at hand; then will I slay my brother Jacob.
Genesis 27:41

*J*acob and Rebekah succeeded in their purpose, but they gained only trouble and sorrow by their deception... Rebekah bitterly repented the wrong counsel she had given her son; it was the means of separating him from her, and she never saw his face again. From the hour when he received the birthright, Jacob was weighed down with self-condemnation. He had sinned against his father, his brother, his own soul, and against God. In one short hour he had made work for a lifelong repentance. This scene was vivid before him in afteryears, when the wicked course of his sons oppressed his soul. (*Patriarchs and Prophets*, 180)

Threatened with death by the wrath of Esau, Jacob went out from his father's home a fugitive; but he carried with him the father's blessing; Isaac had renewed to him the covenant promise, and had bidden him, as its inheritor, to seek a wife of his mother's family in Mesopotamia. Yet it was with a deeply troubled heart that Jacob set out on his lonely journey. With only his staff in his hand he must travel hundreds of miles through a country inhabited by wild, roving tribes." (*Patriarchs and Prophets*, 183)

REFLECTION: *Sin can look so appealing, yet once committed, we have great regrets that we had given in so easily. One small sin can cause lifelong consequences.*

FEBRUARY 4

CHRIST THE LADDER

*And he dreamed, and behold a ladder set up on the
earth, and the top of it reached to heaven: and behold the
angels of God ascending and descending on it.*
Genesis 28:12

Wearied with his journey, the wanderer lay down upon the ground, with a stone for his pillow. As he slept he beheld a ladder, bright and shining, whose base rested upon the earth, while the top reached to heaven. Upon this ladder angels were ascending and descending; above it was the Lord of glory, and from the heavens His voice was heard: "I am the Lord God of Abraham thy father, and the God of Isaac. In thee and in thy seed shall all the families of the earth be blessed." This promise had been given to Abraham and to Isaac, and now it was renewed to Jacob. Then in special regard to his present loneliness and distress, the words of comfort and encouragement were spoken: "Behold, I am with thee, and will keep thee in all places whither thou goest, and will bring thee again into this land; for I will not leave thee, until I have done that which I have spoken to thee of." ...

The ladder represents Jesus, the appointed medium of communication. Had He not with His own merits bridged the gulf that sin had made, the ministering angels could have held no communion with fallen man. Christ connects man in his weakness and helplessness with the source of infinite power. (*Patriarchs and Prophets*, 183, 184)

REFLECTION: *Even though sins we have committed seem to separate us from God, we have a Savior, Christ, who will comfort and encourage us when we are lonely and distressed. God is our comfort and encouragement.*

FEBRUARY 5

GRATITUDE TOWARD GOD

And this stone, which I have set for a pillar, shall be God's house: and of all that thou shalt give me I will surely give the tenth unto thee.
Genesis 28:22

Our time, our talents, our property, should be sacredly devoted to Him who has given us these blessings in trust. Whenever a special deliverance is wrought in our behalf, or new and unexpected favors are granted us, we should acknowledge God's goodness, not only by expressing our gratitude in words, but, like Jacob, by gifts and offerings to His cause. As we are continually receiving the blessings of God, so we are to be continually giving.

"Of all that Thou shalt give me," said Jacob, "I will surely give the tenth unto Thee." Shall we who enjoy the full light and privileges of the gospel be content to give less to God than was given by those who lived in the former, less favored dispensation? Nay, as the blessings we enjoy are greater, are not our obligations correspondingly increased? But how small the estimate; how vain the endeavor to measure with mathematical rules, time, money, and love, against a love so immeasurable and a gift of such inconceivable worth. Tithes for Christ! Oh, meager pittance, shameful recompense for that which cost so much! From the cross of Calvary, Christ calls for an unreserved consecration. All that we have, all that we are, should be devoted to God. (*Patriarchs and Prophets*, 187, 188)

REFLECTION: *We must never forget that God owns everything. He only asks us to return a portion of what is His for our own sakes; to build character and faith. God gave His only Son to die for our sins. Shall we, then, give meagerly for the work of the gospel?*

FEBRUARY 6

*J*ACOB *B*ECOMES *I*SRAEL

And he said, Thy name shall be called no more Jacob, but Israel: for as a
prince hast thou power with God and with men, and hast prevailed.
Genesis 32:28

Suddenly a strong hand was laid upon him. He thought that an enemy was seeking his life, and he endeavored to wrest himself from the grasp of his assailant.... The struggle continued until near the break of day, when the stranger placed his finger upon Jacob's thigh, and he was crippled instantly. The patriarch now discerned the character of his antagonist. ...

The error that had led to Jacob's sin in obtaining the birthright by fraud was now clearly set before him. He had not trusted God's promises, but had sought by his own efforts to bring about that which God would have accomplished in His own time and way. As an evidence that he had been forgiven, his name was changed from one that was a reminder of his sin, to one that commemorated his victory. "Thy name," said the Angel, "shall be called no more Jacob [the supplanter], but Israel: for as a prince hast thou power with God and with men, and hast prevailed."

Jacob had received the blessing for which his soul had longed. His sin as a supplanter and deceiver had been pardoned. The crisis in his life was past. (*Patriarchs and Prophets*, 196–198)

REFLECTION: *This night of Jacob's struggle represents the trying circumstances God's people will face at the end of time. We will sense our shortcomings, but must wrestle with God in prayer and be sure we have confessed every sin.*

FEBRUARY 7

JOSEPH THE SON OF JACOB

*And Joseph dreamed a dream, and he told it his
brethren: and they hated him yet the more.*
Genesis 37:5

The sin of Jacob, and the train of events to which it led,
had not failed to exert an influence for evil—an influence
that revealed its bitter fruit in the character and life of
his sons....

There was one, however, of a widely different character—the
elder son of Rachel, Joseph, whose rare personal beauty seemed
but to reflect an inward beauty of mind and heart ... and Jacob's
heart was bound up in this child of his old age. He "loved Joseph
more than all his children." ...

Jacob unwisely manifested his preference for Joseph, and
this excited the jealousy of his other sons.... The father's injudi-
cious gift to Joseph of a costly coat, or tunic, such as was usually
worn by persons of distinction, seemed to them another evidence
of his partiality, and excited a suspicion that he intended to pass
by his elder children, to bestow the birthright upon the son of
Rachel. Their malice was still further increased as the boy one
day told them of a dream that he had had. "Behold," he said, "we
were binding sheaves in the field, and, lo, my sheaf arose, and
also stood upright; and, behold, your sheaves stood round about,
and made obeisance to my sheaf."

"Shalt thou indeed reign over us? or shalt thou indeed have
dominion over us?" exclaimed his brothers in envious anger.
(*Patriarchs and Prophets*, 208–210)

REFLECTION: *As parents we should never play favorites with our children. It will, in most cases, have an effect that can ruin all of the children, not just the disadvantaged one. Remember God is always there to
help us and give us wisdom when we ask.*

Selling Their Brother

Come, and let us sell him to the Ishmeelites, and let not our hand be upon him; for he is our brother and our flesh. And his brethren were content.
Genesis 37:27

The brothers were obliged to move from place to place to secure pasturage for their flocks. ... Some time passed, bringing no tidings from them, and the father began to fear for their safety. ... He therefore sent Joseph to find them, and bring him words as to their welfare. ...

His brothers saw him approaching; but no thought of the long journey he had made to meet them, of his weariness and hunger, of his claims upon their hospitality and brotherly love, softened the bitterness of their hatred. ... "Behold, this dreamer cometh," they cried in mockery. Envy and revenge, long secretly cherished, now controlled them. ...

Soon a company of travelers was seen approaching. It was a caravan of Ishmaelites from beyond Jordan, on their way to Egypt with spices and other merchandise. Judah now proposed to sell their brother to these heathen traders instead of leaving him to die. While he would be effectually put out of their way, they would remain clear of his blood; "for," he urged, "he is our brother and our flesh." To this proposition all agreed, and Joseph was quickly drawn out of the pit. ...

Steeling their hearts against his entreaties, they delivered him into the hands of the heathen traders. (*Patriarchs and Prophets*, 210, 211)

REFLECTION: *When we do one wrong, it usually does not stop there, but multiplies into a succession of more wrongs and untruths. Honesty is always the best policy. Let God work out what we are fearful of. He has a thousand ways to help us. Being honest and doing right is the best way to build a character for heaven.*

FEBRUARY 9

JOSEPH IN EGYPT

And it came to pass after these things, that his master's wife
cast her eyes upon Joseph; and she said, Lie with me.
Genesis 39:7

Joseph's faith and integrity were to be tested by fiery trials. His master's wife endeavored to entice the young man to transgress the law of God. …

Joseph's answer reveals the power of religious principle. He would not betray the confidence of his master on earth, and, whatever the consequences, he would be true to his Master in heaven. Under the inspecting eye of God and holy angels many take liberties of which they would not be guilty in the presence of their fellow men, but Joseph's first thought was of God. "How … can I do this great wickedness, and sin against God?" he said. …

Let the young ever remember that wherever they are, and whatever they do, they are in the presence of God. No part of our conduct escapes observation. We cannot hide our ways from the Most High. … The deepest midnight is no cover for the guilty one. He may think himself alone, but to every deed there is an unseen witness. The very motives of his heart are open to divine inspection. Every act, every word, every thought, is as distinctly marked as though there were only one person in the whole world, and the attention of heaven were centered upon him. (*Patriarchs and Prophets*, 217)

REFLECTION: *We may be able to hide our sins from others, but not from God. Our ideal is to have a constant desire to please God with loving obedience.*

FEBRUARY 10

PHARAOH'S DREAM

And Joseph answered Pharaoh, saying, It is not in me:
God shall give Pharaoh an answer of peace.
Genesis 41:16

"And Pharaoh said unto Joseph, I have dreamed a dream, and there is none that can interpret it: and I have heard say of thee, that thou canst understand a dream to interpret it. And Joseph answered Pharaoh, saying, It is not in me: God shall give Pharaoh an answer of peace." Joseph's reply to the king reveals his humility and his faith in God. He modestly disclaims the honor of possessing in himself superior wisdom. "It is not in me." God alone can explain these mysteries. ...

How was Joseph enabled to make such a record of firmness of character, uprightness, and wisdom? — In his early years he had consulted duty rather than inclination; and the integrity, the simple trust, the noble nature, of the youth bore fruit in the deeds of the man. A pure and simple life had favored the vigorous development of both physical and intellectual powers. Communion with God through His works and the contemplation of the grand truths entrusted to the inheritors of faith had elevated and ennobled his spiritual nature, broadening and strengthening the mind as no other study could do. Faithful attention to duty in every station, from the lowliest to the most exalted, had been training every power for its highest service. (*Patriarchs and Prophets*, 220–222)

REFLECTION: *Joseph became successful not from one single, great thing. He had learned to stand for right principles on a daily basis and in the small things; especially when wronged and sent to prison. Our everyday duties and responsibilities, in the end, make us who we are. These "ho-hum" duties, performed faithfully, build a beautiful character.*

FEBRUARY 11

CORN IN EGYPT

And Joseph's ten brethren went down to buy corn in Egypt.
Genesis 42:3

*A*t the very opening of the fruitful years began the preparation for the approaching famine. Under the direction of Joseph, immense storehouses were erected in all the principal places throughout the land of Egypt, and ample arrangements were made for preserving the surplus of the expected harvest. The same policy was continued during the seven years of plenty, until the amount of grain laid in store was beyond computation.

And now the seven years of dearth began to come, according to Joseph's prediction. "And the dearth was in all lands; but in all the land of Egypt there was bread." ...

Hearing of the abundant provision made by the king of Egypt, ten of Jacob's sons journeyed thither to purchase grain. On their arrival they were directed to the king's deputy, and with other applicants they came to present themselves before the ruler of the land. And they "bowed down themselves before him with their faces to the earth." "Joseph knew his brethren, but they knew not him." His Hebrew name had been exchanged for the one bestowed upon him by the king, and there was little resemblance between the prime minister of Egypt and the stripling whom they had sold to the Ishmaelites. As Joseph saw his brothers stooping and making obeisance, his dreams came to his mind, and the scenes of the past rose vividly before him. His keen eye, surveying the group, discovered that Benjamin was not among them. (*Patriarchs and Prophets*, 224)

REFLECTION: *The dream of Joseph had come true. Often, when we ask God for things, we want them NOW! Many times, as in Joseph's circumstance, it takes time for our prayers to be answered.*

JOSEPH BROTHERS IN PRISON

And he put them all together into ward three days.
Genesis 42:17

is keen eye, surveying the group, discovered that Benjamin was not among them. Had he also fallen a victim to the treacherous cruelty of those savage men? He determined to learn the truth. "Ye are spies," he said sternly; "to see the nakedness of the land ye are come." ...

The three days in the Egyptian prison were days of bitter sorrow as the brothers reflected upon their past sins. Unless Benjamin could be produced their conviction as spies appeared certain, and they had little hope of gaining their father's consent to Benjamin's absence. On the third day Joseph caused the brothers to be brought before him. He dared not detain them longer. ...

Again they journeyed to Egypt and presented themselves before Joseph. As his eye fell upon Benjamin, his own mother's son, he was deeply moved. He concealed his emotion, however, but ordered that they be taken to his house, and that preparation be made for them to dine with him. ...

Joseph was satisfied. He had seen in his brothers the fruits of true repentance. Upon hearing Judah's noble offer he gave orders that all but these men should withdraw; then, weeping aloud, he cried, "I am Joseph; doth my father yet live?"

Seeing their confusion, he said kindly, "Come near to me, I pray you;" and as they came near, he continued, "I am Joseph your brother, whom ye sold into Egypt. Now therefore be not grieved, nor angry with yourselves, that ye sold me hither: for God did send me before you to preserve life." (*Patriarchs and Prophets*, 224–230)

REFLECTION: *God is able to take bad and turn it into good.*

SLAVERY IN EGYPT

Now there arose up a new king over Egypt, which knew not Joseph.
Exodus 1:8

The Israelites had already become very numerous; they "were fruitful, and increased abundantly, and multiplied, and waxed exceeding mighty; and the land was filled with them." Under Joseph's fostering care, and the favor of the king who was then ruling, they had spread rapidly over the land. But they had kept themselves a distinct race, having nothing in common with the Egyptians in customs or religion; and their increasing numbers now excited the fears of the king and his people, lest in case of war they should join themselves with the enemies of Egypt. Yet policy forbade their banishment from the country. Many of them were able and understanding workmen, and they added greatly to the wealth of the nation; the king needed such laborers for the erection of his magnificent palaces and temples. Accordingly he ranked them with the Egyptians who had sold themselves with their possessions to the kingdom. Soon taskmasters were set over them, and their slavery became complete. "And the Egyptians made the children of Israel to serve with rigor: and they made their lives bitter with hard bondage, in mortar, and in brick, and in all manner of service in the field: all their service, wherein they made them serve, was with rigor." "But the more they afflicted them, the more they multiplied and grew." (*Patriarchs and Prophets*, 241, 242)

REFLECTION: *The Egyptians not only took the wealth of the Hebrews, but hoped to crush their independent spirit. So shall it be in the end of time when God's people cannot buy and sell.*

THE BIRTH OF MOSES

And the woman conceived, and bare a son: and when she saw him
that he [was a] goodly [child], she hid him three months.
Exodus 2:2

Orders were issued to the women whose employment gave them opportunity for executing the command, to destroy the Hebrew male children at their birth. Satan was the mover in this matter. He knew that a deliverer was to be raised up among the Israelites; and by leading the king to destroy their children he hoped to defeat the divine purpose. But the women feared God, and dared not execute the cruel mandate. The Lord approved their course, and prospered them. The king, angry at the failure of his design, made the command more urgent and extensive. The whole nation was called upon to hunt out and slaughter his helpless victims. "And Pharaoh charged all his people, saying, Every son that is born ye shall cast into the river, and every daughter ye shall save alive."

While this decree was in full force a son was born to Amram and Jochebed, devout Israelites of the tribe of Levi. The babe was "a goodly child;" and the parents, believing that the time of Israel's release was drawing near, and that God would raise up a deliverer for His people, determined that their little one should not be sacrificed. Faith in God strengthened their hearts,"'and they were not afraid of the king's commandment" (Hebrews 11:23). (*Patriarchs and Prophets*, 242)

REFLECTION: *Women who feared God chose to save the babies. Those under the spirit of Satan chose to slay them. No matter the consequence, we must obey God rather than men.*

FEBRUARY 15

A Faithful Mother

And Pharaoh's daughter said unto her, Take this child
away, and nurse it for me, and I will give thee thy wages.
And the woman took the child, and nursed it.
Exodus 2:9

Angels directed Pharaoh's daughter thither. Her curiosity was excited by the little basket, and as she looked upon the beautiful child within, she read the story at a glance. The tears of the babe awakened her compassion, and her sympathies went out to the unknown mother who had resorted to this means to preserve the life of her precious little one. She determined that he should be saved; she would adopt him as her own.

Miriam had been secretly noting every movement; perceiving that the child was tenderly regarded, she ventured nearer, and at last said, "Shall I go and call thee a nurse of the Hebrew women, that she may nurse the child for thee?" And permission was given.

The sister hastened to her mother with the happy news, and without delay returned with her to the presence of Pharaoh's daughter. "Take this child away, and nurse it for me, and I will give thee thy wages," said the princess.

God had heard the mother's prayers; her faith had been rewarded. It was with deep gratitude that she entered upon her now safe and happy task. She faithfully improved her opportunity to educate her child for God. (*Patriarchs and Prophets*, 243)

REFLECTION: *Jochebed's prayers for her baby were only the beginning of her responsibility as a mother. She would then train him to be devoted to God even amid the surrounding evils of the day.*

ℳOSES 𝒦ILLS AN ℰGYPTIAN

And it came to pass in those days, when Moses was grown, that
he went out unto his brethren, and looked on their burdens: and
he spied an Egyptian smiting an Hebrew, one of his brethren.
Exodus 2:11

Angels instructed Moses also that Jehovah had chosen him to break the bondage of His people. He, supposing that they were to obtain their freedom by force of arms, expected to lead the Hebrew host against the armies of Egypt. ...

One day, while thus abroad, seeing an Egyptian smiting an Israelite, he sprang forward and slew the Egyptian. Except the Israelite, there had been no witness to the deed, and Moses immediately buried the body in the sand. ... On the following day Moses saw two Hebrews striving together, one of them evidently at fault. Moses reproved the offender, who at once retaliated upon the reprover, denying his right to interfere, and basely accusing him of crime: "Who made thee a prince and a judge over us?" he said. "Intendest thou to kill me, as thou killedst the Egyptian?"

The whole matter was quickly made known to the Egyptians. ...It was represented to the king that this act meant much; that Moses designed to lead his people against the Egyptians, to overthrow the government. ... It was at once determined by the monarch that he should die; but, becoming aware of his danger, he made his escape and fled toward Arabia. (*Patriarchs and Prophets*, 245–247)

REFLECTION: *The Bible account is that Moses looked to the left then to the right. When he thought no one was watching he slew the Egyptian. We should never look to the left or right, but only to God. Our strength is not to be found in carnal weapons, but in the power of God; His love, wisdom and humility.*

FEBRUARY 17

MOSES, ALONE WITH GOD

Now Moses kept the flock of Jethro his father in law, the priest
of Midian: and he led the flock to the backside of the desert,
and came to the mountain of God, even to Horeb.
Exodus 3:1

The Lord directed his course, and he found a home with Jethro, the priest and prince of Midian, who was also a worshiper of God. After a time Moses married one of the daughters of Jethro; and here, in the service of his father-in-law, as keeper of his flocks, he remained forty years. ...

Moses was not prepared for his great work. He had yet to learn the same lesson of faith that Abraham and Jacob had been taught—not to rely upon human strength or wisdom, but upon the power of God for the fulfillment of His promises. And there were other lessons that, amid the solitude of the mountains, Moses was to receive. In the school of self-denial and hardship he was to learn patience, to temper his passions. Before he could govern wisely, he must be trained to obey. His own heart must be fully in harmony with God before he could teach the knowledge of His will to Israel. ...

Shut in by the bulwarks of the mountains, Moses was alone with God. ... Here his pride and self-sufficiency were swept away. ... Moses became patient, reverent, and humble, "very meek, above all the men which were upon the face of the earth" (Numbers 12:3), yet strong in faith in the mighty God of Jacob. (*Patriarchs and Prophets*, 247, 248)

REFLECTION: *Moses became patient, reverent, and humble. Those three qualities are the very essence of our characters. They represent the physical, mental and spiritual qualities of our being. You may not live in the mountains, but it's still important to find the time and place to commune with God alone.*

FEBRUARY 18

Holy Ground

And he said, Draw not nigh hither: put off thy shoes from off thy
feet, for the place whereon thou standest is holy ground.
Exodus 3:5

Moses saw a bush in flames, branches, foliage, and trunk, all burning, yet seeming not to be consumed. He drew near to view the wonderful sight, when a voice from out of the flame called him by name. With trembling lips he answered, "Here am I." He was warned not to approach irreverently: "Put off thy shoes from off thy feet; for the place whereon thou standest is holy ground.... I am the God of thy father, the God of Abraham, the God of Isaac, and the God of Jacob." It was He who, as the Angel of the covenant, had revealed Himself to the fathers in ages past. "And Moses hid his face; for he was afraid to look upon God."

Humility and reverence should characterize the deportment of all who come into the presence of God. In the name of Jesus we may come before Him with confidence, but we must not approach Him with the boldness of presumption, as though He were on a level with ourselves.... These should remember that they are in His sight whom seraphim adore, before whom angels veil their faces. (*Patriarchs and Prophets*, 251, 252)

REFLECTION: *To reverence God is to honor God. To honor Him is to obey Him. If there is no reverence for God, there is no honor toward Him, and therefore, no restraint from evil.*

Who Am I?

*And Moses said unto God, Who am I, that I should go unto Pharaoh,
and that I should bring forth the children of Israel out of Egypt?*
Exodus 3:11

*A*mazed and terrified at the command, Moses drew
back, saying, "Who am I, that I should go unto
Pharaoh, and that I should bring forth the children
of Israel out of Egypt?" The reply was, "Certainly I will be with
thee; and this shall be a token unto thee, that I have sent thee:
When thou hast brought forth the people out of Egypt, ye shall
serve God upon this mountain."

Moses thought of the difficulties to be encountered, of the
blindness, ignorance, and unbelief of his people, many of whom
were almost destitute of a knowledge of God. "Behold," he said,
"when I come unto the children of Israel, and shall say unto
them, The God of your fathers hath sent me unto you; and they
shall say to me, What is His name? What shall I say unto them?"
The answer was—

"I AM THAT I AM." "Thus shalt thou say unto the children of Israel, I AM hath sent me unto you." (*Patriarchs and
Prophets*, 252, 253)

REFLECTION: *Often God will ask us to do tasks that seem impossible.
Perhaps we feel that we do not have the talent or necessary resources.
Moses was correct in acknowledging his own limitations. The important question is, however, "What has God asked us to do?" All God's
biddings are His "enablings." He will supply all our needs to fulfill the
tasks He has requested of us.*

MOSES BEFORE PHARAOH

*And the LORD said unto Moses, When thou goest to return into Egypt, see
that thou do all those wonders before Pharaoh, which I have put in thine
hand: but I will harden his heart, that he shall not let the people go.*

Exodus 4:21

God had declared concerning Pharaoh, "I will harden his
heart, that he shall not let the people go" (Exodus 4:21).
There was no exercise of supernatural power to harden the heart of the king. God gave to Pharaoh the most striking
evidence of divine power, but the monarch stubbornly refused to
heed the light. Every display of infinite power rejected by him,
rendered him the more determined in his rebellion. The seeds of
rebellion that he sowed when he rejected the first miracle, produced their harvest. ...

God speaks to men through His servants, giving cautions and
warnings, and rebuking sin. He gives to each an opportunity to
correct his errors before they become fixed in the character; but if
one refuses to be corrected, divine power does not interpose to
counteract the tendency of his own action. He finds it more easy
to repeat the same course. He is hardening the heart against the
influence of the Holy Spirit. A further rejection of light places
him where a far stronger influence will be ineffectual to make an
abiding impression. (*Patriarchs and Prophets*, 268)

REFLECTION: *When we yield to temptation, we are more inclined to repeat that sin. Our hearts harden to spiritual things.*

FEBRUARY 21

Sorry for the Results

And Pharaoh sent, and called for Moses and Aaron, and said unto them, I have sinned this time: the Lord is righteous, and I and my people are wicked.
Exodus 9:27

There are many who fail to understand the true nature of repentance. Multitudes sorrow that they have sinned and even make an outward reformation because they fear that their wrongdoing will bring suffering upon themselves. But this is not repentance in the Bible sense. They lament the suffering rather than the sin. Such was the grief of Esau when he saw that the birthright was lost to him forever. ...

Pharaoh, when suffering under the judgments of God, acknowledged his sin in order to escape further punishment, but returned to his defiance of Heaven as soon as the plagues were stayed. These all lamented the results of sin, but did not sorrow for the sin itself.

But when the heart yields to the influence of the Spirit of God, the conscience will be quickened, and the sinner will discern something of the depth and sacredness of God's holy law, the foundation of His government in heaven and on earth. ... The sinner has a sense of the righteousness of Jehovah and feels the terror of appearing, in his own guilt and uncleanness, before the Searcher of hearts. He sees the love of God, the beauty of holiness, the joy of purity; he longs to be cleansed and to be restored to communion with Heaven. (*Steps to Christ*, 23, 24)

REFLECTION: *The prayer of David in Psalm 51 is a perfect example of true sorrow for sin. His repentance was without excuses. He was truly sorry for his actions. Three things must happen to have forgiveness of sin: sorrow for the sin, repentance of the sin, and turning away from the sin.*

The Paschal Lamb

*And they shall take of the blood, and strike it on the two side posts
and on the upper door post of the houses, wherein they shall eat it.*
Exodus 12:7

The Passover was to be both commemorative and typical,
not only pointing back to the deliverance from Egypt,
but forward to the greater deliverance which Christ was
to accomplish in freeing His people from the bondage of sin. The
sacrificial lamb represents "the Lamb of God," in whom is our
only hope of salvation. Says the apostle, "Christ our Passover is
sacrificed for us" (1 Corinthians 5:7). It was not enough that the
paschal lamb be slain; its blood must be sprinkled upon the door-
posts; so the merits of Christ's blood must be applied to the soul.
We must believe, not only that He died for the world, but that He
died for us individually. We must appropriate to ourselves the
virtue of the atoning sacrifice.

The hyssop used in sprinkling the blood was the symbol of
purification, being thus employed in the cleansing of the leper and of those defiled by contact with the dead. In the psalmist's prayer also its significance is seen: "Purge me with hyssop,
and I shall be clean: wash me, and I shall be whiter than snow"
(Psalm 51:7).

The lamb was to be prepared whole, not a bone of it being
broken: so not a bone was to be broken of the Lamb of God, who
was to die for us (John 19:36). Thus was also represented the
completeness of Christ's sacrifice. (*Patriarchs and Prophets, 277*)

REFLECTION: *In the blood Christ shed is forgiveness and purification
from sin. We must always keep before us that it was our sin that caused
the death of our Redeemer. In a spiritual sense, we crucify our Lord
every time we sin. Let us keep present in our minds how evil sin is.*

FEBRUARY 23

$\mathcal{S}$PIRITUAL $\mathcal{S}$TRENGTH

And thus shall ye eat it; with your loins girded, your shoes on your feet, and your staff in your hand; and ye shall eat it in haste: it is the LORD's Passover.
Exodus 12:11

The flesh was to be eaten. It is not enough even that we believe on Christ for the forgiveness of sin; we must by faith be constantly receiving spiritual strength and nourishment from Him through His word. Said Christ, "Except ye eat the flesh of the Son of man, and drink His blood, ye have no life in you. Whoso eateth My flesh, and drinketh My blood, hath eternal life" (John 6:53, 54). And to explain His meaning He said, "The words that I speak unto you, they are spirit, and they are life" (Verse 63). Jesus accepted His Father's law, wrought out its principles in His life, manifested its spirit, and showed its beneficent power in the heart.... The followers of Christ must be partakers of His experience. They must receive and assimilate the word of God so that it shall become the motive power of life and action. By the power of Christ they must be changed into His likeness, and reflect the divine attributes. They must eat the flesh and drink the blood of the Son of God, or there is no life in them. The spirit and work of Christ must become the spirit and work of His disciples. (*Patriarchs and Prophets*, 277)

REFLECTION: *It is not enough to only believe Christ is our Savior. We must be like Him. By His Grace and love we have the great opportunity, and responsibility, to emulate Him. It is by faith and not by sight that we follow Him wherever He goes — eating His flesh and drinking His blood. The impartation of the Holy Spirit is the impartation of the life of Christ. We cannot live the Christian life without the power of the Holy Spirit. Hence we cannot live the Christian life without the life of Christ dwelling in us.*

BITTER HERBS AND UNLEAVENED BREAD

And they shall eat the flesh in that night, roast with fire, and unleavened bread; and with bitter herbs they shall eat it.
Exodus 12:8

The lamb was to be eaten with bitter herbs, as pointing back to the bitterness of the bondage in Egypt. So when we feed upon Christ, it should be with contrition of heart, because of our sins. The use of unleavened bread also was significant. It was expressly enjoined in the law of the Passover, and as strictly observed by the Jews in their practice, that no leaven should be found in their houses during the feast. In like manner the leaven of sin must be put away from all who would receive life and nourishment from Christ. So Paul writes to the Corinthian church, "Purge out therefore the old leaven, that ye may be a new lump. … For even Christ our Passover is sacrificed for us: therefore let us keep the feast, not with old leaven, neither with the leaven of malice and wickedness; but with the unleavened bread of sincerity and truth" (1 Corinthians 5:7,8). …

As Moses rehearsed to Israel the provisions of God for their deliverance, "the people bowed the head and worshiped." The glad hope of freedom, the awful knowledge of the impending judgment upon their oppressors, the cares and labors incident to their speedy departure—all were for the time swallowed up in gratitude to their gracious Deliverer. (*Patriarchs and Prophets*, 278, 279)

REFLECTION: *The Israelite was saved by the blood, not by works, yet he was required to comply with all God expected them to do. By following God's commands he showed both love and trust in God.*

DELIVERED AT THE RED SEA

*And Moses said unto the people, Fear ye not, stand still, and see
the salvation of the LORD, which he will show to you to day: for the
Egyptians whom ye have seen to day, ye shall see them again no more
for ever. The LORD shall fight for you, and ye shall hold your peace.*
Exodus 14:13, 14

God in His providence brought the Hebrews into the mountain fastnesses before the sea, that He might manifest His power in their deliverance and signally humble the pride of their oppressors. He might have saved them in any other way, but He chose this method in order to test their faith and strengthen their trust in Him. The people were weary and terrified, yet if they had held back when Moses bade them advance, God would never have opened the path for them. It was "by faith" that "they passed through the Red Sea as by dry land" (Hebrews 11:29). In marching down to the very water, they showed that they believed the word of God as spoken by Moses. They did all that was in their power to do, and then the Mighty One of Israel divided the sea to make a path for their feet.

The great lesson here taught is for all time. Often the Christian life is beset by dangers, and duty seems hard to per-form. The imagination pictures impending ruin before and bond-age or death behind. Yet the voice of God speaks clearly, "Go forward." We should obey this command, even though our eyes cannot penetrate the darkness, and we feel the cold waves about our feet. (*Patriarchs and Prophets*, 290)

REFLECTION: *God does not eliminate the obstacles, but He gives us the strength to overcome them.*

*M*OSES' *S*ONG

Then sang Moses and the children of Israel this song unto the LORD,
and spake, saying, I will sing unto the LORD, for he hath triumphed
gloriously: the horse and his rider hath he thrown into the sea.
Exodus 15:1

*T*he dealings of God with His people should be often repeated. How frequently were the waymarks set up by
the Lord in His dealings with ancient Israel! Lest they
should forget the history of the past, He commanded Moses to
frame these events into song, that parents might teach them to
their children. They were to gather up memorials and to lay them
up in sight. Special pains were taken to preserve them, that when
the children should inquire concerning these things, the whole
story might be repeated. Thus the providential dealings and the
marked goodness and mercy of God in His care and deliverance
of His people were kept in mind. We are exhorted to call to "remembrance the former days, in which, after ye were illuminat-
ed, ye endured a great fight of afflictions" (Hebrews 10:32). For
His people in this generation the Lord has wrought as a won-
der-working God. The past history of the cause of God needs
to be often brought before the people, young and old. We need
often to recount God's goodness and to praise Him for His wonderful works.

"Sing unto the Lord, O ye saints of His, and give thanks at
the remembrance of His holiness" (Psalm 30:4). (*Testimonies for
the Church*, volume 6, 364, 365)

REFLECTION: *We have nothing to fear in the future except we forget how*
God has led us in the past. Remember and share God's past providences
with your spouses and children.

MANNA

And the house of Israel called the name thereof Manna: and it was like coriander seed, white; and the taste of it was like wafers made with honey.
Exodus 16:31

Every week during their long sojourn in the wilderness the Israelites witnessed a threefold miracle, designed to impress their minds with the sacredness of the Sabbath: a double quantity of manna fell on the sixth day, none on the seventh, and the portion needed for the Sabbath was preserved sweet and pure, when if any were kept over at any other time it became unfit for use.

In the circumstances connected with the giving of the manna, we have conclusive evidence that the Sabbath was not instituted, as many claim, when the law was given at Sinai. Before the Israelites came to Sinai they understood the Sabbath to be obligatory upon them. In being obliged to gather every Friday a double portion of manna in preparation for the Sabbath, when none would fall, the sacred nature of the day of rest was continually impressed upon them. And when some of the people went out on the Sabbath to gather manna, the Lord asked, "How long refuse ye to keep My commandments and My laws?" (*Patriarchs and Prophets*, 296)

REFLECTION: *The truth can always stand to be examined. We as humans love to put our slant on things and then claim we are honoring God. The absence of manna on Sabbath was just as miraculous as its provision the other six days of the week. Let us remember always to find and honor truth, instead of tradition.*

UNBELIEF OVER WATER

*And the people thirsted there for water; and the people murmured
against Moses, and said, Wherefore is this that thou hast brought us up
out of Egypt, to kill us and our children and our cattle with thirst?*
Exodus 17:3

After leaving the wilderness of Sin, the Israelites encamped in Rephidim. Here there was no water, and
again they distrusted the providence of God. In their
blindness and presumption the people came to Moses with the
demand, "Give us water that we may drink." But his patience
failed not. "Why chide ye with me?" he said; "wherefore do ye
tempt the Lord?" They cried in anger, "Wherefore is this, that
thou hast brought us up out of Egypt, to kill us and our children
and our cattle with thirst?" When they had been so abundantly
supplied with food, they remembered with shame their unbelief
and murmurings, and promised to trust the Lord in the future; but
they soon forgot their promise, and failed at the first trial of their
faith. The pillar of cloud that was leading them seemed to veil a
fearful mystery. And Moses — who was he? They questioned, and
what could be his object in bringing them from Egypt? Suspicion
and distrust filled their hearts, and they boldly accused him of
designing to kill them and their children by privations and hardships that he might enrich himself with their possessions. In the
tumult of rage and indignation they were about to stone him.
(*Patriarchs and Prophets*, 297)

REFLECTION: *It's so easy to forget God's leading in our everyday lives
when problems arise. These hardships build our faith and character to
trust Him who sees the beginning from the end.*

$\mathcal{C}$OVENANT $\mathcal{A}$GREEMENT

*And all the people answered together, and said, All that the LORD hath spoken
we will do. And Moses returned the words of the people unto the LORD.*
Exodus 19:8

God's favor toward Israel had always been conditional
on their obedience. At the foot of Sinai they had entered into covenant relationship with Him as His "peculiar treasure ... above all people." Solemnly they had promised
to follow in the path of obedience. "All that the Lord hath spoken we will do," they had said (Exodus 19:5, 8). And when, a
few days afterward, God's law was spoken from Sinai, and additional instruction in the form of statutes and judgments was
communicated through Moses, the Israelites with one voice had
again promised, "All the words which the Lord hath said will
we do." At the ratification of the covenant, the people had once
more united in declaring, "All that the Lord hath said will we do,
and be obedient" (Exodus 24:3, 7). God had chosen Israel as His
people, and they had chosen Him as their King.

Near the close of the wilderness wandering the conditions
of the covenant had been repeated ... "Now therefore hearken,"-
Moses had instructed Israel, "unto the statutes and unto the judgments, which I teach you, for to do them, that ye may live, and
go in and possess the land which the Lord God of your fathers
giveth you" (Deuteronomy 4:1–3). (*Prophets and Kings*, 293, 294)

REFLECTION: *Before the Hebrews were given the Ten Commandments,
they agreed to do all that God commanded. In like manner, we should
always be willing to do all that God asks.*

MARCH

THE FIRST COMMANDMENT

Thou shalt have no other gods before me.
Exodus 20:3

The law was not spoken at this time exclusively for the benefit of the Hebrews. God honored them by making them the guardians and keepers of His law, but it was to be held as a sacred trust for the whole world. The precepts of the Decalogue are adapted to all mankind, and they were given for the instruction and government of all. Ten precepts, brief, comprehensive, and authoritative, cover the duty of man to God and to his fellow man; and all based upon the great fundamental principle of love. "Thou shalt love the Lord thy God with all thy heart, and with all thy soul, and with all thy strength, and with all thy mind; and thy neighbor as thyself" (Luke 10:27; See also Deuteronomy 6:4, 5; Leviticus 19:18). In the Ten Commandments these principles are carried out in detail, and made applicable to the condition and circumstances of man.

"Thou shalt have no other gods before Me."

Jehovah, the eternal, self-existent, uncreated One, Himself the Source and Sustainer of all, is alone entitled to supreme reverence and worship. Man is forbidden to give to any other object the first place in his affections or his service. Whatever we cherish that tends to lessen our love for God or to interfere with the service due Him, of that do we make a god. (*Patriarchs and Prophets*, 305)

REFLECTION: *If we could keep the first commandment by always putting God first, we would inevitably keep the other nine commandments.*

MARCH 2

THE SECOND COMMANDMENT

Thou shalt not make unto thee any graven image, or any likeness of anything that is in heaven above, or that is in the earth beneath, or that is in the water under the earth: thou shalt not bow down thyself to them, nor serve them.
Exodus 20:4–6

*T*he second commandment forbids the worship of the true God by images or similitudes. Many heathen nations claimed that their images were mere figures or symbols by which the Deity was worshiped, but God has declared such worship to be sin. The attempt to represent the Eternal One by material objects would lower man's conception of God....

"I the Lord thy God am a jealous God." The close and sacred relation of God to His people is represented under the figure of marriage. Idolatry being spiritual adultery, the displeasure of God against it is fitly called jealousy.

"Visiting the iniquity of the fathers upon the children unto the third and fourth generation of them that hate Me." It is inevitable that children should suffer from the consequences of parental wrongdoing, but they are not punished for the parents' guilt, except as they participate in their sins....

"Showing mercy unto thousands of them that love Me, and keep My commandments." In prohibiting the worship of false gods, the second commandment by implication enjoins the worship of the true God. And to those who are faithful in His service, mercy is promised, not merely to the third and fourth generation as is the wrath threatened against those who hate Him, but to thousands of generations. (*Patriarchs and Prophets*, 306)

REFLECTION: *The first commandment tells us who to worship; the second how to worship Him. We are to worship Him in spirit and in truth.*

THE THIRD COMMANDMENT

Thou shalt not take the name of the LORD thy God in vain: for the
Lord will not hold him guiltless that taketh His name in vain.
Exodus 20:7

This commandment not only prohibits false oaths and common swearing, but it forbids us to use the name of God in a light or careless manner, without regard to its awful significance. By the thoughtless mention of God in common conversation, by appeals to Him in trivial matters, and by the frequent and thoughtless repetition of His name, we dishonor Him. "Holy and reverend is His name" (Psalm 111:9). All should meditate upon His majesty, His purity and holiness, that the heart may be impressed with a sense of His exalted character; and His holy name should be uttered with reverence and solemnity. (*Patriarchs and Prophets*, 306)

REFLECTION: *Many Christians use God's name in vain everyday. We hang crosses on our necks, wear "I love Jesus" pins, and do other things in vain because we really don't live for Him. For to know Him is to worship Him. To know Him is to reverence Him. To know Him is to honor Him. And finally, to know Him is to be like Him.*

MARCH 4

THE FOURTH COMMANDMENT

Remember the Sabbath day, to keep it holy. Six days shalt thou labor, and do all thy work: but the seventh day is the Sabbath of the LORD thy God:…for in six days the LORD made heaven and earth, the sea, and all that in them is, and rested the seventh day: wherefore the LORD blessed the Sabbath day, and hallowed it.
Exodus 20:8–11

The Sabbath is not introduced as a new institution but as having been founded at creation. It is to be remembered and observed as the memorial of the Creator's work. Pointing to God as the Maker of the heavens and the earth, it distinguishes the true God from all false gods. All who keep the seventh day signify by this act that they are worshipers of Jehovah. …

God has given men six days wherein to labor, and He requires that their own work be done in the six working days. Acts of necessity and mercy are permitted on the Sabbath, the sick and suffering are at all times to be cared for; but unnecessary labor is to be strictly avoided. … Those who discuss business matters or lay plans on the Sabbath are regarded by God as though engaged in the actual transaction of business. To keep the Sabbath holy, we should not even allow our minds to dwell upon things of a worldly character. (*Patriarchs and Prophets*, 307)

REFLECTION: *Let us not forget who created the Sabbath. No man, woman or child, however religious they may be, has the right to change what God made Holy. While the first commandment directs us to the true object of worship, the fourth designates a special time purely devoted to worship Him who has given us life.*

THE FIFTH COMMANDMENT

*Honor thy father and thy mother: that thy days may be long
upon the land which the LORD thy God giveth thee.*
Exodus 20:12

*P*arents are entitled to a degree of love and respect which is due to no other person. God Himself, who has placed upon them a responsibility for the souls committed to their charge, has ordained that during the earlier years of life, parents shall stand in the place of God to their children. And he who rejects the rightful authority of his parents is rejecting the authority of God. The fifth commandment requires children not only to yield respect, submission, and obedience to their parents, but also to give them love and tenderness, to lighten their cares, to guard their reputation, and to succor and comfort them in old age. It also enjoins respect for ministers and rulers and for all others to whom God has delegated authority.

This, says the apostle, "is the first commandment with promise" (Ephesians 6:2). To Israel, expecting soon to enter Canaan, it was a pledge to the obedient, of long life in that good land; but it has a wider meaning, including all the Israel of God, and promising eternal life upon the earth when it shall be freed from the curse of sin. (*Patriarchs and Prophets*, 308)

REFLECTION: *The second table of the Decalogue deals with human relationships. The family is the most important and fundamental unit in society, and therefore it is the first of the last six commandments.*

MARCH 6

The Sixth Commandment

Thou shalt not kill.
Exodus 20:13

*A*ll acts of injustice that tend to shorten life; the spirit of hatred and revenge, or the indulgence of any passion that leads to injurious acts toward others, or causes us even to wish them harm (for "whosoever hateth his brother is a murderer"'); a selfish neglect of caring for the needy or suffering; all self-indulgence or unnecessary deprivation or excessive labor that tends to injure health—all these are, to a greater or less degree, violations of the sixth commandment. (*Patriarchs and Prophets*, 308)

REFLECTION: *Talking evil of someone behind their back is murder. We must realize that "Thou shalt not kill" is much greater than physically killing someone. This is a commandment that needs to be more fully understood by Christians. More Christians will lose eternal life by disregarding this commandment than we can imagine. Let us ask the Lord to take hatred from our hearts. Only He can accomplish this.*

The Seventh Commandment

Thou shalt not commit adultery.
Exodus 20:14

*T*his commandment forbids not only acts of impurity, but sensual thoughts and desires, or any practice that tends to excite them. Purity is demanded not only in the outward life but in the secret intents and emotions of the heart. Christ, who taught the far-reaching obligation of the law of God, declared the evil thought or look to be as truly sin as is the unlawful deed. (*Patriarchs and Prophets*, 308)

When the thought of evil is loved and cherished, however secretly, said Jesus, it shows that sin still reigns in the heart. The soul is still in the gall of bitterness and in the bond of iniquity. He who finds pleasure in dwelling upon scenes of impurity, who indulges the evil thought, the lustful look, may behold in the open sin, with its burden of shame and heart-breaking grief, the true nature of the evil which he has hidden in the chambers of the soul. The season of temptation, under which, it may be, one falls into grievous sin, does not create the evil that is revealed, but only develops or makes manifest that which was hidden and latent in the heart. As a man "thinketh in his heart, so is he;" for out of the heart "are the issues of life" (Proverbs 23:7; 4:23). (*Thoughts from the Mount of Blessing*, 60)

REFLECTION: *The devil will put thoughts into our minds but we don't have to dwell on them. We need to be like Jesus and say, "Get behind me Satan." When these sinful thoughts come into the mind, think of something else. Singing a Christian song, even if sung in the mind and not out loud, will change your thoughts and feelings.*

THE EIGHTH COMMANDMENT

Thou shalt not steal.
Exodus 20:15

Both public and private sins are included in this prohibition. The eighth commandment condemns manstealing and slave dealing, and forbids wars of conquest. It condemns theft and robbery. It demands strict integrity in the minutest details of the affairs of life. It forbids overreaching in trade, and requires the payment of just debts or wages. It declares that every attempt to advantage oneself by the ignorance, weakness, or misfortune of another is registered as fraud in the books of heaven. (*Patriarchs and Prophets*, 309)

Those who thus shorten their lives and unfit themselves for service by disregarding nature's laws, are guilty of robbery toward God. And they are robbing their fellow men also. The opportunity of blessing others, the very work for which God sent them into the world, has by their own course of action been cut short.... The Lord holds us guilty when by our injurious habits we thus deprive the world of good. (*Christ's Object Lessons*, 346)

REFLECTION: *Often we think of stealing only in a monetary sense; However, to steal because we could have helped someone in need, but didn't, is for most, a new thought. Today, let us make better choices in our temperance.*

MARCH 9

T*HE* N*INTH* C*OMMANDMENT*

Thou shalt not bear false witness against thy neighbor.
Exodus 20:16

*F*alse speaking in any matter, every attempt or purpose to deceive our neighbor, is here included. An intention to deceive is what constitutes falsehood. By a glance of the eye, a motion of the hand, an expression of the countenance, a falsehood may be told as effectually as by words. All intentional overstatement, every hint or insinuation calculated to convey an erroneous or exaggerated impression, even the statement of facts in such a manner as to mislead, is falsehood. This precept forbids every effort to injure our neighbor's reputation by misrepresentation or evil surmising, by slander or tale bearing. Even the intentional suppression of truth, by which injury may result to others, is a violation of the ninth commandment. (*Patriarchs and Prophets*, 309)

REFLECTION: *Even silence, under circumstances when you know the slander to be false but don't speak in defense of the victim, is false witnessing. By holding our peace when it is in our power to defend, by failing to mention the good when evil is spoken, by encouraging evil with undue attention and eager ears, we assault the reputation of our neighbor.*

THE TENTH COMMANDMENT

*Thou shalt not covet thy neighbor's house, thou shalt not covet
thy neighbor's wife, nor his manservant, nor his maidservant,
nor his ox, nor his ass, nor anything that is thy neighbor's.*
Exodus 20:17

The tenth commandment strikes at the very root of all sins, prohibiting the selfish desire, from which springs the sinful act. He who in obedience to God's law refrains from indulging even a sinful desire for that which belongs to another will not be guilty of an act of wrong toward his fellow creatures.

Such were the sacred precepts of the Decalogue, spoken amid thunder and flame, and with a wonderful display of the power and majesty of the great Lawgiver. God accompanied the proclamation of His law with exhibitions of His power and glory, that His people might never forget the scene, and that they might be impressed with profound veneration for the Author of the law, the Creator of heaven and earth. He would also show to all men the sacredness, the importance, and the permanence of His law.

The people of Israel were overwhelmed with terror. The awful power of God's utterances seemed more than their trembling hearts could bear. For as God's great rule of right was presented before them, they realized as never before the offensive character of sin, and their own guilt in the sight of a holy God. (*Patriarchs and Prophets*, 309)

REFLECTION: *To covet is to desire. It is not an outward act, but may lead to one. This makes covetousness a state of mind, a condition of the heart.*

LAW CONCERNING THE POOR

But the seventh year thou shalt let it rest and lie still; that the poor of thy people may eat: and what they leave the beasts of the field shall eat. In like manner thou shalt deal with thy vineyard, and with thy oliveyard.
Exodus 23:11

The law of God gave the poor a right to a certain portion of the produce of the soil. When hungry, a man was at liberty to go to his neighbor's field or orchard or vineyard, and eat of the grain or fruit to satisfy his hunger. It was in accordance with this permission that the disciples of Jesus plucked and ate of the standing grain as they passed through a field upon the Sabbath day. ...

Every seventh year special provision was made for the poor. The sabbatical year, as it was called, began at the end of the harvest. At the seedtime, which followed the ingathering, the people were not to sow; they should not dress the vineyard in the spring; and they must expect neither harvest nor vintage. Of that which the land produced spontaneously they might eat while fresh, but they were not to lay up any portion of it in their storehouses. The yield of this year was to be free for the stranger, the fatherless, and the widow, and even for the creatures of the field (Exodus 23:10, 11; Leviticus 25:5). (*Patriarchs and Prophets*, 531)

REFLECTION: *Just think, even the creatures of the field were at liberty to eat freely! When we have this kind of love, we'll be forming the characters God has intended us to have from the beginning.*

THE SANCTUARY

And let them make me a sanctuary; that I may dwell among them.
Exodus 25:8

God commanded Moses for Israel, "Let them make Me a sanctuary; that I may dwell among them" (Exodus 25:8), and He abode in the sanctuary, in the midst of His people. Through all their weary wandering in the desert, the symbol of His presence was with them. So Christ set up His tabernacle in the midst of our human encampment. He pitched His tent by the side of the tents of men, that He might dwell among us, and make us familiar with His divine character and life. "The Word became flesh, and tabernacled among us (and we beheld His glory, glory as of the Only Begotten from the Father), full of grace and truth" (John 1:14, R. V., margin). (*The Desire of Ages*, 23)

The sanctuary in heaven, in which Jesus ministers in our behalf, is the great original, of which the sanctuary built by Moses was a copy. God placed His Spirit upon the builders of the earthly sanctuary. The artistic skill displayed in its construction was a manifestation of divine wisdom. The walls had the appearance of massive gold, reflecting in every direction the light of the seven lamps of the golden candlestick. The table of shewbread and the altar of incense glittered like burnished gold. The gorgeous curtain which formed the ceiling, inwrought with figures of angels in blue and purple and scarlet, added to the beauty of the scene. And beyond the second veil was the holy Shekinah, the visible manifestation of God's glory, before which none but the high priest could enter and live. (*Great Controversy*, 414)

REFLECTION: *The sanctuary services illustrated God's great plan of salvation. Even in the book of Revelation Jesus is described walking in the Sanctuary. To know His plan of salvation more fully, we must learn all we can about the Sanctuary.*

MARCH 13

THE OFFERING FOR SIN

Speak unto the children of Israel, and say unto them, If any man of you bring an offering unto the LORD, ye shall bring your offering of the cattle, even of the herd, and of the flock.
Leviticus 1:2

When man fell by transgression the law was not changed, but a remedial system was established to bring him back to obedience. The promise of a Saviour was given, and sacrificial offerings pointing forward to the death of Christ as the great sin offering were established. But had the law of God never been transgressed, there would have been no death, and no need of a Saviour; consequently there would have been no need of sacrifices....

The sacrificial system, committed to Adam, was also perverted by his descendants. Superstition, idolatry, cruelty, and licentiousness corrupted the simple and significant service that God had appointed. Through long intercourse with idolaters the people of Israel had mingled many heathen customs with their worship; therefore the Lord gave them at Sinai definite instruction concerning the sacrificial service. (*Patriarchs and Prophets*, 363, 364)

REFLECTION: *The sanctuary service had become necessary because men had strayed far from God. Man's mind had become so darkened that a simple illustration of the gospel needed to be instituted.*

Symbolic Transfer of Sin

*And he shall lay his hand upon the head of the sin offering, and
slay the sin offering in the place of the burnt offering.*
Leviticus 4:29

The most important part of the daily ministration was the
service performed in behalf of individuals. The repentant sinner brought his offering to the door of the tabernacle, and, placing his hand upon the victim's head, confessed
his sins, thus in figure transferring them from himself to the innocent sacrifice. By his own hand the animal was then slain, and
the blood was carried by the priest into the holy place and sprinkled before the veil, behind which was the ark containing the law
that the sinner had transgressed. By this ceremony the sin was,
through the blood, transferred in figure to the sanctuary. In some
cases the blood was not taken into the holy place; but the flesh
was then to be eaten by the priest, as Moses directed the sons of
Aaron, saying, "God hath given it you to bear the iniquity of the
congregation" (Leviticus 10:17). Both ceremonies alike symbolized the transfer of the sin from the penitent to the sanctuary.

Such was the work that went on day by day throughout the
year. The sins of Israel being thus transferred to the sanctuary,
the holy places were defiled, and a special work became necessary for the removal of the sins. God commanded that an atonement be made for each of the sacred apartments, as for the altar,
to "cleanse it, and hallow it from the uncleanness of the children
of Israel" (Leviticus 16:19). (*Patriarchs and Prophets,*354,355)

REFLECTION: *As the penitent placed his hands upon the sacrifice, he was
transferring the full burden of his sin to Christ.*

MARCH 15

CLEAN AND UNCLEAN FOODS

Speak unto the children of Israel, saying, These are the beasts
which ye shall eat among all the beasts that are on the earth.
Leviticus 11:2

The diet appointed man in the beginning did not include animal food. Not till after the Flood, when every green thing on the earth had been destroyed, did man receive permission to eat flesh.

In choosing man's food in Eden, the Lord showed what was the best diet; in the choice made for Israel He taught the same lesson. He brought the Israelites out of Egypt and undertook their training, that they might be a people for His own possession. Through them He desired to bless and teach the world. He provided them with the food best adapted for this purpose, not flesh, but manna, "the bread of heaven." It was only because of their discontent and their murmuring for the fleshpots of Egypt that animal food was granted them, and this only for a short time. Its use brought disease and death to thousands. Yet the restriction to a nonflesh diet was never heartily accepted...." (*Ministry of Healing*, 311)

There are few who realize as they should how much their habits of diet have to do with their health, their character, their usefulness in this world, and their eternal destiny. The appetite should ever be in subjection to the moral and intellectual powers. The body should be servant to the mind, and not the mind to the body. (*Patriarchs and Prophets*, 562)

REFLECTION: *If there was ever a time to glorify God in our bodies, it is, no doubt, today. We must understand that when we claim to be His, then we have a responsibility to glorify Him with our choices. Our eating habits will honor or dishonor God.*

PREVENTING THE SPREAD OF DISEASE

*And the vessel of earth, that he toucheth which hath the issue, shall
be broken: and every vessel of wood shall be rinsed in water.*
Leviticus 15:12

In the teaching that God gave to Israel, the preservation
of health received careful attention. The people who had
come from slavery with the uncleanly and unhealthful
habits which it engenders, were subjected to the strictest training
in the wilderness before entering Canaan. Health principles were
taught and sanitary laws enforced.

Not only in their religious service, but in all the affairs of
daily life was observed the distinction between clean and unclean. All who came in contact with contagious or contaminating
diseases were isolated from the encampment, and they were not
permitted to return without thorough cleansing of both the person and the clothing. In the case of one afflicted with a contaminating disease, the direction was given:

"Every bed, whereon he lieth, ... is unclean: and everything,
whereon he sitteth, shall be unclean. And whosoever toucheth
his bed shall wash his clothes, and bathe himself in water,
and be unclean until the even" (Leviticus 15:4–6). (*Ministry of
Healing*, 277, 278)

REFLECTION: *By learning these lessons concerning our physical health,
we may better understand God's moral law concerning our spiritual
health. What an awesome God we serve!*

TAKING ADVANTAGE OF OTHERS

*Thou shalt not defraud thy neighbour, neither rob him: the wages of him
that is hired shall not abide with thee all night until the morning.*
Leviticus 19:13

God's word sanctions no policy that will enrich one class by the oppression and suffering of another. In all our business transactions it teaches us to put ourselves in the place of those with whom we are dealing, to look not only on our own things, but also on the things of others. He who would take advantage of another's misfortunes in order to benefit himself, or who seeks to profit himself through another's weakness or incompetence, is a transgressor both of the principles and of the precepts of the word of God.

The plan of life that God gave to Israel was intended as an object lesson for all mankind. If these principles were carried out today, what a different place this world would be! (*Ministry of Healing*, 187, 188)

REFLECTION: *If we loved others as much as ourselves, the government would never have to take care of the poor. How different the world would be if everyone lived by these principles! Today, think of someone in real need and help them out.*

ℒove 𝒯hy 𝒩eighbor

Thou shalt not avenge, nor bear any grudge against the children of thy people, but thou shalt love thy neighbour as thyself: I am the Lord.
Leviticus 19:18

Through Moses the Lord had said, "Thou shalt not hate thy brother in thine heart. ... Thou shalt not avenge, nor bear any grudge against the children of thy people, but thou shalt love thy neighbor as thyself" (Leviticus 19:17, 18).

The spirit of hatred and revenge originated with Satan, and it led him to put to death the Son of God. Whoever cherishes malice or unkindness is cherishing the same spirit, and its fruit will be unto death. In the revengeful thought the evil deed lies enfolded, as the plant in the seed. "Whosoever hateth his brother is a murderer: and ye know that no murderer hath eternal life abiding in him" (1 John 3:15).

Jesus proceeded to show His hearers what it means to keep the commandments of God—that it is a reproduction in themselves of the character of Christ. For in Him, God was daily made manifest before them. (*Thoughts from the Mount of Blessing*, 55, 56)

REFLECTION: *Loving those who love us is much easier than loving those who don't love us. As we allow the love of Christ to permeate our very souls, we will, in turn, begin to have a love that cannot ever come from us alone — a Christlike love.*

MARCH 19

B̄e Ye Holy

*Sanctify yourselves therefore, and be ye holy: for I am the L*ORD *your God.*
Leviticus 20:7

It is the work of conversion and sanctification to reconcile men to God by bringing them into accord with the principles of His law. In the beginning, man was created in the image of God. He was in perfect harmony with the nature and the law of God; the principles of righteousness were written upon his heart. But sin alienated him from his Maker. He no longer reflected the divine image. His heart was at war with the principles of God's law. "The carnal mind is enmity against God: for it is not subject to the law of God, neither indeed can be" (Romans 8:7). But "God so loved the world, that He gave His only-begotten Son," that man might be reconciled to God. Through the merits of Christ he can be restored to harmony with his Maker. His heart must be renewed by divine grace; he must have a new life from above. This change is the new birth, without which, says Jesus, "he cannot see the kingdom of God." (*The Great Controversy*, 467)

REFLECTION: *We can only have the righteousness the law demands by receiving the righteousness of Christ.*

MARCH 20

$\mathcal{L}$EVITES

But the Levites after the tribe of their fathers were not numbered among them.
Numbers 1:47

$\mathcal{B}$y divine direction the tribe of Levi was set apart for the service of the sanctuary. In the earliest times every man was the priest of his own household…Now… the Lord accepted the tribe of Levi for the work of the sanctuary. By this signal honor He manifested His approval of their fidelity, both in adhering to His service and in executing His judgments when Israel apostatized in the worship of the golden calf. The priesthood, however, was restricted to the family of Aaron. Aaron and his sons alone were permitted to minister before the Lord; the rest of the tribe were entrusted with the charge of the tabernacle and its furniture, and they were to attend upon the priests in their ministration, but they were not to sacrifice, to burn incense, or to see the holy things till they were covered. …

Moses at the burning bush was directed to put off his sandals, for the ground whereon he stood was holy. So the priests were not to enter the sanctuary with shoes upon their feet. Particles of dust cleaving to them would desecrate the holy place. They were to leave their shoes in the court before entering the sanctuary, and also to wash both their hands and their feet before ministering in the tabernacle or at the altar of burnt offering. Thus was constantly taught the lesson that all defilement must be put away from those who would approach into the presence of God. (*Patriarchs and Prophets*, 350)

REFLECTION: *God has a plan for us. The way He wants things done — though we might not agree or understand — is always the best plan. From the beginning, He has set in motion a way of conducting our lives and who should do certain things. Let us learn to follow his plan more and more each day.*

PASSOVER'S PERFECT SACRIFICE

*They shall leave none of it unto the morning, nor break any bone of it:
according to all the ordinances of the passover they shall keep it.*
Numbers 9:12

The Passover was to be both commemorative and typical, not only pointing back to the deliverance from Egypt, but forward to the greater deliverance which Christ was to accomplish in freeing His people from the bondage of sin. The sacrificial lamb represents "the Lamb of God," in whom is our only hope of salvation. Says the apostle, "Christ our Passover is sacrificed for us" (1 Corinthians 5:7). It was not enough that the paschal lamb be slain; its blood must be sprinkled upon the door-posts; so the merits of Christ's blood must be applied to the soul. We must believe, not only that He died for the world, but that He died for us individually. We must appropriate to ourselves the virtue of the atoning sacrifice.

The hyssop used in sprinkling the blood was the symbol of purification, being thus employed in the cleansing of the leper and of those defiled by contact with the dead. In the psalmist's prayer also its significance is seen: "Purge me with hyssop, and I shall be clean: wash me, and I shall be whiter than snow" (Psalm 51:7).

"The lamb was to be prepared whole, not a bone of it being broken: so not a bone was to be broken of the Lamb of God, who was to die for us (John 19:36). Thus was also represented the completeness of Christ's sacrifice. (*Patriarchs and Prophets*, 277)

REFLECTION: *To think that Christ died for me personally. Oh what a thought! As we contemplate how much Christ loves us individually, we will want to serve Him more fully.*

MARCH 22

CONTAGIOUS COMPLAINING

*And when the people complained, it displeased the LORD: and the LORD
heard it; and his anger was kindled; and the fire of the LORD burnt among
them, and consumed them that were in the uttermost parts of the camp.*
Numbers 11:1

After three days' journey open complaints were heard.
These originated with the mixed multitude, many of
whom were not fully united with Israel, and were
continually watching for some cause of censure. The complainers were not pleased with the direction of the march, and they
were continually finding fault with the way in which Moses was
leading them, though they well knew that he, as well as they, was
following the guiding cloud. Dissatisfaction is contagious, and
it soon spread in the encampment. (*Patriarchs and Prophets*, 377)

REFLECTION: *Complainers generally keep complaining. Tragically, dissatisfaction has a terrible way of spreading. Today, make a decision to
not complain. Don't even allow someone in your presence to get you
into that situation. Take the high road.*

*M*EEKEST *M*AN

Now the man Moses was very meek, above all the
men which were upon the face of the earth.
Numbers 12:3

*P*atience and gentleness under wrong were not characteristics prized by the heathen or by the Jews. The statement made by Moses under the inspiration of the Holy Spirit, that he was the meekest man upon the earth, would not have been regarded by the people of his time as a commendation; it would rather have excited pity or contempt. But Jesus places meekness among the first qualifications for His kingdom. In His own life and character the divine beauty of this precious grace is revealed.

Jesus, the brightness of the Father's glory, thought "it not a thing to be grasped to be on an equality with God, but emptied Himself, taking the form of a servant" (Philippians 2:6, 7, R.V., margin). Through all the lowly experiences of life He consented to pass, walking among the children of men, not as a king, to demand homage, but as one whose mission it was to serve others. There was in His manner no taint of bigotry, no cold austerity. The world's Redeemer had a greater than angelic nature, yet united with His divine majesty were meekness and humility that attracted all to Himself.

Jesus emptied Himself, and in all that He did, self did not appear. He subordinated all things to the will of His Father." (*Thoughts from the Mount of Blessing*, 14)

REFLECTION: *Jesus bids us, "Learn of Me; for I am meek and lowly in heart." "If any man will come after Me, let him deny himself." (Matthew 11:29, Matthew 16:24)*

Unbelief Limits God's Power

And wherefore hath the LORD brought us unto this land, to fall by the sword, that our wives and our children should be a prey? Were it not better for us to return into Egypt?
Numbers 14:3

*I*n their unbelief they limited the power of God and distrusted the hand that had hitherto safely guided them. And they repeated their former error of murmuring against Moses and Aaron. "This, then, is the end of our high hopes," they said. "This is the land we have traveled all the way from Egypt to possess." They accused their leaders of deceiving the people and bringing trouble upon Israel.

The people were desperate in their disappointment and despair. A wail of agony arose and mingled with the confused murmur of voices. Caleb comprehended the situation, and, bold to stand in defense of the word of God, he did all in his power to counteract the evil influence of his unfaithful associates. For an instant the people were stilled to listen to his words of hope and courage respecting the goodly land. He did not contradict what had already been said; the walls were high and the Canaanites strong. But God had promised the land to Israel. "Let us go up at once and possess it," urged Caleb; "for we are well able to overcome it." (*Patriarchs and Prophets*, 388)

REFLECTION: *Like Caleb, we should all stand boldly for the Lord. God never promised that everything would be easy, but He did promise that by faith He would get us through it.*

A Spirit of Jealousy

And they gathered themselves together against Moses and against Aaron, and said unto them, Ye take too much upon you, seeing all the congregation are holy, every one of them, and the LORD is among them: wherefore then lift ye up yourselves above the congregation of the LORD?
Numbers 16:3

Korah, the leading spirit in this movement, was a Levite, of the family of Kohath, and a cousin of Moses; he was a man of ability and influence. Though appointed to the service of the tabernacle, he had become dissatisfied with his position and aspired to the dignity of the priesthood. The bestowal upon Aaron and his house of the priestly office, which had formerly devolved upon the first-born son of every family, had given rise to jealousy and dissatisfaction, and for some time Korah had been secretly opposing the authority of Moses and Aaron, though he had not ventured upon any open act of rebellion. He finally conceived the bold design of overthrowing both the civil and the religious authority. He did not fail to find sympathizers. (*Patriarchs and Prophets*, 395)

REFLECTION: *So often we get jealous of others and think we have the same right as they have. Korah had tremendous abilities. In his own eyes he felt more capable than Aaron and his sons. With God, it's not all about capabilities, but how and who should perform the duties. If we will do it God's way and trust in Him, we will be developing a most important part of our characters.*

The Brazen Serpent

And Moses made a serpent of brass, and put it upon a
pole, and it came to pass, that if a serpent had bitten any
man, when he beheld the serpent of brass, he lived.
Numbers 21:9

The people well knew that there was no power in the serpent of brass to cause such a change in those who looked upon it. The healing virtue was from God alone. In His wisdom He chose this way of displaying His power. By this simple means the people were made to realize that this affliction had been brought upon them by their sins. They were also assured that while obeying God they had no reason to fear, for He would preserve them.

The lifting up of the brazen serpent was to teach Israel an important lesson. They could not save themselves from the fatal effect of the poison in their wounds. God alone was able to heal them. Yet they were required to show their faith in the provision which He had made. They must look in order to live. It was their faith that was acceptable with God, and by looking upon the serpent their faith was shown. They knew that there was no virtue in the serpent itself, but it was a symbol of Christ; and the necessity of faith in His merits was thus presented to their minds. (*Patriarchs and Prophets*, 430)

REFLECTION: *The Bible says that faith without works is dead. Our characters can only grow by our trust and faith in Jesus. We, like God's people of old, must look in order to live. In the end it will be our faith through Christ that is acceptable to God.*

MARCH 27

DALLYING WITH TEMPTATION

And God said unto Balaam, Thou shalt not go with them;
thou shalt not curse the people: for they are blessed.
Numbers 22:12

B alaam was once a good man and a prophet of God; but he had apostatized, and had given himself up to covetousness; yet he still professed to be a servant of the Most High. He was not ignorant of God's work in behalf of Israel; and when the messengers announced their errand, he well knew that it was his duty to refuse the rewards of Balak and to dismiss the ambassadors. But he ventured to dally with temptation, and urged the messengers to tarry with him that night, declaring that he could give no decided answer till he had asked counsel of the Lord. Balaam knew that his curse could not harm Israel. God was on their side, and so long as they were true to Him no adverse power of earth or hell could prevail against them. But his pride was flattered by the words of the ambassadors, 'He whom thou blessest is blessed, and he whom thou cursest is cursed.' The bribe of costly gifts and prospective exaltation excited his covetousness. He greedily accepted the offered treasures, and then, while professing strict obedience to the will of God, he tried to comply with the desires of Balak. (*Patriarchs and Prophets*, 439)

REFLECTION: *Very often we profess to be Christians, but in our every day lives we serve self. Let us learn that serving self will only harm us, as it did Balaam. When these temptations arise, which they will, Let our hearts say, "I would rather obey God than man."*

ISRAEL IS SEDUCED

And Israel abode in Shittim, and the people began to commit whoredom with the daughters of Moab. And they called the people unto the sacrifices of their gods: and the people did eat, and bowed down to their gods. And Israel joined himself unto Baalpeor: and the anger of the Lord was kindled against Israel.
Numbers 25:1–3

At first there was little intercourse between the Israelites and their heathen neighbors, but after a time Midianitish women began to steal into the camp. Their appearance excited no alarm, and so quietly were their plans conducted that the attention of Moses was not called to the matter. It was the object of these women, in their association with the Hebrews, to seduce them into transgression of the law of God, to draw their attention to heathen rites and customs, and lead them into idolatry. These motives were studiously concealed under the garb of friendship, so that they were not suspected, even by the guardians of the people....

It was not long before the poison had spread, like a deadly infection, through the camp of Israel. Those who would have conquered their enemies in battle were overcome by the wiles of heathen women. The people seemed to be infatuated. The rulers and the leading men were among the first to transgress, and so many of the people were guilty that the apostasy became national. "Israel joined himself unto Baalpeor." (*Patriarchs and Prophets*, 454)

REFLECTION: *Although we should always respect leadership, we must also be certain they are reflecting God's will. We are able to do this from the Bible. Leadership is of no value unless God directs it. This story would have read differently if the leadership had stayed true to God.*

*T*RAITORS ON THE *I*NSIDE

*And Israel joined himself unto Baalpeor: and the anger
of the LORD was kindled against Israel.*
Numbers 25:3

*I*t was when the Israelites were in a condition of outward ease and security that they were led into sin. They failed to keep God ever before them, they neglected prayer and cherished a spirit of self-confidence. Ease and self-indulgence left the citadel of the soul unguarded, and debasing thoughts found entrance. It was the traitors within the walls that overthrew the strongholds of principle and betrayed Israel into the power of Satan. It is thus that Satan still seeks to compass the ruin of the soul. A long preparatory process, unknown to the world, goes on in the heart before the Christian commits open sin. The mind does not come down at once from purity and holiness to depravity, corruption, and crime. It takes time to degrade those formed in the image of God to the brutal or the satanic. By beholding we become changed. By the indulgence of impure thoughts man can so educate his mind that sin which he once loathed will become pleasant to him. (*Patriarchs and Prophets*, 459)

REFLECTION: *When things go well for us there is greater danger that we will put the Lord on the back burner, yet it's really a time we need Him the most. Satan will, if we let him, ruin us one day at a time. Don't fall for it.*

THE PROMISED LAND

*And the LORD said unto Moses, Get thee up into this mount Abarim,
and see the land which I have given unto the children of Israel.*
Numbers 27:12

The Lord announced to Moses that the appointed time for the possession of Canaan was at hand; and as the aged prophet stood upon the heights overlooking the river Jordan and the Promised Land, he gazed with deep interest upon the inheritance of his people. Would it be possible that the sentence pronounced against him for his sin at Kadesh might be revoked? With deep earnestness he pleaded, "O Lord God, Thou hast begun to show Thy servant Thy greatness, and Thy mighty hand; for what god is there in heaven or in earth, that can do according to Thy works, and according to Thy might? I pray Thee, let me go over, and see the good land that is beyond Jordan, that goodly mountain, and Lebanon" (Deuteronomy 3:24-27).

The answer was, "Let it suffice thee; speak no more unto Me of this matter. Get thee up into the top of Pisgah, and lift up thine eyes westward, and northward, and southward, and eastward, and behold it with thine eyes; for thou shalt not go over this Jordan."

Without a murmur Moses submitted to the decree of God. (*Patriarchs and Prophets*, 462)

REFLECTION: *What a disappointment Moses must have felt when he asked God to let him go into the promised land but God replied, "Speak no more unto Me of this matter." When Moses heard this he did not murmur or complain. Even in his great disappointment he would not let go of his Savior. Let us learn this most important lesson.*

WHAT ONE CHERISHED SIN WILL DO

And they slew the kings of Midian, beside the rest of them that were slain; namely, Evi, and Rekem, and Zur, and Hur, and Reba, five kings of Midian: Balaam also the son of Beor they slew with the sword.
Numbers 31:8

The fate of Balaam was similar to that of Judas, and their characters bear a marked resemblance to each other. Both these men tried to unite the service of God and mammon, and met with signal failure. Balaam acknowledged the true God, and professed to serve Him; Judas believed in Jesus as the Messiah, and united with His followers. ...Judas expected by his connection with Christ to secure wealth and promotion in that worldly kingdom which, as he believed, the Messiah was about to set up. The failure of his hopes drove him to apostasy and ruin. Both Balaam and Judas had received great light and enjoyed special privileges, but a single cherished sin poisoned the entire character and caused their destruction.

It is a perilous thing to allow an unchristian trait to live in the heart. One cherished sin will, little by little, debase the character, bringing all its nobler powers into subjection to the evil desire. The removal of one safeguard from the conscience, the indulgence of one evil habit, one neglect of the high claims of duty, breaks down the defenses of the soul and opens the way for Satan to come in and lead us astray." (*Patriarchs and Prophets*, 452)

REFLECTION: *The only safe course for us is to pray daily from a sincere heart as did David, "Hold up my goings in Thy paths, that my footsteps slip not" (Psalm 17:5). (Patriarchs and Prophets, 452)*

April

$\mathscr{H}$OLINESS $\mathscr{D}$EFINED

*And he humbled thee, and suffered thee to hunger, and fed thee with
manna, which thou knewest not, neither did thy fathers know; that he
might make thee know that man doth not live by bread only, but by every
word that proceedeth out of the mouth of the LORD doth man live.*
Deuteronomy 8:3

*I*t is not a conclusive evidence that a man is a Christian
because he manifests spiritual ecstasy under extraordi-
nary circumstances. Holiness is not rapture: it is an entire
surrender of the will to God; it is living by every word that proceeds from the mouth of God; it is doing the will of our heavenly
Father; it is trusting God in trial, in darkness as well as in the
light; it is walking by faith and not by sight; it is relying on God
with unquestioning confidence, and resting in His love. (*Acts of
the Apostles*, 51)

REFLECTION: *Today, more than ever, we are in danger of calling
Christianity something it isn't. Just because we go to church or quote
scriptures does not make us Christians. Many charming pastors and
TV evangelists mention God or read some scripture and we automat-
ically believe they are Christians. Don't be fooled. Let's live by every
word that proceeds from the mouth of God.*

GOD EXPRESSLY FORBIDS SPIRITUALISM

*There shall not be found among you any one that maketh his son or
his daughter to pass through the fire, or that useth divination, or an
observer of times, or an enchanter, or a witch, Or a charmer, or a consulter
with familiar spirits, or a wizard, or a necromancer. For all that do
these things are an abomination unto the* LORD*: and because of these
abominations the* LORD *thy God doth drive them out from before thee.*
Deuteronomy 18:10–12

The Bible declares that the dead know not anything, that
their thoughts have perished; they have no part in anything that is done under the sun; they know nothing of
the joys or sorrows of those who were dearest to them on earth.

Furthermore, God has expressly forbidden all pretend-
ed communication with departed spirits. In the days of the
Hebrews there was a class of people who claimed, as do the
spiritualists of today, to hold communication with the dead.
But the "familiar spirits," as these visitants from other worlds
were called, are declared by the Bible to be "the spirits of devils."
(Compare Numbers 25:1–3; Psalm 106:28; 1 Corinthians 10:20;
Revelation 16:14.) The work of dealing with familiar spirits was
pronounced an abomination to the Lord, and was solemnly forbidden under penalty of death (Leviticus 19:31; 20:27).… But
spiritualism, which numbers its converts by hundreds of thousands, yea, by millions, which has made its way into scientific
circles, which has invaded churches, and has found favor in leg-
islative bodies, and even in the courts of kings—this mammoth
deception is but a revival, in a new disguise, of the witchcraft
condemned and prohibited of old. *(The Great Controversy,* 556)

REFLECTION: *From the very beginning, the devil has tried to brainwash
us into believing that no matter what we do, will never die. He is a liar
and deceiver*

BLESSING OF BIBLE STUDY

*The secret things belong unto the LORD our God: but those
things which are revealed belong unto us and to our children
for ever, that we may do all the words of this law.*
Deuteronomy 29:29

The more we search the Bible, the deeper is our conviction that it is the word of the living God, and human reason bows before the majesty of divine revelation.

God intends that to the earnest seeker the truths of His word shall be ever unfolding. While "the secret things belong unto the Lord our God: ... those things which are revealed belong unto us and to our children" (Deuteronomy 29:29). The idea that certain portions of the Bible cannot be understood has led to neglect of some of its most important truths. The fact needs to be emphasized, and often repeated, that the mysteries of the Bible are not such because God has sought to conceal truth, but because our own weakness or ignorance makes us incapable of comprehending or appropriating truth. The limitation is not in His purpose, but in our capacity. Of those very portions of Scripture often passed by as impossible to be understood, God desires us to understand as much as our minds are capable of receiving. "All Scripture is given by inspiration of God," that we may be "thoroughly furnished unto all good works" (2 Timothy 3:16, 17). (*Education*, 170)

REFLECTION: *The Bible is very complex. Behind each verse is an endless sea of spiritual food. God so desires us to learn more and more about Him as we search the scriptures like we would mine for gold. Our goal should be to dig deeper every day and then practice what God has shown us.*

APRIL 4

*L*IFE AND *D*EATH

See, I have set before thee this day life and good, and death and evil.
Deuteronomy 30:15

"The wages of sin is death; but the gift of God is eternal life through Jesus Christ our Lord" (Romans 6:23). While life is the inheritance of the righteous, death is the portion of the wicked. Moses declared to Israel: "I have set before thee this day life and good, and death and evil" (Deuteronomy 30:15). The death referred to in these scriptures is not that pronounced upon Adam, for all mankind suffer the penalty of his transgression. It is "the second death" that is placed in contrast with everlasting life.

In consequence of Adam's sin, death passed upon the whole human race. All alike go down into the grave. And through the provisions of the plan of salvation, all are to be brought forth from their graves. "There shall be a resurrection of the dead, both of the just and unjust;" … "for as in Adam all die, even so in Christ shall all be made alive" (Acts 24:15; 1 Corinthians 15:22). But a distinction is made between the two classes that are brought forth. "All that are in the graves shall hear His voice, and shall come forth; they that have done good, unto the resurrection of life; and they that have done evil, unto the resurrection of damnation" (John 5:28, 29). They who have been "accounted worthy" of the resurrection of life are "Blessed and holy; … on such the second death hath no power" (Revelation 20:6). (*The Great Controversy*, 544)

REFLECTION: *But those who have not, through repentance and faith, secured pardon, must receive the penalty of transgression – "the wages of sin."* (The Great Controversy, 544)

THE GREAT PROPHET

*And there arose not a prophet since in Israel like unto
Moses, whom the LORD knew face to face.*
Deuteronomy 34:10

Moses gained that which went with him throughout the years of his toilsome and care-burdened life—a sense of the personal presence of the Divine One. Not merely did he look down the ages for Christ to be made manifest in the flesh; he saw Christ accompanying the host of Israel in all their travels. When misunderstood and misrepresented, when called to bear reproach and insult, to face danger and death, he was able to endure "as seeing Him who is invisible" (Hebrews 11:27).

Moses did not merely think of God, he saw Him. God was the constant vision before him. Never did he lose sight of His face.

To Moses faith was no guesswork; it was a reality. He believed that God ruled his life in particular; and in all its details he acknowledged Him. For strength to withstand every temptation, he trusted in Him.

The great work assigned him he desired to make in the highest degree successful, and he placed his whole dependence upon divine power. He felt his need of help, asked for it, by faith grasped it, and in the assurance of sustaining strength went forward. (*Education*, 63)

REFLECTION: *Those who do the greatest work for God are those who feel the greatest need for divine help. For forty years in the wilderness, this was the experience of Moses.*

The Nations Feared

And as soon as we had heard [these things], our hearts did melt, neither
did there remain any more courage in any man, because of you: for the
Lord your God, he is God in heaven above, and in earth beneath.
Joshua 2:11

This exercise of divine power in behalf of Israel was designed also to increase the fear with which they were
regarded by the surrounding nations, and thus prepare
the way for their easier and complete triumph. When the tidings
that God had stayed the waters of Jordan before the children of
Israel, reached the kings of the Amorites and of the Canaanites,
their hearts melted with fear. The Hebrews had already slain the
five kings of Midian, the powerful Sihon, king of the Amorites,
and Og of Bashan, and now the passage over the swollen and im-
petuous Jordan filled all the surrounding nations with terror. To
the Canaanites, to all Israel, and to Joshua himself, unmistakable
evidence had been given that the living God, the King of heaven
and earth, was among His people, and that He would not fail
them nor forsake them.

Heathen nations had reproached the Lord and His people
because the Hebrews had failed to take possession of Canaan, as
they expected, soon after leaving Egypt. Their enemies had triumphed because Israel had wandered so long in the wilderness,
and they had mockingly declared that the God of the Hebrews
was not able to bring them into the Promised Land. The Lord
had now signally manifested His power and favor in opening
the Jordan before His people, and their enemies could no longer
reproach them. (*Patriarchs and Prophets*, 485, 486)

REFLECTION: *Their desert wanderings were over; they would now come*
to possess the land by the power of God. We, like Israel of old, have
plenty of evidence that He is real and still as powerful as in those days.

GOD TESTS HIS PEOPLE'S FAITH

And it shall come to pass, as soon as the soles of the feet of the priests that bear the ark of the LORD, the Lord of all the earth, shall rest in the waters of Jordan, that the waters of Jordan shall be cut off from the waters that come down from above; and they shall stand upon an heap.
Joshua 3:13

In the upbuilding of His work the Lord does not always make everything plain before His servants. He sometimes tries the confidence of His people by bringing about circumstances which compel them to move forward in faith. Often He brings them into strait and trying places, and bids them advance when their feet seem to be touching the waters of Jordan. It is at such times, when the prayers of His servants ascend to Him in earnest faith, that God opens the way before them and brings them out into a large place. (*The Acts of the Apostles*, 357)

REFLECTION: *As we exercise our faith, it will grow. Faith comes by hearing, and hearing by the word of God. When things look most discouraging, we need to remember Joshua 3. We might have to get our feet wet, but it will be worth it all.*

CIRCLING JERICHO

*And ye shall compass the city, all ye men of war, and go round about the
city once. Thus shalt thou do six days. And seven priests shall bear before
the ark seven trumpets of rams' horns: and the seventh day ye shall compass
the city seven times, and the priests shall blow with the trumpets.*
Joshua 6:3, 4

*I*n obedience to the divine command Joshua marshaled
the armies of Israel. No assault was to be made. They
were simply to make the circuit of the city, bearing the
ark of God and blowing upon trumpets. First came the warriors,
a body of chosen men, not now to conquer by their own skill
and prowess, but by obedience to the directions given them from
God. Seven priests with trumpets followed. Then the ark of God,
surrounded by a halo of divine glory, was borne by priests clad
in the dress denoting their sacred office. The army of Israel followed, each tribe under its standard. Such was the procession
that compassed the doomed city. No sound was heard but the
tread of that mighty host and the solemn peal of the trumpets,
echoing among the hills and resounding through the streets of
Jericho. The circuit completed, the army returned in silence to
their tents, and the ark was restored to its place in the tabernacle.

With wonder and alarm the watchmen of the city marked
every move, and reported to those in authority.(*Patriarchs and
Prophets,* 488)

REFLECTION: *The soldiers of Jericho inspected their defenses, but what
might this God of the Hebrews, who parted the Red Sea, do to their city?*

APRIL 9

THE BLAST OF THE TRUMPETS

*And it shall come to pass, that when they make a long blast with the
ram's horn, and when ye hear the sound of the trumpet, all the people
shall shout with a great shout; and the wall of the city shall fall down
flat, and the people shall ascend up every man straight before him.*
Joshua 6:5

For six days the host of Israel made the circuit of the
city. The seventh day came, and with the first dawn of
light, Joshua marshaled the armies of the Lord. Now
they were directed to march seven times around Jericho, and at
a mighty peal from the trumpets to shout with a loud voice, for
God had given them the city.

The vast army marched solemnly around the devoted walls.
All was silent, save the measured tread of many feet, and the oc-
casional sound of the trumpet, breaking the stillness of the early
morning. The massive walls of solid stone seemed to defy the
siege of men. The watchers on the walls looked on with rising
fear, as, the first circuit ended, there followed a second, then a
third, a fourth, a fifth, a sixth. What could be the object of these
mysterious movements? What mighty event was impending?
They had not long to wait. As the seventh circuit was completed,
the long procession paused, the trumpets, which for an interval
had been silent, now broke forth in a blast that shook the very
earth. (*Patriarchs and Prophets*, 491)

REFLECTION: *The watchers on the wall would soon tumble with the
wall, but knew it not.*

God Will Fight Our Battles

And it came to pass at the seventh time, when the priests
blew with the trumpets, Joshua said unto the people,
Shout; for the LORD hath given you the city.
Joshua 6:16

The simple act of blowing a blast upon the trumpet by the army of Joshua around Jericho, and by Gideon's little band about the hosts of Midian, was made effectual, through the power of God, to overthrow the might of His enemies. The most complete system that men have ever devised, apart from the power and wisdom of God, will prove a failure, while the most unpromising methods will succeed when divinely appointed and entered upon with humility and faith. Trust in God and obedience to His will are as essential to the Christian in the spiritual warfare as to Gideon and Joshua in their battles with the Canaanites. By the repeated manifestations of His power in behalf of Israel, God would lead them to have faith in Him—with confidence to seek His help in every emergency. He is just as willing to work with the efforts of His people now and to accomplish great things through weak instrumentalities. All heaven awaits our demand upon its wisdom and strength. God is "able to do exceeding abundantly above all that we ask or think" (Ephesians 3:20). (*Patriarchs and Prophets*, 554)

The Israelites had not gained the victory by their own power; the conquest had been wholly the Lord's; and as the first fruits of the land, the city, with all that it contained, was to be devoted as a sacrifice to God. (*Patriarchs and Prophets*, 491)

REFLECTION: *The Battle of Jericho proved that God would fight battles for His people. He is just as willing now to fight your battles. Our responsibility is to be submitted and committed to His will, daily.*

A DEADLY SIN

And Achan answered Joshua, and said, Indeed I have sinned
against the LORD *God of Israel, and thus and thus have I done.*
Joshua 7:20

Achan's sin was committed in defiance of the most direct and solemn warnings and the most mighty manifestations of God's power. "Keep yourselves from the accursed thing, lest ye make yourselves accursed," had been the proclamation to all Israel. The command was given immediately after the miraculous passage of the Jordan, and the recognition of God's covenant by the circumcision of the people—after the observance of the Passover, and the appearance of the Angel of the covenant, the Captain of the Lord's host. It had been followed by the overthrow of Jericho, giving evidence of the destruction which will surely overtake all transgressors of God's law. The fact that divine power alone had given the victory to Israel, that they had not come into possession of Jericho by their own strength, gave solemn weight to the command prohibiting them from partaking of the spoils. God, by the might of His own word, had overthrown this stronghold; the conquest was His, and to Him alone the city with all that it contained was to be devoted.

Of the millions of Israel there was but one man who, in that solemn hour of triumph and of judgment, had dared to transgress the command of God. (*Patriarchs and Prophets, 495, 496*)

REFLECTION: *Achan's deadly sin was rooted in covetousness — the most common sin and the one most lightly regarded.*

APRIL 12

PROVIDENCE CONVINCED THE HEATHEN

And Joshua made peace with them, and made a league with them, to
let them live: and the princes of the congregation sware unto them.
Joshua 9:15

The marvelous providences connected with Israel's deliverance from Egyptian bondage and with their occupancy of the Promised Land led many of the heathen to recognize the God of Israel as the Supreme Ruler. "The Egyptians shall know," had been the promise, "that I am the Lord, when I stretch forth Mine hand upon Egypt, and bring out the children of Israel from among them" (Exodus 7:5). Even proud Pharaoh was constrained to acknowledge Jehovah's power. "Go, serve the Lord," he urged Moses and Aaron, "and bless me also" (Exodus 12:31, 32).

The advancing hosts of Israel found that knowledge of the mighty workings of the God of the Hebrews had gone before them, and that some among the heathen were learning that He alone was the true God. In wicked Jericho the testimony of a heathen woman was, "The Lord your God, He is God in heaven above, and in earth beneath" (Joshua 2:11). The knowledge of Jehovah that had thus come to her, proved her salvation. By faith "Rahab perished not with them that believed not" (Hebrews 11:31). And her conversion was not an isolated case of God's mercy toward idolaters who acknowledged His divine authority. In the midst of the land a numerous people — the Gibeonites — renounced their heathenism and united with Israel, sharing in the blessings of the covenant. (*Prophets and Kings*, 369)

REFLECTION: *God is the Maker of all. With Him there is no distinction of nationality, race, or caste. He loves everyone, but He hates all sin. Let us renounce our sins to Him today.*

APRIL 13

The Sun Stood Still

Then spake Joshua to the LORD in the day when the LORD delivered up the Amorites before the children of Israel, and he said in the sight of Israel, Sun, stand thou still upon Gibeon; and thou, Moon, in the valley of Ajalon.
Joshua 10:13

By marching all night he brought his forces before Gibeon in the morning. Scarcely had the confederate princes mustered their armies about the city when Joshua was upon them. The attack resulted in the utter discomfiture of the assailants. The immense host fled before Joshua up the mountain pass to Beth-horon; and having gained the height, they rushed down the precipitous descent upon the other side. Here a fierce hailstorm burst upon them. "The Lord cast down great stones from heaven … they were more which died with hailstones than they whom the children of Israel slew with the sword."

While the Amorites were continuing their headlong flight, intent on finding refuge in the mountain strongholds, Joshua, looking down from the ridge above, saw that the day would be too short for the accomplishment of his work. If not fully routed, their enemies would again rally, and renew the struggle. "Then spake Joshua to the Lord, … and he said in the sight of Israel, Sun, stand thou still upon Gibeon; and thou, Moon, in the valley of Ajalon. And the sun stood still, and the moon stayed, until the people had avenged themselves upon their enemies. … The sun stood still in the midst of heaven, and hasted not to go down about a whole day." (*Patriarchs and Prophets*, 508)

REFLECTION: *Before evening the enemy had fallen, showing that men of prayer receive power from above. This miracle was preserved for us that we may know what He did for His people then and what He will do for us now.*

APRIL 14

*L*ACKING *C*OURAGE

And the children of Joseph said, The hill is not enough for us: and all the Canaanites that dwell in the land of the valley have chariots of iron, both they who are of Bethshean and her towns, and they who are of the valley of Jezreel.
Joshua 17:16

nother claim concerning the division of the land revealed a spirit widely different from that of Caleb. It was presented by the children of Joseph, the tribe of Ephraim with the half tribe of Manasseh. In consideration of their superior numbers, these tribes demanded a double portion of territory. The lot designated for them was the richest in the land, including the fertile Plain of Sharon; but many of the principal towns in the valley were still in possession of the Canaanites, and the tribes shrank from the toil and danger of conquering their possessions, and desired an additional portion in territory already subdued. The tribe of Ephraim was one of the largest in Israel, as well as the one to which Joshua himself belonged, and its members naturally regarded themselves as entitled to special consideration. "Why hast thou given me but one lot and one portion to inherit," they said, "seeing I am a great people?" But no departure from strict justice could be won from the inflexible leader.

His answer was, "If thou be a great people, then get thee up to the wood country, and cut down for thyself there in the land of the Perizzites and of the giants, if Mount Ephraim be too narrow for thee." (*Patriarchs and Prophets*, 513)

REFLECTION: *Their reply showed their lack of faith and courage to drive out the Canaanites. But God had pledged His power; all they needed was faith in that power. (Patriarchs and Prophets, 514)*

CHOOSE THE RIGHT

And if it seem evil unto you to serve the LORD, choose you this day
whom ye will serve; whether the gods which your fathers served that
were on the other side of the flood, or the gods of the Amorites, in whose
land ye dwell: but as for me and my house, we will serve the LORD.
Joshua 24:15

Every child should understand the true force of the will. He should be led to see how great is the responsibility involved in this gift. The will is the governing power in the nature of man, the power of decision, or choice. Every human being possessed of reason has power to choose the right. In every experience of life, God's word to us is, "Choose you this day whom ye will serve" (Joshua 24:15). Everyone may place his will on the side of the will of God, may choose to obey Him, and by thus linking himself with divine agencies, he may stand where nothing can force him to do evil. In every youth, every child, lies the power, by the help of God, to form a character of integrity and to live a life of usefulness.

The parent or teacher who by such instruction trains the child to self-control will be the most useful and permanently successful. To the superficial observer his work may not appear to the best advantage; it may not be valued so highly as that of the one who holds the mind and will of the child under absolute authority; but after years will show the result of the better method of training. (*Education*, 289)

REFLECTION: *Forcing the will almost never works for the good. Although we need to be lovingly firm at times, we should never force. God never forces but always has consequences for good or for evil.*

DEATH OF JOSHUA

*And it came to pass after these things, that Joshua the son of Nun,
the servant of the LORD, died, being an hundred and ten years old.*
Joshua 24:29

Joshua endeavored to lead his hearers to weigh well their words, and refrain from vows which they would be unprepared to fulfill. With deep earnestness they repeated the declaration: "Nay; but we will serve the Lord." Solemnly consenting to the witness against themselves that they had chosen Jehovah, they once more reiterated their pledge of loyalty: "The Lord our God will we serve, and His voice will we obey."

"So Joshua made a covenant with the people that day, and set them a statute and an ordinance in Shechem." Having written an account of this solemn transaction, he placed it, with the book of the law, in the side of the ark. And he set up a pillar as a memorial, saying, "Behold, this stone shall be a witness unto us; for it hath heard all the words of the Lord which He spake unto us; it shall be therefore a witness unto you, lest ye deny your God. So Joshua let the people depart, every man unto his inheritance."

Joshua's work for Israel was done. He had "wholly followed the Lord;" and in the book of God he is written, "The servant of Jehovah." The noblest testimony to his character as a public leader is the history of the generation that had enjoyed his labors: "Israel served the Lord all the days of Joshua, and all the days of the elders that overlived Joshua." (*Patriarchs and Prophets*, 524)

REFLECTION: *Joshua was a faithful leader who directed the people to God, not to himself. Let us be like faithful Joshua in all the areas of our life. His character was one we should emulate.*

THE EARLY JUDGES

*And it came to pass, when Israel was strong, that they put the
Canaanites to tribute, and did not utterly drive them out.*
Judges 1:28

After the settlement in Canaan the tribes made no vigorous effort to complete the conquest of the land. Satisfied with the territory already gained, their zeal soon flagged, and the war was discontinued. "When Israel was strong, ... they put the Canaanites to tribute, and did not utterly drive them out" (Judges 1:28).

The Lord had faithfully fulfilled, on His part, the promises made to Israel; Joshua had broken the power of the Canaanites, and had distributed the land to the tribes. It only remained for them, trusting in the assurance of divine aid, to complete the work of dispossessing the inhabitants of the land. But this they failed to do. By entering into league with the Canaanites they directly transgressed the command of God, and thus failed to fulfill the condition on which He had promised to place them in possession of Canaan.

From the very first communication of God with them at Sinai, they had been warned against idolatry. Immediately after the proclamation of the law the message was sent them by Moses concerning the nations of Canaan: "Thou shalt not bow down to their gods, nor serve them, nor do after their works: but thou shalt utterly overthrow them, and quite break down their images. And ye shall serve the Lord your God, and He shall bless thy bread, and thy water; and I will take sickness away from the midst of thee" (Exodus 23:24, 25). (*Patriarchs and Prophets*, 543)

REFLECTION: *As long as Israel remained faithful to God, He would subdue their foes. From the beginning God gave us a blueprint. By beholding we become changed. We should always be careful who our friends are. Choose them wisely.*

No Half-Hearted Warriors

*And the LORD said unto Gideon, The people are yet too many;
bring them down unto the water, and I will try them for thee
there: and it shall be, that of whom I say unto thee, This shall go
with thee, the same shall go with thee; and of whomsoever I say
unto thee, This shall not go with thee, the same shall not go.*

Judges 7:4

"All the Midianites and the Amalekites and the children of the east were gathered together, and went over, and pitched in the valley of Jezreel." The entire force under Gideon's command numbered only thirty-two thousand men; but with the vast host of the enemy spread out before him, the word of the Lord came to him: "The people that are with thee are too many for Me to give the Midianites into their hands, lest Israel vaunt themselves against Me, saying, Mine own hand hath saved me. Now therefore go to, proclaim in the ears of the people, saying, Whosoever is fearful and afraid, let him return and depart early from Mount Gilead." Those who were unwilling to face danger and hardships, or whose worldly interests would draw their hearts from the work of God, would add no strength to the armies of Israel. Their presence would prove only a cause of weakness. (*Patriarchs and Prophets*, 548)

REFLECTION: *Had Israel triumphed with their many soldiers, even the cowards would have taken credit for the victory. So God greatly reduced their numbers. Let us never forget that it is trust and faith in the One who is mighty that wins battles.*

TRUE AND FALSE REPENTANCE

And the children of Israel cried unto the LORD, saying, We have sinned against thee, both because we have forsaken our God, and also served Baalim.
Judges 10:10

A gain the people sought help from Him whom they had so forsaken and insulted. 'The children of Israel cried unto the Lord, saying, We have sinned against Thee, both because we have forsaken our God, and also served Baalim.' But sorrow had not worked true repentance. The people mourned because their sins had brought suffering upon themselves, but not because they had dishonored God by transgression of His holy law. True repentance is more than sorrow for sin. It is a resolute turning away from evil.

The Lord answered them through one of His prophets: "Did I not deliver you from the Egyptians, and from the Amorites, from the children of Ammon, and from the Philistines? The Zidonians also, and the Amalekites, and the Maonites, did oppress you; and ye cried to Me, and I delivered you out of their hand. Yet ye have forsaken Me, and served other gods: wherefore I will deliver you no more. Go and cry unto the gods which ye have chosen; let them deliver you in the time of your tribulation."

These solemn and fearful words carry the mind forward to another scene—the great day of final judgment—when the rejecters of God's mercy and the despisers of His grace shall be brought face to face with His justice. (*Patriarchs and Prophets*, 557)

REFLECTION: *We too can forsake the Lord for other gods. They may be in the form of celebrities, money, fame, fashion, or even our cherished opinions. These are not idols of metal, stone, or wood, but they're idols nonetheless.*

*N*EAREST *K*INSMAN

*And Naomi said unto her daughter in law, Blessed be he of the L*ORD*, who*
hath not left off his kindness to the living and to the dead. And Naomi
said unto her, The man is near of kin unto us, one of our next kinsmen.
Ruth 2:20

Of Christ's relation to His people, there is a beautiful illustration in the laws given to Israel. When through poverty a Hebrew had been forced to part with his patrimony,
and to sell himself as a bondservant, the duty of redeeming him
and his inheritance fell to the one who was nearest of kin. (See
Leviticus 25:25, 47–49; Ruth 2:20.) So the work of redeeming us
and our inheritance, lost through sin, fell upon Him who is "near
of kin" unto us. It was to redeem us that He became our kinsman.
Closer than father, mother, brother, friend, or lover is the Lord
our Saviour. "Fear not," He says, "for I have redeemed thee, I
have called thee by thy name; thou art Mine." "Since thou wast
precious in My sight, thou hast been honorable, and I have loved
thee: therefore will I give men for thee, and people for thy life"
(Isaiah 43:1, 4).

Christ loves the heavenly beings that surround His throne;
but what shall account for the great love wherewith He has loved
us? We cannot understand it, but we can know it true in our own
experience. (*The Desire of Ages*, 327)

REFLECTION: *If we claim Christ as our Elder Brother, we should also*
regard one another as brothers and sisters of our Lord.

APRIL 21

Two Wives

And he had two wives; the name of the one was Hannah, and the name of the other Peninnah: and Peninnah had children, but Hannah had no children.

1 Samuel 1:2

Elkanah, a Levite of Mount Ephraim, was a man of wealth and influence, and one who loved and feared the Lord. His wife, Hannah, was a woman of fervent piety. Gentle and unassuming, her character was marked with deep earnestness and a lofty faith.

The blessing so earnestly sought by every Hebrew was denied this godly pair; their home was not gladdened by the voice of childhood; and the desire to perpetuate his name led the husband—as it had led many others—to contract a second marriage. But this step, prompted by a lack of faith in God, did not bring happiness. Sons and daughters were added to the household; but the joy and beauty of God's sacred institution had been marred and the peace of the family was broken. Peninnah, the new wife, was jealous and narrow-minded, and she bore herself with pride and insolence. To Hannah, hope seemed crushed and life a weary burden; yet she met the trial with uncomplaining meekness.

The burden which she could share with no earthly friend she cast upon God. Earnestly she pleaded that He would take away her reproach and grant her the precious gift of a son to nurture and train for Him. And she made a solemn vow that if her request were granted, she would dedicate her child to God, even from its birth. (*Patriarchs and Prophets*, 569)

REFLECTION: *Hannah's prayer was granted: she would bear a son, and she would name him Samuel. Hannah would also keep her promise to the Lord. Let us remember to keep our promises also.*

A Mother's Vow

Therefore also I have lent him to the LORD; as long as he liveth he shall be lent to the LORD. And he worshipped the LORD there.

1 Samuel 1:28

As soon as the little one was old enough to be separated from his mother, she fulfilled her vow. She loved her child with all the devotion of a mother's heart; day by day, as she watched his expanding powers and listened to his childish prattle, her affections entwined about him more closely. He was her only son, the special gift of Heaven; but she had received him as a treasure consecrated to God, and she would not withhold from the Giver His own.

Once more Hannah journeyed with her husband to Shiloh and presented to the priest, in the name of God, her precious gift, saying, "For this child I prayed; and the Lord hath given me my petition which I asked of Him: therefore also I have lent him to the Lord; as long as he liveth he shall be lent to the Lord." Eli was deeply impressed by the faith and devotion of this woman of Israel. Himself an overindulgent father, he was awed and humbled as he beheld this mother's great sacrifice in parting with her only child, that she might devote him to the service of God. He felt reproved for his own selfish love, and in humiliation and reverence he bowed before the Lord and worshiped. (*Patriarchs and Prophets*, 571)

REFLECTION: *Hannah trained Samuel to love and reverence God as a young child; now she would leave him with the high priest to receive instruction. The promise she made was not easy to keep. Even Eli was awed and humbled. Today, let us build a noble character in promise-keeping, no matter how difficult it may be.*

APRIL 23

Eli's Sons

Now the sons of Eli were sons of Belial; they knew not the Lord.
1 Samuel 2:12

*E*li was priest and judge in Israel. He held the highest and most responsible positions among the people of God. As a man divinely chosen for the sacred duties of the priesthood, and set over the land as the highest judicial authority, he was looked up to as an example, and he wielded a great influence over the tribes of Israel. But although he had been appointed to govern the people, he did not rule his own household. Eli was an indulgent father. Loving peace and ease, he did not exercise his authority to correct the evil habits and passions of his children. Rather than contend with them or punish them, he would submit to their will and give them their own way. Instead of regarding the education of his sons as one of the most important of his responsibilities, he treated the matter as of little consequence. The priest and judge of Israel had not been left in darkness as to the duty of restraining and governing the children that God had given to his care. But Eli shrank from this duty, because it involved crossing the will of his sons, and would make it necessary to punish and deny them. Without weighing the terrible consequences that would follow his course, he indulged his children in whatever they desired and neglected the work of fitting them for the service of God and the duties of life" (*Patriarchs and Prophets*, 575)

REFLECTION: *While Abraham commanded his children, Eli allowed his children to control him. Never should we allow our children to rule us. Let us, as parents, work together in the love of Christ and teach our children the principles of God's love.*

Israel Wants a King

And said unto him, Behold, thou art old, and thy sons walk not in
thy ways: now make us a king to judge us like all the nations.
1 Samuel 8:5

*I*n the rejection of the ways of God for the ways of men, the
downfall of Israel began. Thus also it continued, until the
Jewish people became a prey to the very nations whose
practices they had chosen to follow.

As a nation the children of Israel failed of receiving the benefits that God desired to give them. They did not appreciate His
purpose or co-operate in its execution. But though individuals
and peoples may thus separate themselves from Him, His purpose for those who trust Him is unchanged. "Whatsoever God
doeth, it shall be forever" (Ecclesiastes 3:14).

While there are different degrees of development and different manifestations of His power to meet the wants of men in the
different ages, God's work in all time is the same. The Teacher is
the same. God's character and His plan are the same. With Him
"is no variableness, neither shadow of turning" (James 1:17).

The experiences of Israel were recorded for our instruction.
"All these things happened unto them for ensamples: and they
are written for our admonition, upon whom the ends of the
world are come" (1 Corinthians 10:11). With us, as with Israel of
old, success in education depends on fidelity in carrying out the
Creator's plan. Adherence to the principles of God's word will
bring as great blessings to us as it would have brought to the
Hebrew people. (*Education*, 50)

REFLECTION: *Even today, we readily turn to men for direction instead*
of the Lord. God's word will bring great blessings to us and build our
character for the heavenly kingdom.

APRIL 25

$\mathcal{S}$AUL IS $\mathcal{K}$ING

*And Samuel said to all the people, See ye him whom the L*ORD
hath chosen, that there is none like him among all the people?
And all the people shouted, and said, God save the king.
1 Samuel 10:24

*I*n Saul, God had given to Israel a king after their own heart,
as Samuel said when the kingdom was confirmed to Saul
at Gilgal, "Behold the king whom ye have chosen, and
whom ye have desired" (1 Samuel 12:13). Comely in person, of
noble stature and princely bearing, his appearance accorded with
their conceptions of royal dignity; and his personal valor and his
ability in the conduct of armies were the qualities which they regarded as best calculated to secure respect and honor from other
nations. They felt little solicitude that their king should possess
those higher qualities which alone could fit him to rule with justice and equity. They did not ask for one who had true nobility of
character, who possessed the love and fear of God. They had not
sought counsel from God as to the qualities a ruler should possess, in order to preserve their distinctive, holy character as His
chosen people. They were not seeking God's way, but their own
way. Therefore God gave them such a king as they desired — one
whose character was a reflection of their own. Their hearts were
not in submission to God, and their king also was unsubdued by
divine grace. Under the rule of this king they would obtain the
experience necessary in order that they might see their error, and
return to their allegiance to God. (*Patriarchs and Prophets*, 636)

REFLECTION: *Often God, out of love, will allow us to have what we
want even though it's not good; but He even uses this for our character
building and learning process.*

A Stubborn King

And Saul said, Bring hither a burnt offering to me, and
peace offerings. And he offered the burnt offering.
1 Samuel 13:9

At Gilgal, but a short time before, Saul had presumed to officiate as priest, contrary to the command of God. When reproved by Samuel, he had stubbornly justified himself. Now, when his own command was disobeyed — though the command was unreasonable and had been violated through ignorance — the king and father sentenced his son to death.

The people refused to allow the sentence to be executed. Braving the anger of the king, they declared, "Shall Jonathan die, who hath wrought this great salvation in Israel? God forbid: as the Lord liveth, there shall not one hair of his head fall to the ground; for he hath wrought with God this day." The proud monarch dared not disregard this unanimous verdict, and the life of Jonathan was preserved.

Saul could not but feel that his son was preferred before him, both by the people and by the Lord. Jonathan's deliverance was a severe reproof to the king's rashness. He felt a presentiment that his curses would return upon his own head. He did not longer continue the war with the Philistines, but returned to his home, moody and dissatisfied. (*Patriarchs and Prophets*, 625)

REFLECTION: *Those who excuse and justify their own sins are often the most severe in judging and condemning others (Patriarchs and Prophets, 625). We would do well to remember Jesus' words, "With what judgment ye judge, ye shall be judged: and with what measure ye mete, it shall be measured to you again" (Matthew 7:2).*

God Rejects Saul as King

It repenteth me that I have set up Saul to be king: for he is turned back from following me, and hath not performed my commandments. And it grieved Samuel; and he cried unto the LORD all night.
1 Samuel 15:11

When called to the throne, Saul had a humble opinion of his own capabilities, and was willing to be instructed. He was deficient in knowledge and experience and had serious defects of character. But the Lord granted him the Holy Spirit as a guide and helper, and placed him in a position where he could develop the qualities requisite for a ruler of Israel. Had he remained humble, seeking constantly to be guided by divine wisdom, he would have been enabled to discharge the duties of his high position with success and honor. Under the influence of divine grace every good quality would have been gaining strength, while evil tendencies would have lost their power. This is the work which the Lord proposes to do for all who consecrate themselves to Him. There are many whom He has called to positions in His work because they have a humble and teachable spirit. In His providence He places them where they may learn of Him. He will reveal to them their defects of character, and to all who seek His aid He will give strength to correct their errors. (*Patriarchs and Prophets*, 632)

REFLECTION: *Success made Saul self-confident. Victory in battle, from the very beginning, had kindled pride in his heart. How easy it is for the prideful heart to turn from the reproofs of God.*

APRIL 28

$\mathcal{G}$od $\mathcal{C}$hooses $\mathcal{D}$avid

And he sent, and brought him in. Now he was ruddy, and
withal of a beautiful countenance, and goodly to look to.
And the LORD said, Arise, anoint him: for this is he.
1 Samuel 16:12

A few miles south of Jerusalem, 'the city of the great King,' is Bethlehem, where David, the son of Jesse, was born more than a thousand years before the infant Jesus was cradled in the manger and worshiped by the Wise Men from the East. Centuries before the advent of the Saviour, David, in the freshness of boyhood, kept watch of his flocks as they grazed on the hills surrounding Bethlehem. The simple shepherd boy sang the songs of his own composing, and the music of his harp made a sweet accompaniment to the melody of his fresh young voice. The Lord had chosen David, and was preparing him, in his solitary life with his flocks, for the work He designed to commit to his trust in after years.

While David was thus living in the retirement of his humble shepherd's life, the Lord God was speaking about him to the prophet Samuel. "And the Lord said unto Samuel, How long wilt thou mourn for Saul, seeing I have rejected him from reigning over Israel? fill thine horn with oil, and go, I will send thee to Jesse the Bethlehemite: for I have provided Me a king among his sons." (Patriarchs and Prophets, 637)

REFLECTION: *Our characters are built through the responsibilities we perform every day. Let us never think that God is not working on us because, in our minds, we believe we are doing some menial task. So it was with David. God was preparing him to be the next king by herding sheep.*

APRIL 29

FEELINGS OF JEALOUSY

*And Eliab his eldest brother heard when he spake unto the men; and
Eliab's anger was kindled against David, and he said, Why camest
thou down hither? ...I know thy pride, and the naughtiness of thine
heart; for thou art come down that thou mightest see the battle.*
1 Samuel 17:28

The armies of Israel were depressed. Their courage failed. They said one to another, "Have ye seen this man that is come up? Surely to defy Israel is he come up." In shame and indignation, David exclaimed, "Who is this uncircumcised Philistine, that he should defy the armies of the living God?"

Eliab, David's eldest brother, when he heard these words, knew well the feelings that were stirring the young man's soul. Even as a shepherd, David had manifested daring, courage, and strength but rarely witnessed; and the mysterious visit of Samuel to their father's house, and his silent departure, had awakened in the minds of the brothers suspicions of the real object of his visit. Their jealousy had been aroused as they saw David honored above them … and now the question which he asked was regarded by Eliab as a censure upon his own cowardice in making no attempt to silence the giant of the Philistines. The elder brother exclaimed angrily, "Why camest thou down hither?" (*Patriarchs and Prophets*, 645)

REFLECTION: *One character trait we must overcome is being jealous of others. Jealousy is a terrible disease. It started with Satan. David's brothers should have prayed with and encouraged David. We should do the same and never entertain jealousy.*

David Slays Goliath

Therefore David ran, and stood upon the Philistine, and took his sword, and drew it out of the sheath thereof, and slew him, and cut off his head therewith. And when the Philistines saw their champion was dead, they fled.
1 Samuel 17:51

There was a ring of fearlessness in his tone, a look of triumph and rejoicing upon his fair countenance. This speech, given in a clear, musical voice, rang out on the air, and was distinctly heard by the listening thousands marshaled for war. The anger of Goliath was roused to the very highest heat. In his rage he pushed up the helmet that protected his forehead and rushed forward to wreak vengeance upon his opponent. The son of Jesse was preparing for his foe. "And it came to pass, when the Philistine arose, and came and drew nigh to meet David, that David hasted, and ran toward the army to meet the Philistine. And David put his hand in his bag, and took thence a stone, and slang it, and smote the Philistine in the forehead, that the stone sunk into his forehead; and he fell upon his face to the earth."

Amazement spread along the lines of the two armies. They had been confident that David would be slain; but when the stone went whizzing through the air, straight to the mark, they saw the mighty warrior tremble, and reach forth his hands, as if he were struck with sudden blindness. The giant reeled, and staggered, and like a smitten oak, fell to the ground. (*Patriarchs and Prophets*, 648)

REFLECTION: *David had learned to put his whole trust in the Lord and charged Goliath like he was the giant. David did not hesitate to take Goliath's sword and sever his head. The Philistines were smitten with terror and all of Israel rejoiced.*

MAY

MAY 1

$\mathcal{S}$AUL'S $\mathcal{J}$EALOUSY OF $\mathcal{D}$AVID

And the women answered one another as they played, and said,
Saul hath slain his thousands, and David his ten thousands.
1 Samuel 18:7

One company sang, "Saul hath slain his thousands," while another company took up the strain, and responded, "And David his ten thousands." The demon of jealousy entered the heart of the king. He was angry because David was exalted above himself in the song of the women of Israel. In place of subduing these envious feelings, he displayed the weakness of his character, and exclaimed. "They have ascribed unto David ten thousands, and to me they have ascribed but thousands: and what can he have more but the kingdom?"

One great defect in the character of Saul was his love of approbation. This trait had had a controlling influence over his actions and thoughts; everything was marked by his desire for praise and self-exaltation. His standard of right and wrong was the low standard of popular applause. No man is safe who lives that he may please men, and does not seek first for the approbation of God. It was the ambition of Saul to be first in the estimation of men; and when this song of praise was sung, a settled conviction entered the mind of the king that David would obtain the hearts of the people and reign in his stead. (*Patriarchs and Prophets*, 650)

REFLECTION: *Saul may have ruled a nation, but he didn't know how to rule his own spirit. We have this lesson that we may not fall into the same trap as Saul. Today, many try to be people pleasers instead of pleasing God. We must always keep our eyes on the One who is most important.*

MAY 2

SPIRITUALISM AND SAUL

Then said Saul unto his servants, Seek me a woman that hath a familiar spirit, that I may go to her, and inquire of her. And his servants said to him, Behold, there is a woman that hath a familiar spirit at Endor.
1 Samuel 28:7

Through spiritualism many of the sick, the bereaved, the curious, are communicating with evil spirits. All who venture to do this are on dangerous ground. The word of truth declares how God regards them. In ancient times He pronounced a stern judgment on a king who had sent for counsel to a heathen oracle: "Is it not because there is not a God in Israel, that ye go to inquire of Baal-zebub the god of Ekron? Now therefore thus saith the Lord, Thou shalt not come down from that bed on which thou art gone up, but shalt surely die" (2 Kings 1:3, 4).

The magicians of heathen times have their counterpart in the spiritualistic mediums, the clairvoyants, and the fortune-tellers of today. The mystic voices that spoke at Endor and at Ephesus are still by their lying words misleading the children of men. Could the veil be lifted from before our eyes, we should see evil angels employing all their arts to deceive and to destroy. Wherever an influence is exerted to cause men to forget God, there Satan is exercising his bewitching power. ... The apostle's admonition to the Ephesian church should be heeded by the people of God today: "Have no fellowship with the unfruitful works of darkness, but rather reprove them" (Ephesians 5:11). (*The Acts of the Apostles*, 290)

REFLECTION: *It wasn't Samuel that appeared to Saul, but a demon impersonating Samuel. What a sad story. Saul, the first king of Israel, continued on a path that led to his demise. We mustn't allow any form of media-or anything else, for that matter-to turn our minds from the explicit word of God.*

Saul Dies

Then said Saul unto his armour bearer, Draw thy sword, and thrust me through therewith; lest these uncircumcised come and thrust me through, and abuse me. But his armour bearer would not; for he was sore afraid. Therefore Saul took a sword, and fell upon it.

1 Samuel 31:4

On the plain of Shunem and the slopes of Mount Gilboa the armies of Israel and the hosts of the Philistines closed in mortal combat. Though the fearful scene in the cave of Endor had driven all hope from his heart, Saul fought with desperate valor for his throne and his kingdom. But it was in vain. "The men of Israel fled from before the Philistines, and fell down slain in Mount Gilboa." Three brave sons of the king died at his side. The archers pressed upon Saul. He had seen his soldiers falling around him and his princely sons cut down by the sword. Himself wounded, he could neither fight nor fly. Escape was impossible, and determined not to be taken alive by the Philistines, he bade his armor-bearer, "Draw thy sword, and thrust me through therewith." When the man refused to lift his hand against the Lord's anointed, Saul took his own life by falling upon his sword.

Thus the first king of Israel perished, with the guilt of self-murder upon his soul. His life had been a failure, and he went down in dishonor and despair, because he had set up his own perverse will against the will of God. (*Patriarchs and Prophets*, 682)

REFLECTION: *The start of Saul's downfall was when he began to reign independently from God.*

MAY 4

SINCERE GRIEF

And they mourned, and wept, and fasted until even, for Saul,
and for Jonathan his son, and for the people of the LORD, and for
the house of Israel; because they were fallen by the sword.
2 Samuel 1:12

Twice David had had Saul in his power; but when urged to slay him, he had refused to lift his hand against him who had been consecrated by the command of God to rule over Israel. Yet the Amalekite feared not to boast that he had slain the king of Israel. He had accused himself of a crime worthy of death, and the penalty was inflicted at once. David said, "Thy blood be upon thy head; for thy mouth hath testified against thee, saying, I have slain the Lord's anointed" (2 Samuel 1:16).

David's grief at the death of Saul was sincere and deep, evincing the generosity of a noble nature. He did not exult in the fall of his enemy. The obstacle that had barred his access to the throne of Israel was removed, but at this he did not rejoice. Death had obliterated the remembrance of Saul's distrust and cruelty, and now nothing in his history was thought of but that which was noble and kingly. The name of Saul was linked with that of Jonathan, whose friendship had been so true and so unselfish. (*Patriarchs and Prophets*, 695)

REFLECTION: *Though we must stand for truth as it is found in scripture, we should be like David when it comes to our so-called enemies. Let us pray for them and not try to hurt them in any way. This is part of having a noble character like Christ's.*

MAY 5

DAVID BECOMES KING

So all the elders of Israel came to the king to Hebron; and king David made a league with them in Hebron before the LORD: and they anointed David king over Israel.

2 Samuel 5:3

"Then came all the tribes of Israel to David unto Hebron, and spake, saying, Behold, we are thy bone and thy flesh." They declared, "Thou wast he that leddest out and broughtest in Israel: and the Lord said to thee, Thou shalt feed My people Israel, and thou shalt be a captain over Israel. So all the elders of Israel came to the king to Hebron; and King David made a league with them in Hebron before the Lord." Thus through the providence of God the way had been opened for him to come to the throne. He had no personal ambition to gratify, for he had not sought the honor to which he had been brought.

More than eight thousand of the descendants of Aaron and of the Levites waited upon David. The change in the sentiments of the people was marked and decisive. The revolution was quiet and dignified, befitting the great work they were doing. Nearly half a million souls, the former subjects of Saul, thronged Hebron and its environs.... The hour for the coronation was appointed; the man who had been expelled from the court of Saul, who had fled to the mountains and hills and to the caves of the earth to preserve his life, was about to receive the highest honor that can be conferred upon man by his fellow man. (*Patriarchs and Prophets*, 701)

REFLECTION: *David had been running for his life for years. From a human standpoint, it seemed as though he would never be king, but he had waited patiently upon the Lord. Now David was the King of Israel, scepter in hand. It was a divine appointment.*

The Great Temple

That the king said unto Nathan the prophet, See now, I dwell in an
house of cedar, but the ark of God dwelleth within curtains.
2 Samuel 7:2

The tabernacle built by Moses, with all that appertained to the sanctuary service, except the ark, was still at Gibeah. It was David's purpose to make Jerusalem the religious center of the nation. He had erected a palace for himself, and he felt that it was not fitting for the ark of God to rest within a tent. He determined to build for it a temple of such magnificence as should express Israel's appreciation of the honor granted the nation in the abiding presence of Jehovah their King. Communicating his purpose to the prophet Nathan, he received the encouraging response, "Do all that is in thine heart; for the Lord is with thee."

But that same night the word of the Lord came to Nathan, giving him a message for the king. David was to be deprived of the privilege of building a house for God, but he was granted an assurance of the divine favor to him, to his posterity, and to the kingdom of Israel. (Patriarchs and Prophets, 711, 712)

Reflection: *Even though David was not to build the temple, he gathered much of the materials. Likewise, we may work very hard for something, but never enjoy the fruits of our labor; they may come after we die. Let us never become discouraged when things don't happen exactly the way we want them to. May we be content with what God has given us to do today.*

MAY 7

SUBMITTING TO GOD'S WILL

*Then went king David in, and sat before the LORD, and he said, Who am I,
O Lord GOD? and what is my house, that thou hast brought me hitherto?*
2 Samuel 7:18

David knew that it would be an honor to his name and would bring glory to his government to perform the work that he had purposed in his heart to do, but he was ready to submit his will to the will of God. The grateful resignation thus manifested is rarely seen, even among Christians. How often do those who have passed the strength of manhood cling to the hope of accomplishing some great work upon which their hearts are set, but which they are unfitted to perform! God's providence may speak to them, as did His prophet to David, declaring that the work which they so much desire is not committed to them. It is theirs to prepare the way for another to accomplish it. But instead of gratefully submitting to the divine direction, many fall back as if slighted and rejected, feeling that if they cannot do the one thing which they desire to do, they will do nothing. Many cling with desperate energy to responsibilities which they are incapable of bearing, and vainly endeavor to accomplish a work for which they are insufficient, while that which they might do, lies neglected. And because of this lack of co-operation on their part the greater work is hindered or frustrated. (*Patriarchs and Prophets*, 712)

REFLECTION: *We are the body of Christ, and each one has a specific duty in the Lord's work. May each one of us rejoice in the abilities of others and show our appreciation for their contributions. God has a purpose for us each and every day. May we come to know His will for our lives more fully.*

Solomon Prays for Wisdom

Give therefore thy servant an understanding heart to judge
thy people, that I may discern between good and bad: for
who is able to judge this thy so great a people?
1 Kings 3:9

hose who today occupy positions of trust should seek to learn the lesson taught by Solomon's prayer. The higher the position a man occupies, the greater the responsibility that he has to bear, the wider will be the influence that he exerts and the greater his need of dependence on God. Ever should he remember that with the call to work comes the call to walk circumspectly before his fellow men. He is to stand before God in the attitude of a learner. Position does not give holiness of character. It is by honoring God and obeying His commands that a man is made truly great.

The God whom we serve is no respecter of persons. He who gave to Solomon the spirit of wise discernment is willing to impart the same blessing to His children today. "If any of you lack wisdom," His word declares, "let him ask of God, that giveth to all men liberally, and upbraideth not; and it shall be given him" (James 1:5). When a burden bearer desires wisdom more than he desires wealth, power, or fame, he will not be disappointed. Such a one will learn from the Great Teacher not only what to do, but how to do it in a way that will meet with the divine approval. (*Prophets and Kings*, 31)

REFLECTION: *We are not to strive for supremacy. We are to ask for an understanding heart, to discern between good and evil, and to receive strength and enlightenment.*

Solomon's Temple

*And the house which king Solomon built for the LORD, the
length thereof was threescore cubits, and the breadth thereof
twenty cubits, and the height thereof thirty cubits.*
1 Kings 6:2

O f surpassing beauty and unrivaled splendor was the
palatial building which Solomon and his associates
erected for God and His worship. Garnished with precious stones, surrounded by spacious courts with magnificent
approaches, and lined with carved cedar and burnished gold,
the temple structure, with its broidered hangings and rich furnishings, was a fit emblem of the living church of God on earth,
which through the ages has been building in accordance with the
divine pattern, with materials that have been likened to "gold,
silver, precious stones," … "polished after the similitude of a palace" (1 Corinthians 3:12; Psalm 144:12). Of this spiritual temple
Christ is "the chief Cornerstone; in whom all the building fitly framed together groweth unto an holy temple in the Lord"
(Ephesians 2:20, 21).

At last the temple planned by King David, and built by
Solomon his son, was completed. "All that came into Solomon's
heart to make in the house of the Lord," he had "prosperously effected" (2 Chronicles 7:11). And now, in order that the palace crowning the heights of Mount Moriah might indeed be, as
David had so much desired, a dwelling place "'not for man, but
for the Lord God" (1 Chronicles 29:1), there remained the solemn
ceremony of formally dedicating it to Jehovah and His worship.
(*Prophets and Kings*, 36)

REFLECTION: *On this very spot Abraham was willing to offer his son in
obedience to God. Here God renewed His covenant with Abraham. Here
was also the crucifixion of God's own Son. What an awesome thought!
Through all the ages, no man or woman could have devised such a plan.*

MAY 10

THE LAW IN THE ARK

There was nothing in the ark save the two tables of stone, which
Moses put there at Horeb, when the LORD made a covenant with
the children of Israel, when they came out of the land of Egypt.
1 Kings 8:9

The ark in the tabernacle on earth contained the two tables of stone, upon which were inscribed the precepts of the law of God. The ark was merely a receptacle for the tables of the law, and the presence of these divine precepts gave to it its value and sacredness. When the temple of God was opened in heaven, the ark of His testament was seen. Within the holy of holies, in the sanctuary in heaven, the divine law is sacredly enshrined—the law that was spoken by God Himself amid the thunders of Sinai and written with His own finger on the tables of stone.

The law of God in the sanctuary in heaven is the great original, of which the precepts inscribed upon the tables of stone and recorded by Moses in the Pentateuch were an unerring transcript. Those who arrived at an understanding of this important point were thus led to see the sacred, unchanging character of the divine law. They saw, as never before, the force of the Saviour's words: "Till heaven and earth pass, one jot or one tittle shall in no wise pass from the law" (Matthew 5:18). (*The Great Controversy*, 434)

REFLECTION: *The Law of God is a revelation of His character. Since God does not change, His Law will endure forever.*

Solomon's Fall

But king Solomon loved many strange women, together
with the daughter of Pharaoh, women of the Moabites,
Ammonites, Edomites, Zidonians, and Hittites.
1 Kings 11:1

So gradual was Solomon's apostasy that before he was aware of it; he had wandered far from God. Almost imperceptibly he began to trust less and less in divine guidance and blessing, and to put confidence in his own strength. Little by little he withheld from God that unswerving obedience which was to make Israel a peculiar people, and he conformed more and more closely to the customs of the surrounding nations. Yielding to the temptations incident to his success and his honored position, he forgot the Source of his prosperity. An ambition to excel all other nations in power and grandeur led him to pervert for selfish purposes the heavenly gifts hitherto employed for the glory of God. The money which should have been held in sacred trust for the benefit of the worthy poor and for the extension of principles of holy living throughout the world was selfishly absorbed in ambitious projects.

Engrossed in an overmastering desire to surpass other nations in outward display, the king overlooked the need of acquiring beauty and perfection of character. In seeking to glorify himself before the world, he sold his honor and integrity. (*Prophets and Kings*, 55)

REFLECTION: *Solomon equated greatness with wealth and luxury, but the greatest thing we can ever possess is a noble character.*

AHAB THE WICKED KING

And Ahab the son of Omri did evil in the sight of
the LORD above all that were before him.
1 Kings 16:30

Taking to wife Jezebel, "the daughter of Ethbaal king of the Zidonians" and high priest of Baal, Ahab "served Baal, and worshiped him. And he reared up an altar for Baal in the house of Baal, which he had built in Samaria" (Verses 31, 32).

Not only did Ahab introduce Baal worship at the capital city, but under the leadership of Jezebel he erected heathen altars in many "high places," where in the shelter of surrounding groves the priests and others connected with this seductive form of idolatry exerted their baleful influence, until well-nigh all Israel were following after Baal. "There was none like unto Ahab," who "did sell himself to work wickedness in the sight of the Lord, whom Jezebel his wife stirred up. And he did very abominably in following idols, according to all things as did the Amorites, whom the Lord cast out before the children of Israel" (1 Kings 21:25, 26).

Ahab was weak in moral power. His union by marriage with an idolatrous woman of decided character and positive temperament resulted disastrously both to himself and to the nation. Unprincipled, and with no high standard of rightdoing, his character was easily molded by the determined spirit of Jezebel. His selfish nature was incapable of appreciating the mercies of God to Israel and his own obligations as the guardian and leader of the chosen people. (*Prophets and Kings*, 115)

REFLECTION: *Ahab's influence as king led much of the nation into apostasy; whereby they lost their sense of reverence and godly fear.*

MAY 13

ELIJAH THE PROPHET

*And Elijah the Tishbite, who was of the inhabitants of Gilead, said
unto Ahab, As the LORD God of Israel liveth, before whom I stand, there
shall not be dew nor rain these years, but according to my word.*
1 Kings 17:1

Among the mountains of Gilead, east of the Jordan, there dwelt in the days of Ahab a man of faith and prayer whose fearless ministry was destined to check the rapid spread of apostasy in Israel. Far removed from any city of renown, and occupying no high station in life, Elijah the Tishbite nevertheless entered upon his mission confident in God's purpose to prepare the way before him and to give him abundant success. The word of faith and power was upon his lips, and his whole life was devoted to the work of reform. His was the voice of one crying in the wilderness to rebuke sin and press back the tide of evil. And while he came to the people as a reprover of sin, his message offered the balm of Gilead to the sin-sick souls of all who desired to be healed.

As Elijah saw Israel going deeper and deeper into idolatry, his soul was distressed and his indignation aroused. God had done great things for His people. He had delivered them from bondage and given them "the lands of the heathen, ... that they might observe His statutes, and keep His laws" (Psalm 105:44, 45). (*Prophets and Kings*, 119)

REFLECTION: *Elijah was in great sorrow over the apostasy of Israel. He knew that if the people did not repent, there would be neither dew nor rain.*

MAY 14

WIDOW AT ZAREPHATH

And the woman said to Elijah, Now by this I know that thou art a man of God, and that the word of the LORD in thy mouth is truth.
1 Kings 17:24

The widow of Zarephath shared her morsel with Elijah, and in return her life and that of her son were preserved. And to all who, in time of trial and want, give sympathy and assistance to others more needy, God has promised great blessing. He has not changed. His power is no less now than in the days of Elijah. No less sure now than when spoken by our Saviour is the promise, "He that receiveth a prophet in the name of a prophet shall receive a prophet's reward" (Matthew 10:41).

"Be not forgetful to entertain strangers: for thereby some have entertained angels unawares" (Hebrews 13:2). These words have lost none of their force through the lapse of time. Our heavenly Father still continues to place in the pathway of His children opportunities that are blessings in disguise; and those who improve these opportunities find great joy. "If thou draw out thy soul to the hungry, and satisfy the afflicted soul; then shall thy light rise in obscurity, and thy darkness be as the noonday: and the Lord shall guide thee continually, and satisfy thy soul in drought, and make fat thy bones: and thou shalt be like a watered garden, and like a spring of water, whose waters fail not" (Isaiah 58:10, 11). (*Prophets and Kings*, 132)

REFLECTION: *To His faithful servants today Christ says, "He that receiveth you receiveth Me, and he that receiveth Me receiveth Him that sent Me." Every kindness is recognized by the Lord.*

MAY 15

*F*EARLESS *P*ROPHET

*And he answered, I have not troubled Israel; but thou, and thy
father's house, in that ye have forsaken the commandments
of the LORD, and thou hast followed Baalim.*
1 Kings 18:18

*T*he king and the prophet stand face to face. Though Ahab
is filled with passionate hatred, yet in the presence of
Elijah he seems unmanned, powerless. In his first falter-
ing words, "Art thou he that troubleth Israel?" he unconsciously
reveals the inmost feelings of his heart. Ahab knew that it was
by the word of God that the heavens had become as brass, yet
he sought to cast upon the prophet the blame for the heavy judgments resting on the land. ...

Standing in conscious innocence before Ahab, Elijah makes
no attempt to excuse himself or to flatter the king. Nor does
he seek to evade the king's wrath by the good news that the
drought is almost over. He has no apology to offer. Indignant,
and jealous for the honor of God, he casts back the imputation
of Ahab, fearlessly declaring to the king that it is his sins, and
the sins of his fathers, that have brought upon Israel this terrible calamity. "I have not troubled Israel," Elijah boldly asserts,
"but thou, and thy father's house, in that ye have forsaken the
commandments of the Lord, and thou hast followed Baalim."
(*Prophets and Kings*, 140)

REFLECTION: *Smooth sermons destroy the people. Today we need voices
of stern rebuke for the grievous sins committed by the professed people
of God.*

May 16

A Still Small Voice

And after the earthquake a fire; but the LORD *was not in the fire: and after the fire a still small voice.*
1 Kings 19:12

Not in mighty manifestations of divine power, but by "a still small voice," did God choose to reveal Himself to His servant. He desired to teach Elijah that it is not always the work that makes the greatest demonstration that is most successful in accomplishing His purpose. While Elijah waited for the revelation of the Lord, a tempest rolled, the lightning flashed, and a devouring fire swept by; but God was not in all this. Then there came a still, small voice, and the prophet covered his head before the presence of the Lord. His petulance was silenced, his spirit softened and subdued. He now knew that a quiet trust, a firm reliance on God, would ever find for him a present help in time of need.

Not by eloquence or logic are men's hearts reached, but by the sweet influences of the Holy Spirit, which operate quietly yet surely in transforming and developing character. It is the still, small voice of the Spirit of God that has power to change the heart. *(Prophets and Kings,* 168, 169)

REFLECTION: *More than ever, we need to have quiet time with God. We need to be ever listening to that still small voice of the Holy Spirit. Our success depends on this.*

ELIJAH TAKEN TO HEAVEN

And it came to pass, as they still went on, and talked, that, behold,
there appeared a chariot of fire, and horses of fire, and parted them
both asunder; and Elijah went up by a whirlwind into heaven.
2 Kings 2:11

Elijah was a type of the saints who will be living on the earth at the time of the second advent of Christ and who will be "changed, in a moment, in the twinkling of an eye, at the last trump," without tasting of death (1 Corinthians 15:51, 52). It was as a representative of those who shall be thus translated that Elijah, near the close of Christ's earthly ministry, was permitted to stand with Moses by the side of the Saviour on the mount of transfiguration. In these glorified ones, the disciples saw in miniature a representation of the kingdom of the redeemed. They beheld Jesus clothed with the light of heaven; they heard the "voice out of the cloud" (Luke 9:35), acknowledging Him as the Son of God; they saw Moses, representing those who will be raised from the dead at the time of the second advent; and there also stood Elijah, representing those who at the close of earth's history will be changed from mortal to immortal and be translated to heaven without seeing death. (*Prophets and Kings*, 227)

REFLECTION: *Whether we live or die before Jesus returns, may we each be found faithful.*

KING HEZEKIAH

He removed the high places, and brake the images, and cut down the groves,
and brake in pieces the brazen serpent that Moses had made: for unto those
days the children of Israel did burn incense to it: and he called it Nehushtan.
2 Kings 18:4

In sharp contrast with the reckless rule of Ahaz was the reformation wrought during the prosperous reign of his son. Hezekiah came to the throne determined to do all in his power to save Judah from the fate that was overtaking the northern kingdom. The messages of the prophets offered no encouragement to halfway measures. Only by most decided reformation could the threatened judgments be averted.

In the crisis, Hezekiah proved to be a man of opportunity. No sooner had he ascended the throne than he began to plan and to execute. He first turned his attention to the restoration of the temple services, so long neglected; and in this work he earnestly solicited the co-operation of a band of priests and Levites who had remained true to their sacred calling. Confident of their loyal support, he spoke with them freely concerning his desire to institute immediate and far-reaching reforms. "Our fathers have trespassed," he confessed, "and done that which was evil in the eyes of the Lord our God, and have forsaken Him, and have turned away their faces from the habitation of the Lord." "Now it is in mine heart to make a covenant with the Lord God of Israel, that His fierce wrath may turn away from us" (2 Chronicles 29:6, 10). (*Prophets and Kings*, 331)

REFLECTION: *Let us be like Hezekiah, a man of opportunity. He did not wait around to do that which needed to be done right away. Many times waiting only makes it more difficult to carry out the necessary duty. Today, let us promptly obey the Lord.*

*F*AITH *I*NSPIRES

*With him is an arm of flesh; but with us is the L*ORD *our God*
to help us, and to fight our battles. And the people rested
themselves upon the words of Hezekiah king of Judah.
2 Chronicles 32:8

*A*t the time of Hezekiah's accession to the throne of Judah, the Assyrians had already carried captive a large number of the children of Israel from the northern kingdom; and a few years after he had begun to reign, and while he was still strengthening the defenses of Jerusalem, the Assyrians besieged and captured Samaria and scattered the ten tribes among the many provinces of the Assyrian realm. The borders of Judah were only a few miles distant, with Jerusalem less than fifty miles away; and the rich spoils to be found within the temple would tempt the enemy to return.

But the king of Judah had determined to do his part in preparing to resist the enemy; and, having accomplished all that human ingenuity and energy could do, he had assembled his forces and had exhorted them to be of good courage. "Great is the Holy One of Israel in the midst of thee" had been the message of the prophet Isaiah to Judah; and the king with unwavering faith now declared, "With us is the Lord our God to help us, and to fight our battles" (Isaiah 12:6; 2 Chronicles 32:8). (*Prophets and Kings*, 351)

REFLECTION: *Active faith inspires more faith. In preparation for the coming crisis, King Hezekiah encouraged the people to believe in God's Word.*

ONE ANGEL DESTROYS ASSYRIAN ARMY

And the LORD sent an angel, which cut off all the mighty men of valour, and the leaders and captains in the camp of the king of Assyria. So he returned with shame of face to his own land. And when he was come into the house of his god, they that came forth of his own bowels slew him there with the sword.
2 Chronicles 32:21

"Therefore thus saith the Lord concerning the king of Assyria, He shall not come into this city, nor shoot an arrow there, nor come before it with shield, nor cast a bank against it. By the way that he came, by the same shall he return, and shall not come into this city, saith the Lord. For I will defend this city, to save it, for Mine own sake, and for My servant David's sake" (Verses 29–34).

That very night deliverance came. "The angel of the Lord went out, and smote in the camp of the Assyrians an hundred fourscore and five thousand" (Verse 35). …

Tidings of this terrible judgment upon the army that had been sent to take Jerusalem, soon reached Sennacherib, who was still guarding the approach to Judea from Egypt. Stricken with fear, the Assyrian king hasted to depart and "returned with shame of face to his own land" (Verse 21). But he had not long to reign. In harmony with the prophecy that had been uttered concerning his sudden end, he was assassinated by those of his own home, "and Esarhaddon his son reigned in his stead" (Isaiah 37:38). (*Prophets and Kings,* 361)

REFLECTION: *The honor of God was vindicated before the surrounding nations. The boastful Assyrian king and his army were defeated.*

MAY 21

JOSIAH'S REFORMS

Josiah was eight years old when he began to reign, and
he reigned in Jerusalem one and thirty years.
2 Chronicles 34:1

Thus Josiah, from his earliest manhood, had endeavored to take advantage of his position as king to exalt the principles of God's holy law. And now, while Shaphan the scribe was reading to him out of the book of the law, the king discerned in this volume a treasure of knowledge, a powerful ally, in the work of reform he so much desired to see wrought in the land. He resolved to walk in the light of its counsels, and also to do all in his power to acquaint his people with its teachings and to lead them, if possible, to cultivate reverence and love for the law of heaven.

But was it possible to bring about the needed reform? Israel had almost reached the limit of divine forbearance; soon God would arise to punish those who had brought dishonor upon His name. Already the anger of the Lord was kindled against the people. Overwhelmed with sorrow and dismay, Josiah rent his garments and bowed before God in agony of spirit, seeking pardon for the sins of an impenitent nation. (*Prophets and Kings*, 398).

REFLECTION: *Because the king humbled his heart before God, and sought mercy and forgiveness, the message was sent to him, "Because thine heart was tender, and thou hast humbled thyself before the Lord ...and hast rent thy clothes, and wept before Me... Behold therefore, I will gather thee unto thy fathers, and thou shalt be gathered into thy grave in peace; and thine eyes shall not see all the evil which I will bring upon this place" (Verses 19, 20). (Prophets and Kings, 399)*

JERUSALEM DESTROYED

Nebuchadnezzar also carried of the vessels of the house of the
LORD to Babylon, and put them in his temple at Babylon.
2 Chronicles 36:7

The first years of Jehoiakim's reign were filled with warnings of approaching doom.... The Assyrian power to the northward, long supreme, was no longer to rule the nations. Egypt on the south, in whose power the king of Judah was vainly placing his trust, was soon to receive a decided check. All unexpectedly a new world power, the Babylonian Empire, was rising to the eastward and swiftly overshadowing all other nations.

Within a few short years the king of Babylon was to be used as the instrument of God's wrath upon impenitent Judah. Again and again Jerusalem was to be invested and entered by the besieging armies of Nebuchadnezzar. Company after company—at first a few only, but later on thousands and tens of thousands—were to be taken captive to the land of Shinar, there to dwell in enforced exile. Jehoiakim, Jehoiachin, Zedekiah—all these Jewish kings were in turn to become vassals of the Babylonian ruler, and all in turn were to rebel. Severer and yet more severe chastisements were to be inflicted upon the rebellious nation, until at last the entire land was to become a desolation, Jerusalem was to be laid waste and burned with fire, the temple that Solomon had built was to be destroyed, and the kingdom of Judah was to fall, never again to occupy its former position among the nations of earth. (*Prophets and Kings*, 422)

REFLECTION: *Through the prophet Jeremiah, God had given the children of Judah many opportunities to avoid the coming controversy and calamity with Babylon. They chose to put their trust in man rather than God and inevitable consequences followed.*

THE LAW OF THE LORD IS PERFECT

The law of the LORD is perfect, converting the soul: the testimony of the LORD is sure, making wise the simple.
Psalm 19:7

*I*s he now free to transgress God's law? Says Paul: "Do we then make void the law through faith? God forbid: yea, we establish the law." "How shall we, that are dead to sin, live any longer therein?" And John declares: "This is the love of God, that we keep His commandments: and His commandments are not grievous" (Romans 3:31; 6:2; 1 John 5:3). In the new birth the heart is brought into harmony with God, as it is brought into accord with His law. When this mighty change has taken place in the sinner, he has passed from death unto life, from sin unto holiness, from transgression and rebellion to obedience and loyalty. The old life of alienation from God has ended; the new life of reconciliation, of faith and love, has begun. Then "the righteousness of the law" will "be fulfilled in us, who walk not after the flesh, but after the Spirit" (Romans 8:4). And the language of the soul will be: "O how I love Thy law! It is my meditation all the day" (Psalm 119:97).

"The law of the Lord is perfect, converting the soul" (Psalm 19:7). Without the law, men have no just conception of the purity and holiness of God or of their own guilt and uncleanness. (*The Great Controversy*, 468)

REFLECTION: *With a shallow understanding of God's Law, men will have a lower concept of righteousness. Oh to be like King David and love to meditate upon His law.*

THE GOOD SHEPHERD

The LORD is my shepherd; I shall not want.
Psalm 23:1

"I am the Good Shepherd: the good shepherd giveth his life for the sheep." "I am the Good Shepherd, and know My sheep, and am known of Mine. As the Father knoweth Me, even so know I the Father: and I lay down My life for the sheep."

Again Jesus found access to the minds of His hearers by the pathway of their familiar associations. He had likened the Spirit's influence to the cool, refreshing water. He had represented Himself as the light, the source of life and gladness to nature and to man. Now in a beautiful pastoral picture He represents His relation to those that believe on Him. No picture was more familiar to His hearers than this, and Christ's words linked it forever with Himself. Never could the disciples look on the shepherds tending their flocks without recalling the Saviour's lesson. They would see Christ in each faithful shepherd. They would see themselves in each helpless and dependent flock.

This figure the prophet Isaiah had applied to the Messiah's mission, in the comforting words, "O Zion, that bringest good tidings, get thee up into the high mountain; O Jerusalem, that bringest good tidings, lift up thy voice with strength; lift it up, be not afraid; say unto the cities of Judah, Behold your God! ... He shall feed His flock like a shepherd: He shall gather the lambs with His arm, and carry them in His bosom" (Isaiah 40:9–11). David had sung, "The Lord is my shepherd; I shall not want" (Psalm 23:1). (*The Desire of Ages*, 476)

REFLECTION: *The Holy Spirit through Ezekiel had declared: "I will set up one Shepherd over them, and He shall feed them" (Ezekiel 34:23). (The Desire of Ages, 476)*

MAY 25

*M*Y *H*IDING *P*LACE

For in the time of trouble he shall hide me in his pavilion: in the secret of his tabernacle shall he hide me; he shall set me up upon a rock.

Psalm 27:5

The eye of God, looking down the ages, was fixed upon the crisis which His people are to meet, when earthly powers shall be arrayed against them. Like the captive exile, they will be in fear of death by starvation or by violence. But the Holy One who divided the Red Sea before Israel, will manifest His mighty power and turn their captivity. "They shall be Mine, saith the Lord of hosts, in that day when I make up My jewels; and I will spare them, as a man spareth his own son that serveth him" (Malachi 3:17). If the blood of Christ's faithful witnesses were shed at this time, it would not, like the blood of the martyrs, be as seed sown to yield a harvest for God. Their fidelity would not be a testimony to convince others of the truth; for the obdurate heart has beaten back the waves of mercy until they return no more. If the righteous were now left to fall a prey to their enemies, it would be a triumph for the prince of darkness. Says the psalmist: "In the time of trouble He shall hide me in His pavilion: in the secret of His tabernacle shall He hide me" (Psalm 27:5). (*The Great Controversy*, 635)

REFLECTION: *Christ has spoken: "Come, My people, enter thou into thy chambers, and shut thy doors about thee: hide thyself as it were for a little moment, until the indignation be overpast. For behold, the Lord cometh out of His place to punish the inhabitants of the earth for their iniquity" (Isaiah 26:20, 21). (The Great Controversy, 635)*

MAY 26

BEHOLDING CHRIST

They looked unto him, and were lightened: and their faces were not ashamed.
Psalm 34:5

In the secret place of prayer, where no eye but God's can see, no ear but His can hear, we may pour out our most hidden desires and longings to the Father of infinite pity, and in the hush and silence of the soul that voice which never fails to answer the cry of human need will speak to our hearts.

"The Lord is very pitiful, and of tender mercy" (James 5:11). He waits with unwearied love to hear the confessions of the wayward and to accept their penitence. He watches for some return of gratitude from us, as the mother watches for the smile of recognition from her beloved child. He would have us understand how earnestly and tenderly His heart yearns over us. He invites us to take our trials to His sympathy, our sorrows to His love, our wounds to His healing, our weakness to His strength, our emptiness to His fullness. Never has one been disappointed who came unto Him. "They looked unto Him, and were lightened: and their faces were not ashamed" (Psalm 34:5). (*Thoughts from the Mount of Blessing*, 84)

REFLECTION: *As we make Christ our daily companion we shall feel that the powers of an unseen world are all around us; and by looking unto Jesus we shall become assimilated to His image. By beholding we become changed. The character is softened, refined, and ennobled for the heavenly kingdom. (Thoughts from the Mount of Blessing, 85)*

MAY 27

CONTRITE HEART

The LORD is nigh unto them that are of a broken heart;
and saveth such as be of a contrite spirit.
Psalm 34:18

The proud heart strives to earn salvation; but both our title to heaven and our fitness for it are found in the righteousness of Christ. The Lord can do nothing toward the recovery of man until, convinced of his own weakness, and stripped of all self-sufficiency, he yields himself to the control of God. Then he can receive the gift that God is waiting to bestow. From the soul that feels his need, nothing is withheld. He has unrestricted access to Him in whom all fullness dwells. "For thus saith the high and lofty One that inhabiteth eternity, whose name is Holy; I dwell in the high and holy place, with him also that is of a contrite and humble spirit, to revive the spirit of the humble, and to revive the heart of the contrite ones" (Isaiah 57:15).

"Blessed are they that mourn: for they shall be comforted." By these words Christ does not teach that mourning in itself has power to remove the guilt of sin. He gives no sanction to pretense or to voluntary humility. The mourning of which He speaks does not consist in melancholy and lamentation. While we sorrow on account of sin, we are to rejoice in the precious privilege of being children of God. (*The Desire of Ages*, 300)

REFLECTION: *We often sorrow because our evil deeds bring unpleasant consequences to ourselves, but this is not repentance. Real sorrow for sin is the result of the working of the Holy Spirit. The tears of the penitent are only the raindrops that precede the sunshine of holiness. (The Desire of Ages, 300)*

TRUST IN THE LORD

Trust in the LORD, and do good; so shalt thou dwell
in the land, and verily thou shalt be fed.
Psalm 37:3

The psalmist says, "Trust in the Lord, and do good; so shalt thou dwell in the land, and verily thou shalt be fed" (Psalm 37:3). "Trust in the Lord." Each day has its burdens, its cares and perplexities; and when we meet how ready we are to talk of our difficulties and trials. So many borrowed troubles intrude, so many fears are indulged, such a weight of anxiety is expressed, that one might suppose we had no pitying, loving Saviour ready to hear all our requests and to be to us a present help in every time of need.

Some are always fearing, and borrowing trouble. Every day they are surrounded with the tokens of God's love; every day they are enjoying the bounties of His providence; but they overlook these present blessings. Their minds are continually dwelling upon something disagreeable which they fear may come; or some difficulty may really exist which, though small, blinds their eyes to the many things that demand gratitude. The difficulties they encounter, instead of driving them to God, the only source of their help, separate them from Him because they awaken unrest and repining. (*Steps to Christ*, 121)

REFLECTION: *Do all you can to bring about favorable results. Jesus has promised His aid, but not apart from our effort. When, relying upon our Helper, you have done all you can, accept the result cheerfully. (Steps to Christ, 122)*

MAY 29

LAW WRITTEN ON THE HEART

I delight to do thy will, O my God: yea, thy law is within my heart.
Psalm 40:8

Only those who devote themselves to His service, saying, "Here am I; send me" (Isaiah 6:8), to open blind eyes, to turn men "from darkness to light and from the power of Satan unto God, that they may receive forgiveness of sins and inheritance among them which are sanctified" (Acts 26:18) — they alone pray in sincerity, "Thy kingdom come."

"Thy will be done in earth, as it is in heaven" (Matthew 6:10). The will of God is expressed in the precepts of His holy law, and the principles of this law are the principles of heaven. The angels of heaven attain unto no higher knowledge than to know the will of God, and to do His will is the highest service that can engage their powers.

But in heaven, service is not rendered in the spirit of legality. When Satan rebelled against the law of Jehovah, the thought that there was a law came to the angels almost as an awakening to something unthought of. In their ministry the angels are not as servants, but as sons. There is perfect unity between them and their Creator. Obedience is to them no drudgery. Love for God makes their service a joy. So in every soul wherein Christ, the hope of glory, dwells, His words are re-echoed, "I delight to do Thy will, O My God: yea, Thy law is within My heart" (Psalm 40:8). (*Thoughts from the Mount of Blessing*, 108, 109)

REFLECTION: *A sign of true conversion is our desire to please God through willing obedience to His commands.*

MAY 30

$\mathcal{T}$HE $\mathcal{S}$ECRET OF $\mathcal{S}$TRENGTH

*Be still, and know that I am God: I will be exalted among
the heathen, I will be exalted in the earth.*
Psalm 46:10

An intensity such as never before was seen is taking possession of the world. In amusement, in moneymaking, in the contest for power, in the very struggle for existence, there is a terrible force that engrosses body and mind and soul. In the midst of this maddening rush, God is speaking. He bids us come apart and commune with Him. "Be still, and know that I am God" (Psalm 46:10).

Many, even in their seasons of devotion, fail of receiving the blessing of real communion with God. They are in too great haste. With hurried steps they press through the circle of Christ's loving presence, pausing perhaps a moment within the sacred precincts, but not waiting for counsel. They have no time to remain with the divine Teacher. With their burdens they return to their work.

These workers can never attain the highest success until they learn the secret of strength. They must give themselves time to think, to pray, to wait upon God for a renewal of physical, mental, and spiritual power. They need the uplifting influence of His Spirit. Receiving this, they will be quickened by fresh life. The wearied frame and tired brain will be refreshed, the burdened heart will be lightened. (*Education*, 260)

REFLECTION: *Personal contact with Christ is the strength of the soul. In this world we live in, everything is a mad rush. We must not allow Satan to keep us so busy — even in religious things — that we lose our vital connection with God.*

May 31

A Clean Heart

Create in me a clean heart, O God; and renew a right spirit within me.
Psalm 51:10

"Man looketh on the outward appearance, but the Lord looketh on the heart"—the human heart, with its conflicting emotions of joy and sorrow; the wandering, wayward heart, which is the abode of so much impurity and deceit (1 Samuel 16:7). He knows its motives, its very intents and purposes. Go to Him with your soul all stained as it is. Like the psalmist, throw its chambers open to the all-seeing eye, exclaiming, "Search me, O God, and know my heart: try me, and know my thoughts: and see if there be any wicked way in me, and lead me in the way everlasting" (Psalm 139:23, 24).

Many accept an intellectual religion, a form of godliness, when the heart is not cleansed. Let it be your prayer, "Create in me a clean heart, O God; and renew a right spirit within me" (Psalm 51:10). Deal truly with your own soul. Be as earnest, as persistent, as you would be if your mortal life were at stake. This is a matter to be settled between God and your own soul, settled for eternity. A supposed hope, and nothing more, will prove your ruin. (*Steps to Christ*, 34)

REFLECTION: *As you see the enormity of sin, as you see yourself clearly, do not give in to despair. Christ wants us to realize our sin so that we may call on Him. It was sinners He came to save.*

JUNE

KNEELING BEFORE GOD

O come, let us worship and bow down: let us kneel before the LORD our maker.
Psalm 95:6

oth in public and in private worship it is our privilege to bow on our knees before God when we offer our petitions to Him. Jesus, our example, "kneeled down, and prayed" (Luke 22:41). Of his disciples it is recorded that they, too, "kneeled down, and prayed" (Acts 9:40). Paul declared, "I bow my knees unto the Father of our Lord Jesus Christ" (Ephesians 3:14). In confessing before God the sins of Israel, Ezra knelt. (See Ezra 9:5.) Daniel "kneeled upon his knees three times a day, and prayed, and gave thanks before his God" (Daniel 6:10).

True reverence for God is inspired by a sense of His infinite greatness and a realization of His presence. With this sense of the Unseen, every heart should be deeply impressed. The hour and place of prayer are sacred, because God is there. And as reverence is manifested in attitude and demeanor, the feeling that inspires it will be deepened. "Holy and reverend is His name," the psalmist declares (Psalm 111:9). Angels, when they speak that name, veil their faces. With what reverence, then, should we, who are fallen and sinful, take it upon our lips! (*Prophets and Kings*, 48)

REFLECTION: *Well would it be for old and young to ponder those words of Scripture that show how the place marked by God's special presence should be regarded. "Put off thy shoes from off thy feet," He commanded Moses at the burning bush, "for the place whereon thou standest is holy ground" (Exodus 3:5). (Prophets and Kings, 48)*

JUNE 2

$\mathscr{G}$RATITUDE

*What shall I render unto the L*ORD *for all his benefits toward me?*
Psalm 116:12

he Christian should often review his past life and recall
with gratitude the precious deliverances that God has
wrought for him, supporting him in trial, opening ways
before him when all seemed dark and forbidding, refreshing him
when ready to faint. He should recognize all of them as evidences of the watchcare of heavenly angels. In view of these innumerable blessings he should often ask, with subdued and grateful
heart, "What shall I render unto the Lord for all His benefits toward me?" (Psalm 116:12).

Our time, our talents, our property, should be sacredly devoted to Him who has given us these blessings in trust.
Whenever a special deliverance is wrought in our behalf, or
new and unexpected favors are granted us, we should acknowledge God's goodness, not only by expressing our gratitude in
words, but, like Jacob, by gifts and offerings to His cause. As we
are continually receiving the blessings of God, so we are to be
continually giving.

"Of all that Thou shalt give me," said Jacob, "I will surely
give the tenth unto Thee." Shall we who enjoy the full light and
privileges of the gospel be content to give less to God than was
given by those who lived in the former, less favored dispensation? (*Patriarchs and Prophets*, 187, 188)

REFLECTION: *As the blessings we enjoy grow, shouldn't our obligations
correspondingly increase? All that we have, all that we are, should be
devoted to God.*

*U*NITY

Behold, how good and how pleasant it is for
brethren to dwell together in unity!
Psalm 133:1

*I*t is the will of God that union and brotherly love should exist among His people. The prayer of Christ just before His crucifixion was that His disciples might be one as He is one with the Father, that the world might believe that God had sent Him. This most touching and wonderful prayer reaches down the ages, even to our day; for His words were, "Neither pray I for these alone, but for them also which shall believe on Me through their word" (John 17:20). While we are not to sacrifice one principle of truth, it should be our constant aim to reach this state of unity. This is the evidence of our discipleship. Said Jesus, "By this shall all men know that ye are My disciples, if ye have love one to another" (John 13:35). The apostle Peter exhorts the church, "Be ye all of one mind, having compassion one of another; love as brethren, be pitiful, be courteous: not rendering evil for evil, or railing for railing: but contrariwise blessing; knowing that ye are thereunto called, that ye should inherit a blessing" (1 Peter 3:8, 9). (*Patriarchs and Prophets*, 520)

REFLECTION: *When we call ourselves Christians — followers of Christ — we need to pray more for the mind of Christ. Loving our neighbor unconditionally can only come from above. When this happens, people will know we have a love that only the Lord can give.*

TRUE EDUCATION

*The fear of the LORD is the beginning of wisdom: and
the knowledge of the holy is understanding.*
Proverbs 9:10

The great work of life is character building, and a knowledge of God is the foundation of all true education. To impart this knowledge and to mold the character in harmony with it should be the object of the teacher's work. The law of God is a reflection of His character. Hence the psalmist says, "All Thy commandments are righteousness;" and "through Thy precepts I get understanding" (Psalm 119:172,104). God has revealed Himself to us in His word and in the works of creation. Through the volume of inspiration and the book of nature we are to obtain a knowledge of God.

It is a law of the mind that it gradually adapts itself to the subjects upon which it is trained to dwell. If occupied with commonplace matters only, it will become dwarfed and enfeebled. If never required to grapple with difficult problems, it will after a time almost lose the power of growth. As an educating power the Bible is without a rival. In the word of God the mind finds subject for the deepest thought, the loftiest aspiration. The Bible is the most instructive history that men possess. It came fresh from the fountain of eternal truth, and a divine hand has preserved its purity through all the ages. (*Patriarchs and Prophets*, 596)

REFLECTION: *In the reverent contemplation of the truths presented in His word the mind of the student is brought into communion with the infinite mind. Such a study will not only refine and ennoble the character, but it cannot fail to expand and invigorate the mental powers. (Patriarchs and Prophets, 596)*

JUNE 5

*H*UMILITY

The fear of the LORD is the instruction of wisdom;
and before honour is humility.
Proverbs 15:33

od does not always choose for His work men of the
greatest talents, but He selects those whom He can best
use. "Before honor is humility" (Proverbs 15:33). The
Lord can work most effectually through those who are most sen-
sible of their own insufficiency, and who will rely upon Him as
their leader and source of strength. He will make them strong
by uniting their weakness to His might, and wise by connecting
their ignorance with His wisdom.

If they would cherish true humility, the Lord could do much
more for His people; but there are few who can be trusted with
any large measure of responsibility or success without becoming
self-confident and forgetful of their dependence upon God. This
is why, in choosing the instruments for His work, the Lord passes
by those whom the world honors as great, talented, and brilliant.
They are too often proud and self-sufficient. They feel competent
to act without counsel from God. ...

The most complete system that men have ever devised, apart
from the power and wisdom of God, will prove a failure, while
the most unpromising methods will succeed when divinely appointed and entered upon with humility and faith. (*Patriarchs
and Prophets*, 553, 554)

REFLECTION: *He is just as willing to work with the efforts of His people*
now and to accomplish great things through weak instrumentalities.
All heaven awaits our demand upon its wisdom and strength. God
is "able to do exceeding abundantly above all that we ask or think"
(Ephesians 3:20). (Patriarchs and Prophets, 554)

Good Medicine

A merry heart doeth good like a medicine: but a broken spirit drieth the bones.
Proverbs 17:22

The relation that exists between the mind and the body is very intimate. When one is affected, the other sympathizes. The condition of the mind affects the health to a far greater degree than many realize. Many of the diseases from which men suffer are the result of mental depression. Grief, anxiety, discontent, remorse, guilt, distrust, all tend to break down the life forces and to invite decay and death.

Disease is sometimes produced, and is often greatly aggravated, by the imagination. Many are lifelong invalids who might be well if they only thought so. Many imagine that every slight exposure will cause illness, and the evil effect is produced because it is expected. Many die from disease the cause of which is wholly imaginary.

Courage, hope, faith, sympathy, love, promote health and prolong life. A contented mind, a cheerful spirit, is health to the body and strength to the soul. "A merry [rejoicing] heart doeth good like a medicine." (Proverbs 17:22). (*Ministry of Healing*, 241)

"Rejoice in every good thing which the Lord thy God hath given unto thee, and unto thine house, thou, and the Levite, and the stranger that is among you" (Deuteronomy 26:11).

REFLECTION: *Many of us have made it a habit to worry and be stressed. As one day ends and the next begins, we continue the negative pattern. When we look back, however, we don't even remember yesterday's troubles. Let us ask God to help us get rid of this life-damaging habit and be a positive influence with those we come in contact.*

Heaven's Records

*For God shall bring every work into judgment, with every
secret thing, whether it be good, or whether it be evil.*
Ecclesiastes 12:14

Achan acknowledged his guilt, but when it was too
late for the confession to benefit himself. He had
seen the armies of Israel return from Ai defeated and
disheartened; yet he did not come forward and confess his sin.
He had seen Joshua and the elders of Israel bowed to the earth
in grief too great for words. Had he then made confession, he
would have given some proof of true penitence; but he still kept
silence. He had listened to the proclamation that a great crime
had been committed, and had even heard its character definitely
stated. But his lips were sealed. Then came the solemn investiga-
tion. How his soul thrilled with terror as he saw his tribe pointed
out, then his family and his household! But still he uttered no
confession, until the finger of God was placed upon him. Then,
when his sin could no longer be concealed, he admitted the
truth. How often are similar confessions made. There is a vast
difference between admitting facts after they have been proved
and confessing sins known only to ourselves and to God. Achan
would not have confessed had he not hoped by so doing to avert
the consequences of his crime. But his confession only served to
show that his punishment was just. There was no genuine repentance for sin, no contrition, no change of purpose, no abhorrence
of evil. (*Patriarchs and Prophets*, 497)

REFLECTION: *So long as they can conceal their transgressions from their
fellow men, many, like Achan, feel secure, and flatter themselves that
God will not be strict to mark iniquity. All too late their sins will find
them out in that day when they shall not be purged with sacrifice or
offering forever.* (*Patriarchs and Prophets*, 498)

JUNE 8

Heavenly Treasure

I will make a man more precious than fine gold; even
a man than the golden wedge of Ophir.
Isaiah 13:12

*C*hrist calls upon every one to consider. Make an honest reckoning. Put into one scale Jesus, which means eternal treasure, life, truth, heaven, and the joy of Christ in souls redeemed; put into the other every attraction the world can offer. Into one scale put the loss of your own soul, and the souls of those whom you might have been instrumental in saving; into the other, for yourself and for them, a life that measures with the life of God. Weigh for time and for eternity. While you are thus engaged, Christ speaks: "What shall it profit a man, if he shall gain the whole world, and lose his own soul?" (Mark 8:36).

God desires us to choose the heavenly in place of the earthly. He opens before us the possibilities of a heavenly investment. He would give encouragement to our loftiest aims, security to our choicest treasure. He declares, "I will make a man more precious than fine gold; even a man than the golden wedge of Ophir" (Isaiah 13:12). When the riches that moth devours and rust corrupts shall be swept away, Christ's followers can rejoice in their heavenly treasure, the riches that are imperishable. (*Christ's Object Lessons*, 374)

REFLECTION: *Better than all the friendship of the world is the friendship of Christ's redeemed. Better than a title to the noblest palace on earth is a title to the mansions our Lord has gone to prepare. And better than all the words of earthly praise will be the Saviour's words to His faithful servants, "Come, ye blessed of My Father, inherit the kingdom prepared for you from the foundation of the world"* (Matthew 25:34). (*Christ's Object Lessons*, 374)

*F*ALL OF *L*UCIFER

How art thou fallen from heaven, O Lucifer, son of the morning! How
art thou cut down to the ground, which didst weaken the nations!
Isaiah 14:12

*P*ride in his own glory nourished the desire for supremacy. The high honors conferred upon Lucifer were not
appreciated as the gift of God and called forth no gratitude to the Creator. He gloried in his brightness and exaltation,
and aspired to be equal with God. He was beloved and rever-
enced by the heavenly host. Angels delighted to execute his commands, and he was clothed with wisdom and glory above them
all. Yet the Son of God was the acknowledged Sovereign of heav-
en, one in power and authority with the Father. In all the councils
of God, Christ was a participant, while Lucifer was not permitted
thus to enter into the divine purposes. "Why," questioned this
mighty angel, "should Christ have the supremacy? Why is He
thus honored above Lucifer?"

Leaving his place in the immediate presence of God, Lucifer
went forth to diffuse the spirit of discontent among the angels.
Working with mysterious secrecy, and for a time concealing his
real purpose under an appearance of reverence for God, he endeavored to excite dissatisfaction concerning the laws that governed heavenly beings, intimating that they imposed an unnecessary restraint. Since their natures were holy, he urged that the
angels should obey the dictates of their own will. He sought to
create sympathy for himself by representing that God had dealt
unjustly with him in bestowing supreme honor upon Christ"
(*The Great Controversy*, 495)

REFLECTION: *The central issue of the great controversy is Lucifer's un-*
willingness to submit to the authority of Jesus. Lucifer had it made. It
is easy for us to see how pride caused Lucifer to fall from the heights of
heaven to the pit that is now his domain. The real issue for us to consider
is if pride could be raising its stealthy, ugly head in our lives today.

JUNE 10

SURE FOUNDATION

*Therefore thus saith the Lord GOD, Behold, I lay in Zion for
a foundation a stone, a tried stone, a precious corner stone, a
sure foundation: he that believeth shall not make haste.*
Isaiah 28:16

"Sanctify the Lord of hosts Himself; and let Him be your
fear, and let Him be your dread. And He shall be for a
sanctuary; but for a stone of stumbling and for a rock
of offense to both the houses of Israel, for a gin and for a snare
to the inhabitants of Jerusalem. And many among them shall
stumble, and fall, and be broken, and be snared, and be taken."
Carried down in prophetic vision to the first advent, the prophet is shown that Christ is to bear trials and tests of which the
treatment of the chief cornerstone in the temple of Solomon was
symbolic. "Therefore thus saith the Lord God, Behold, I lay in
Zion for a foundation a stone, a tried stone, a precious cornerstone, a sure foundation: he that believeth shall not make haste"
(Isaiah 8:13–15; 28:16).

In infinite wisdom, God chose the foundation stone, and laid
it Himself. He called it "a sure foundation." The entire world
may lay upon it their burdens and grief; it can endure them all.
With perfect safety they may build upon it. Christ is a "tried
stone." Those who trust in Him, He never disappoints. (*The
Desire of Ages*, 598)

REFLECTION: *To fall upon the Rock and be broken is to give up our
self-righteousness and to go to Christ with the humility of a child, repenting of our transgressions, and believing in His forgiving love. And
so also it is by faith and obedience that we build on Christ as our foundation. (The Desire of Ages, 599)*

God Will Provide

He shall dwell on high: his place of defence shall be the munitions
of rocks: bread shall be given him; his waters shall be sure.
Isaiah 33:16

As the decree issued by the various rulers of Christendom against commandment keepers shall withdraw the protection of government. ... Many will find refuge in the strongholds of the mountains. Like the Christians of the Piedmont valleys, they will make the high places of the earth their sanctuaries and will thank God for "the munitions of rocks" (Isaiah 33:16). But many of all nations and of all classes, high and low, rich and poor, black and white, will be cast into the most unjust and cruel bondage. The beloved of God pass weary days, bound in chains, shut in by prison bars, sentenced to be slain, some apparently left to die of starvation in dark and loathsome dungeons. No human ear is open to hear their moans; no human hand is ready to lend them help.

Will the Lord forget His people in this trying hour? Did He forget faithful Noah when judgments were visited upon the antediluvian world? Did He forget Lot when the fire came down from heaven to consume the cities of the plain? Did He forget Joseph surrounded by idolaters in Egypt? Did He forget Elijah when the oath of Jezebel threatened him with the fate of the prophets of Baal? Did He forget Jeremiah in the dark and dismal pit of his prison house? Did He forget the three worthies in the fiery furnace? or Daniel in the den of lions? (*The Great Controversy*, 626)

REFLECTION: *"Behold, I have graven thee upon the palms of My hands"* *(Isaiah 49:16). The Lord of hosts has said: "He that toucheth you toucheth the apple of His eye" (Zechariah 2:8). (The Great Controversy, 626).The obvious answer to the question of "Will the Lord forget His people" is no, never. He loves us with an everlasting love. If we constantly keep that in our hearts, we overcome trials just as those great men and women in God's Word overcame.*

Sins Blotted Out

I, even I, am he that blotteth out thy transgressions for
mine own sake, and will not remember thy sins.
Isaiah 43:25

A ll who have truly repented of sin, and by faith claimed the blood of Christ as their atoning sacrifice, have had pardon entered against their names in the books of heaven; as they have become partakers of the righteousness of Christ, and their characters are found to be in harmony with the law of God, their sins will be blotted out, and they themselves will be accounted worthy of eternal life. The Lord declares, by the prophet Isaiah: "I, even I, am He that blotteth out thy transgressions for Mine own sake, and will not remember thy sins" (Isaiah 43:25). Said Jesus: "He that overcometh, the same shall be clothed in white raiment; and I will not blot out his name out of the book of life, but I will confess his name before My Father, and before His angels." "Whosoever therefore shall confess Me before men, him will I confess also before My Father which is in heaven. But whosoever shall deny Me before men, him will I also deny before My Father which is in heaven" (Revelation 3:5; Matthew 10:32,33). (*The Great Controversy,*483)

REFLECTION: *What a promise! "All who have repented of sin"… that word, all, means you and me. God has a solution for whatever we may have done to get our lives in a terrible mess. Repent and claim the blood of Christ to wash away our sins. God is truly in the restoration business. Make the decision today to start on a brand new, Christ-washed slate; and through His power you can live a new life.*

174 | JUNE

JUNE 13

$\mathcal{P}$URPOSE OF $\mathcal{T}$RIALS

Behold, I have refined thee, but not with silver; I have
chosen thee in the furnace of affliction.
Isaiah 48:10

$\mathcal{M}$any who sincerely consecrate their lives to God's service are surprised and disappointed to find themselves, as never before, confronted by obstacles and beset by trials and perplexities. They pray for Christlikeness of character, for a fitness for the Lord's work, and they are placed in circumstances that seem to call forth all the evil of their nature. Faults are revealed of which they did not even suspect the existence. Like Israel of old they question, "If God is leading us, why do all these things come upon us?"

It is because God is leading them that these things come upon them. Trials and obstacles are the Lord's chosen methods of discipline and His appointed conditions of success. He who reads the hearts of men knows their characters better than they themselves know them. He sees that some have powers and susceptibilities which, rightly directed, might be used in the advancement of His work. In His providence He brings these persons into different positions and varied circumstances that they may discover in their character the defects which have been concealed from their own knowledge. He gives them opportunity to correct these defects and to fit themselves for His service. Often He permits the fires of affliction to assail them that they may be purified." (*The Ministry of Healing,* 470, 471)

REFLECTION: *"Beloved, think it not strange concerning the fiery trial which is to try you, as though some strange thing happened unto you: but rejoice, inasmuch as ye are partakers of Christ's sufferings; that, when His glory shall be revealed, ye may be glad also with exceeding joy"* (1 Peter 4:12,13). *It's been said we shouldn't tell God about our great big problems; we should tell our problems to our great big God! If we think about the heavenly prize, the difficulties seem smaller.*

JUNE 14

GIVING THE TRUMPET A CERTAIN SOUND

*Cry aloud, spare not, lift up thy voice like a trumpet, and show my
people their transgression, and the house of Jacob their sins.*
Isaiah 58:1

*J*n view of this, what is the duty of the messenger of truth?
Shall he conclude that the truth ought not to be presented, since often its only effect is to arouse men to evade
or resist its claims? No; he has no more reason for withholding
the testimony of God's word, because it excites opposition, than
had earlier Reformers. The confession of faith made by saints and
martyrs was recorded for the benefit of succeeding generations.
Those living examples of holiness and steadfast integrity have
come down to inspire courage in those who are now called to
stand as witnesses for God. They received grace and truth, not for
themselves alone, but that, through them, the knowledge of God
might enlighten the earth. Has God given light to His servants in
this generation? Then they should let it shine forth to the world.

Anciently the Lord declared to one who spoke in His name:
"The house of Israel will not hearken unto thee; for they will not
hearken unto Me." Nevertheless He said: "Thou shalt speak My
words unto them, whether they will hear, or whether they will
forbear" (Ezekiel 3:7; 2:7). To the servant of God at this time is
the command addressed: "Lift up thy voice like a trumpet, and
show My people their transgression, and the house of Jacob their
sins" (*The Great Controversy*, 459)

REFLECTION: *The great obstacle both to the acceptance and to the prom-
ulgation of truth is the fact that it involves inconvenience and reproach
(The Great Controversy, 460). David is a good example of this. Nathan
was sent to David to reprove him of his sin. Because David accepted
the reproach, he repented and was restored. David could not be called
a "man after God's own heart" while he had unconfessed sins in his
heart. We should pray that God will show us where we have made a
wrong turn so that restoration can begin.*

REPAIRERS OF THE BREACH

*And they that shall be of thee shall build the old waste places: thou
shalt raise up the foundations of many generations; and thou shalt be
called, The repairer of the breach, The restorer of paths to dwell in.*
Isaiah 58:12

The prophet here describes a people who, in a time of general departure from truth and righteousness, are seeking to restore the principles that are the foundation of the kingdom of God. They are repairers of a breach that has been made in God's law — the wall that He has placed around His chosen ones for their protection, and obedience to whose precepts of justice, truth, and purity is to be their perpetual safeguard.

In words of unmistakable meaning the prophet points out the specific work of this remnant people who build the wall. "If thou turn away thy foot from the Sabbath, from doing thy pleasure on My holy day; and call the Sabbath a delight, the holy of the Lord, honorable; and shalt honor Him, not doing thine own ways, nor finding thine own pleasure, nor speaking thine own words: then shalt thou delight thyself in the Lord; and I will cause thee to ride upon the high places of the earth, and feed thee with the heritage of Jacob thy father: for the mouth of the Lord hath spoken it" (Isaiah 58:13, 14). (*Prophets and Kings*, 678)

REFLECTION: *God's remnant people, standing before the world as reformers, are to show that the law of God is the foundation of all enduring reform and that the Sabbath of the fourth commandment is to stand as a memorial of creation, a constant reminder of the power of God.* (Prophets and Kings, 678)

WOUNDED FOR OUR TRANSGRESSIONS

*But he was wounded for our transgressions, he was
bruised for our iniquities: the chastisement of our peace
was upon him; and with his stripes we are healed.*
Isaiah 53:5

It was to redeem us that Jesus lived and suffered and died. He became "a Man of Sorrows," that we might be made partakers of everlasting joy. God permitted His beloved Son, full of grace and truth, to come from a world of indescribable glory, to a world marred and blighted with sin, darkened with the shadow of death and the curse. He permitted Him to leave the bosom of His love, the adoration of the angels, to suffer shame, insult, humiliation, hatred, and death. "The chastisement of our peace was upon Him; and with His stripes we are healed" (Isaiah 53:5). Behold Him in the wilderness, in Gethsemane, upon the cross! The spotless Son of God took upon Himself the burden of sin. He who had been one with God, felt in His soul the awful separation that sin makes between God and man. This wrung from His lips the anguished cry, "My God, My God, why hast Thou forsaken Me?" (Matthew 27:46). It was the burden of sin, the sense of its terrible enormity, of its separation of the soul from God—it was this that broke the heart of the Son of God. (*Steps to Christ*, 13)

REFLECTION: *Today would be a good day to reflect on the amazing sacrifice that God made on our behalf. God loved us so much He sent His only Son to save a lost and dying world. That includes you and me. Accept that sacrifice today and form a relationship that will last throughout eternity.*

*M*AN OF *S*ORROWS

He is despised and rejected of men; a man of sorrows, and
acquainted with grief: and we hid as it were our faces from
him; he was despised, and we esteemed him not.
Isaiah 53:3

Let the repenting sinner fix his eyes upon "the Lamb of God, which taketh away the sin of the world" (John 1:29); and by beholding, he becomes changed. His fear is turned to joy, his doubts to hope. Gratitude springs up. The stony heart is broken. A tide of love sweeps into the soul. Christ is in him a well of water springing up unto everlasting life. When we see Jesus, a Man of Sorrows and acquainted with grief, working to save the lost, slighted, scorned, derided, driven from city to city till His mission was accomplished; when we behold Him in Gethsemane, sweating great drops of blood, and on the cross dying in agony,—when we see this, self will no longer clamor to be recognized. Looking unto Jesus, we shall be ashamed of our coldness, our lethargy, our self-seeking. We shall be willing to be anything or nothing, so that we may do heart service for the Master. We shall rejoice to bear the cross after Jesus, to endure trial, shame, or persecution for His dear sake." (*The Desire of Ages*, 439)

REFLECTION: *Sometimes the Christian life can be difficult; but so was the life of Christ. To Christ, every painful drop of blood was worth it because of His love for us. Christ promised that whatever we may have to lose, or leave for His sake, will be returned a hundredfold with eternal life added (Matthew 19:29). I don't know about you, but to me that's a pretty good deal.*

JUNE 18

The Potter and the Clay

But now, O Lord, thou art our father; we are the clay, and
thou our potter; and we all are the work of thy hand.
Isaiah 64:8

Trials and obstacles are the Lord's chosen methods of discipline and His appointed conditions of success. He who reads the hearts of men knows their characters better than they themselves know them. He sees that some have powers and susceptibilities which, rightly directed, might be used in the advancement of His work. In His providence He brings these persons into different positions and varied circumstances that they may discover in their character the defects which have been concealed from their own knowledge. He gives them opportunity to correct these defects and to fit themselves for His service. Often He permits the fires of affliction to assail them that they may be purified.

The fact that we are called upon to endure trial shows that the Lord Jesus sees in us something precious which He desires to develop. If He saw in us nothing whereby He might glorify His name, He would not spend time in refining us. He does not cast worthless stones into His furnace. It is valuable ore that He refines. The blacksmith puts the iron and steel into the fire that he may know what manner of metal they are. The Lord allows His chosen ones to be placed in the furnace of affliction to prove what temper they are of and whether they can be fashioned for His work. (*The Ministry of Healing*, 471)

REFLECTION: *So the great Master Worker desires to mold and fashion us. And as the clay is in the hands of the potter, so are we to be in His hands. (The Ministry of Healing, 471)*

*W*HO *C*AN *K*NOW *J*T?

The heart is deceitful above all things, and
desperately wicked: who can know it?
Jeremiah 17:9

The lips may express a poverty of soul that the heart does not acknowledge. While speaking to God of poverty of spirit, the heart may be swelling with the conceit of its own superior humility and exalted righteousness. In one way only can a true knowledge of self be obtained. We must behold Christ. It is ignorance of Him that makes men so uplifted in their own righteousness. When we contemplate His purity and excellence, we shall see our own weakness and poverty and defects as they really are. We shall see ourselves lost and hopeless, clad in garments of self-righteousness, like every other sinner. We shall see that if we are ever saved, it will not be through our own goodness, but through God's infinite grace.

The prayer of the publican was heard because it showed dependence reaching forth to lay hold upon Omnipotence. Self to the publican appeared nothing but shame. Thus it must be seen by all who seek God. By faith—faith that renounces all self-trust—the needy suppliant is to lay hold upon infinite power. (*Christ's Object Lessons*, 159)

REFLECTION: *The nearer we come to Jesus and the more clearly we discern the purity of His character, the more clearly we shall discern the exceeding sinfulness of sin and the less we shall feel like exalting ourselves. At every advance step in Christian experience our repentance will deepen. (Christ's Object Lessons, 160)*

*U*NFAITHFUL *P*ASTORS

*Woe be unto the pastors that destroy and scatter
the sheep of my pasture! saith the LORD.*
Jeremiah 23:1

"*W*oe be unto the pastors that destroy and scatter the sheep of My pasture!…Behold, I will visit upon you the evil of your doings." "Howl, ye shepherds, and cry; and wallow yourselves in the ashes, ye principal of the flock: for your days for slaughter and of your dispersions are accomplished…and the shepherds shall have no way to flee, nor the principal of the flock to escape" (Jeremiah 23:1, 2; 25:34, 35, margin).

Ministers and people see that they have not sustained the right relation to God. They see that they have rebelled against the Author of all just and righteous law. The setting aside of the divine precepts gave rise to thousands of springs of evil, discord, hatred, iniquity, until the earth became one vast field of strife, one sink of corruption. This is the view that now appears to those who rejected truth and chose to cherish error. No language can express the longing which the disobedient and disloyal feel for that which they have lost forever–eternal life. Men whom the world has worshiped for their talents and eloquence now see these things in their true light. They realize what they have forfeited by transgression, and they fall at the feet of those whose fidelity they have despised and derided, and confess that God has loved them. (*The Great Controversy*, 655)

REFLECTION: *Now, in their despair, these teachers confess before the world their work of deception. The multitudes are filled with fury. "We are lost!" they cry, "and you are the cause of our ruin;" and they turn upon the false shepherds. (The Great Controversy, 655). Paul was truly a man of God, but the Bereans were praised because they listened to him with reserve; then went to the scriptures and checked him out (Acts 17:11). We should never blindly believe, even those that claim to be ministers of Christ. Our only safety is in the Word of God.*

*T*EARFUL *W*ARNINGS

*And the L*ORD *said unto him, Go through the midst of the city, through the midst of Jerusalem, and set a mark upon the foreheads of the men that sigh and that cry for all the abominations that be done in the midst thereof.*
Ezekiel 9:4

*I*n In the time of the end the people of God will sigh and cry for the abominations done in the land. With tears they will warn the wicked of their danger in trampling upon the divine law, and with unutterable sorrow they will humble themselves before the Lord in penitence. The wicked will mock their sorrow and ridicule their solemn appeals. But the anguish and humiliation of God's people is unmistakable evidence that they are regaining the strength and nobility of character lost in consequence of sin. It is because they are drawing nearer to Christ, because their eyes are fixed on His perfect purity, that they discern so clearly the exceeding sinfulness of sin. Meekness and lowliness are the conditions of success and victory. A crown of glory awaits those who bow at the foot of the cross.

God's faithful, praying ones are, as it were, shut in with Him. They themselves know not how securely they are shielded. Urged on by Satan, the rulers of this world are seeking to destroy them; but could the eyes of God's children be opened as were the eyes of Elisha's servant at Dothan, they would see angels of God encamped about them, holding in check the hosts of darkness. (*Prophets and Kings*, 590)

REFLECTION: *Are you crying and sighing for what is going on around us today? Our eyes will see things as they really are as we fix our eyes upon His perfect purity. Today we can experience closeness to Christ. When trials come, look to Jesus for help.*

JUNE 22

Faithful Shepherd

As a shepherd seeketh out his flock in the day that he is among his sheep that are scattered; so will I seek out my sheep, and will deliver them out of all places where they have been scattered in the cloudy and dark day.

Ezekiel 34:12

The wide-spreading tablelands on the east of Jordan afforded abundant pasturage for flocks, and through the gorges and over the wooded hills had wandered many a lost sheep, to be searched for and brought back by the shepherd's care. In the company about Jesus there were shepherds, and also men who had money invested in flocks and herds, and all could appreciate His illustration: "What man of you, having an hundred sheep, if he lose one of them, doth not leave the ninety and nine in the wilderness, and go after that which is lost, until he find it?"...

As the shepherd loves his sheep, and cannot rest if even one be missing, so, in an infinitely higher degree, does God love every outcast soul....He says, "As a shepherd seeketh out his flock in the day that he is among his sheep that are scattered; so will I seek out My sheep, and will deliver them out of all places where they have been scattered in the cloudy and dark day" (Ezekiel 34:12). (*Christ's Object Lessons*, 186, 187)

REFLECTION: *Jesus is looking for you today. Will you stop to listen to His voice, and respond to His call?*

JUNE 23

A New Heart

A new heart also will I give you, and a new spirit will I put within you: and I will take away the stony heart out of your flesh, and I will give you an heart of flesh.
Ezekiel 36:26

You feel that sin has separated you from God, that you are in bondage to the power of evil. The more you struggle to escape, the more you realize your helplessness. Your motives are impure; your heart is unclean. You see that your life has been filled with selfishness and sin. You long to be forgiven, to be cleansed, to be set free. Harmony with God, likeness to Him—what can you do to obtain it?

It is peace that you need—Heaven's forgiveness and peace and love in the soul. Money cannot buy it, intellect cannot procure it, wisdom cannot attain to it; you can never hope, by your own efforts, to secure it. But God offers it to you as a gift, "without money and without price" (Isaiah 55:1). It is yours if you will but reach out your hand and grasp it. The Lord says, "Though your sins be as scarlet, they shall be as white as snow; though they be red like crimson, they shall be as wool" (Isaiah 1:18). "A new heart also will I give you, and a new spirit will I put within you" (Ezekiel 36:26). (*Steps to Christ*, 49)

REFLECTION: *Claim those promises today for the forgiveness, peace, and love that are offered freely.*

JUNE 24

Daniel Taken to Babylon

*Children in whom was no blemish, but well favoured, and skilful in all
wisdom, and cunning in knowledge, and understanding science, and
such as had ability in them to stand in the king's palace, and whom
they might teach the learning and the tongue of the Chaldeans.*
Daniel 1:4

Among the children of Israel who were carried captive
to Babylon at the beginning of the seventy years' captivity were Christian patriots, men who were as true
as steel to principle, who would not be corrupted by selfishness,
but who would honor God at the loss of all things. In the land
of their captivity these men were to carry out God's purpose
by giving to heathen nations the blessings that come through
a knowledge of Jehovah. They were to be His representatives.
Never were they to compromise with idolaters; their faith and
their name as worshipers of the living God they were to bear as
a high honor. And this they did. In prosperity and adversity they
honored God, and God honored them.

The fact that these men, worshipers of Jehovah, were captives in Babylon, and that the vessels of God's house had been
placed in the Temple of the Babylonish gods, was boastfully cited
by the victors as evidence that their religion and customs were
superior to the religion and customs of the Hebrews. Yet through
the very humiliations that Israel's departure from Him had invited, God gave Babylon evidence of His supremacy, of the holiness
of His requirements, and of the sure results of obedience. And
this testimony He gave, as alone it could be given, through those
who were loyal to Him. (*Prophets and Kings*, 479)

REFLECTION: *Among those taken to Babylon were Daniel and his three
Hebrew friends. Though God's people — who were also taken captive —
chose to steep themselves in the customs of Babylon, these four stood
firm for the Lord; and thus God was glorified and blessed them.*

RESULTS OF TEMPERANCE

But Daniel purposed in his heart that he would not defile himself with the portion of the king's meat, nor with the wine which he drank: therefore he requested of the prince of the eunuchs that he might not defile himself.

Daniel 1:8

Daniel and his associates had been trained by their parents to habits of strict temperance. They had been taught that God would hold them accountable for their capabilities, and that they must never dwarf or enfeeble their powers. This education was to Daniel and his companions the means of their preservation amidst the demoralizing influences of the court of Babylon. Strong were the temptations surrounding them in that corrupt and luxurious court, but they remained uncontaminated. No power, no influence, could sway them from the principles they had learned in early life by a study of the word and works of God.

Had Daniel so desired, he might have found in his surroundings a plausible excuse for departing from strictly temperate habits. He might have argued that, dependent as he was on the king's favor and subject to his power, there was no other course for him to pursue than to eat of the king's food and drink of his wine; for should he adhere to the divine teaching, he would offend the king and probably lose his position and his life. (*Prophets and Kings*, 482)

REFLECTION: *These faithful four chose to remain true to God in every circumstance and trial. They reasoned that any compromise here would weaken their resolve and ability to distinguish between right and wrong. This story should encourage each one of us to stand for a "Thus saith the Lord." Today, let us not bend to any kind of peer pressure.*

JUNE 26

THE KING'S DREAM

*And in the second year of the reign of Nebuchadnezzar,
Nebuchadnezzar dreamed dreams, wherewith his spirit
was troubled, and his sleep brake from him.*
Daniel 2:1

Hundreds of years before certain nations came upon the stage of action, the Omniscient One looked down the ages and predicted the rise and fall of the universal kingdoms. God declared to Nebuchadnezzar that the kingdom of Babylon should fall, and a second kingdom would arise, which also would have its period of trial. Failing to exalt the true God, its glory would fade, and a third kingdom would occupy its place. This also would pass away; and a fourth, strong as iron, would subdue the nations of the world.

Had the rulers of Babylon — that richest of all earthly kingdoms — kept always before them the fear of Jehovah, they would have been given wisdom and power which would have bound them to Him and kept them strong. But they made God their refuge only when harassed and perplexed. At such times, failing to find help in their great men, they sought it from men like Daniel — men who they knew honored the living God and were honored by Him. To these men they appealed to unravel the mysteries of Providence; for though the rulers of proud Babylon were men of the highest intellect, they had separated themselves so far from God by transgression that they could not understand the revelations and the warnings given them concerning the future"(*Prophets and Kings*, 501)

REFLECTION: *What led to Babylon's fall? It was their pride and independence from God. The fear of the Lord no longer had a place in their hearts. If we don't keep the fear of the Lord in our hearts, we'll fall too.*

THE GOLDEN IMAGE

*Nebuchadnezzar the king made an image of gold, whose height
was threescore cubits, and the breadth thereof six cubits: he set
it up in the plain of Dura, in the province of Babylon.*
Daniel 3:1

The words, "Thou art this head of gold," had made a deep impression upon the ruler's mind (Verse 38). The wise men of his realm, taking advantage of this and of his return to idolatry, proposed that he make an image similar to the one seen in his dream, and set it up where all might behold the head of gold, which had been interpreted as representing his kingdom.

Pleased with the flattering suggestion, he determined to carry it out, and to go even farther. Instead of reproducing the image as he had seen it, he would excel the original. His image should not deteriorate in value from the head to the feet, but should be entirely of gold—symbolic throughout of Babylon as an eternal, indestructible, all-powerful kingdom, which should break in pieces all other kingdoms and stand forever.

The thought of establishing the empire and a dynasty that should endure forever, appealed very strongly to the mighty ruler before whose arms the nations of earth had been unable to stand. With an enthusiasm born of boundless ambition and selfish pride, he entered into counsel with his wise men as to how to bring this about. (*Prophets and Kings*, 504)

REFLECTION: *How soon we forget the providences of God! This makes us prone to fall back into self-centered living and self-exultation.*

TRUST IN GOD

*If it be so, our God whom we serve is able to deliver us from the burning
fiery furnace, and he will deliver us out of thine hand, O king.*
Daniel 3:17

In vain were the king's threats. He could not turn the men
from their allegiance to the Ruler of the universe. From
the history of their fathers they had learned that disobedience to God results in dishonor, disaster, and death; and that
the fear of the Lord is the beginning of wisdom, the foundation
of all true prosperity. Calmly facing the furnace, they said, "O
Nebuchadnezzar, we are not careful to answer thee in this matter. If it be so [if this is your decision], our God whom we serve
is able to deliver us from the burning fiery furnace, and He will
deliver us out of thine hand, O king." Their faith strengthened as
they declared that God would be glorified by delivering them,
and with triumphant assurance born of implicit trust in God,
they added, "But if not, be it known unto thee, O king, that we
will not serve thy gods, nor worship the golden image which
thou hast set up." (*Prophets and Kings*, 507)

REFLECTION: *Their decision was final; they would not worship that
apostate image. These three Hebrew youth would not even allow the
threat of death to sway them from the right. God was in control, and
they trusted in Him. He's in control today. Where are you putting
your trust?*

JUNE 29

THE SON OF GOD

He answered and said, Lo, I see four men loose, walking in the midst of the fire, and they have no hurt; and the form of the fourth is like the Son of God.
Daniel 3:25

How did that heathen king know what the Son of God was like? The Hebrew captives filling positions of trust in Babylon had in life and character represented before him the truth. When asked for a reason of their faith, they had given it without hesitation. Plainly and simply they had presented the principles of righteousness, thus teaching those around them of the God whom they worshiped. They had told of Christ, the Redeemer to come; and in the form of the fourth in the midst of the fire the king recognized the Son of God.

And now, his own greatness and dignity forgotten, Nebuchadnezzar descended from his throne and, going to the mouth of the furnace, cried out, "Ye servants of the most high God, come forth, and come hither."

Then Shadrach, Meshach, and Abednego came forth before the vast multitude, showing themselves unhurt. The presence of their Saviour had guarded them from harm, and only their fetters had been burned. "And the princes, governors, and captains, and the king's counselors, being gathered together, saw these men, upon whose bodies the fire had no power, nor was an hair of their head singed, neither were their coats changed, nor the smell of fire had passed on them." (*Prophets and Kings*, 509)

REFLECTION: *After this manifestation of the true God, we don't hear of the golden image ever again. What power!*

JUNE 30

A Bad Decree

*Therefore I make a decree, That every people, nation, and language,
which speak any thing amiss against the God of Shadrach, Meshach,
and Abednego, shall be cut in pieces, and their houses shall be made a
dunghill: because there is no other God that can deliver after this sort.*
Daniel 3:29

It was right for the king to make public confession, and to seek to exalt the God of heaven above all other gods; but in endeavoring to force his subjects to make a similar confession of faith and to show similar reverence, Nebuchadnezzar was exceeding his right as a temporal sovereign. He had no more right, either civil or moral, to threaten men with death for not worshiping God, than he had to make the decree consigning to the flames all who refused to worship the golden image. God never compels the obedience of man. He leaves all free to choose whom they will serve.

By the deliverance of His faithful servants, the Lord declared that He takes His stand with the oppressed, and rebukes all earthly powers that rebel against the authority of Heaven. The three Hebrews declared to the whole nation of Babylon their faith in Him whom they worshiped. They relied on God. In the hour of their trial they remembered the promise, "When thou passest through the waters, I will be with thee; and through the rivers, they shall not overflow thee: when thou walkest through the fire, thou shalt not be burned; neither shall the flame kindle upon thee" (Isaiah 43:2). And in a marvelous manner their faith in the living Word had been honored in the sight of all. The tidings of their wonderful deliverance were carried to many countries by the representatives of the different nations that had been invited by Nebuchadnezzar to the dedication. Through the faithfulness of His children, God was glorified in all the earth. (*Prophets and Kings*, 510, 511)

REFLECTION: *History will be repeated. All nations will be required to worship the beast of Revelation chapter thirteen. We too must have a faith that will not falter, even under the threat of death.*

JULY

WEIGHED AND FOUND WANTING

TEKEL: Thou art weighed in the balances, and found wanting.
Daniel 5:27

The righteous and the wicked will still be living upon the earth in their mortal state—men will be planting and building, eating and drinking, all unconscious that the final, irrevocable decision has been pronounced in the sanctuary above. Before the Flood, after Noah entered the ark, God shut him in and shut the ungodly out; but for seven days the people, knowing not that their doom was fixed, continued their careless, pleasure-loving life and mocked the warnings of impending judgment. "So," says the Saviour, "shall also the coming of the Son of man be" (Matthew 24:39). Silently, unnoticed as the midnight thief, will come the decisive hour which marks the fixing of every man's destiny, the final withdrawal of mercy's offer to guilty men.

"Watch ye therefore:...lest coming suddenly He find you sleeping" (Mark 13:35,36). Perilous is the condition of those who, growing weary of their watch, turn to the attractions of the world. While the man of business is absorbed in the pursuit of gain, while the pleasure lover is seeking indulgence, while the daughter of fashion is arranging her adornments—it may be in that hour the Judge of all the earth will pronounce the sentence: "Thou art weighed in the balances, and art found wanting" (Daniel 5:2). *(Great Controversy 491)*

REFLECTION: *No one knows when probation will close. What we do know is that when it does, there will be no more chances. Let us not stray from the One who saves mightily.*

*W*ITHOUT *F*AULT

Then the presidents and princes sought to find occasion
against Daniel concerning the kingdom; but they could
find none occasion nor fault; forasmuch as he was faithful,
neither was there any error or fault found in him.

Daniel 6:4

Unwavering in allegiance to God, unyielding in the mastery of himself, Daniel's noble dignity and courteous deference won for him in his youth the 'favor and tender love' of the heathen officer in whose charge he was. The same characteristics marked his life. Speedily he rose to the position of prime minister of the kingdom. Throughout the reign of successive monarchs, the downfall of the nation, and the establishment of a rival kingdom, such were his wisdom and statesmanship, so perfect his tact, his courtesy, and his genuine goodness of heart, combined with fidelity to principle, that even his enemies were forced to the confession that "they could find none occasion nor fault; forasmuch as he was faithful" (Daniel 6:4).

While Daniel clung to God with unwavering trust, the spirit of prophetic power came upon him. While honored by men with the responsibilities of the court and the secrets of the kingdom, he was honored by God as His ambassador, and taught to read the mysteries of ages to come. Heathen monarchs, through association with Heaven's representative, were constrained to acknowledge the God of Daniel. "Of a truth it is," declared Nebuchadnezzar, "that your God is a God of gods, and a Lord of kings, and a revealer of secrets." (*Education*, 55, 56)

REFLECTION: *Instead of avoiding the wrath of his enemies by obeying the unjust edict, Daniel prayed for strength to endure the inevitable consequences. Let us boldly do that which is right, as did Daniel.*

JULY 3

PROTECTED IN TRIALS

*Then the king commanded, and they brought Daniel, and cast him
into the den of lions. Now the king spake and said unto Daniel,
Thy God whom thou servest continually, he will deliver thee.*

Daniel 6:16

God did not prevent Daniel's enemies from casting him into the lions' den; He permitted evil angels and wicked men thus far to accomplish their purpose; but it was that He might make the deliverance of His servant more marked, and the defeat of the enemies of truth and righteousness more complete. "Surely the wrath of man shall praise Thee" (Psalm 76:10), the psalmist has testified. Through the courage of this one man who chose to follow right rather than policy, Satan was to be defeated, and the name of God was to be exalted and honored.

Early the next morning King Darius hastened to the den and "cried with a lamentable voice, ... O Daniel, servant of the living God, is thy God, whom thou servest continually, able to deliver thee from the lions?"

The voice of the prophet replied: "O king, live forever. My God hath sent His angel, and hath shut the lions' mouths, that they have not hurt me: forasmuch as before Him innocency was found in me; and also before thee, O king, have I done no hurt." (*Prophets and Kings*, 543, 544)

REFLECTION: *In the end, the wicked do not prosper. Truth is eternal, but all that is evil is short lived.*

$uccessful in $usiness

So this Daniel prospered in the reign of Darius,
and in the reign of Cyrus the Persian.
Daniel 6:28

The experience of Daniel as a statesman in the kingdoms of Babylon and Medo-Persia reveals the truth that a businessman is not necessarily a designing, policy man, but that he may be a man instructed by God at every step. Daniel, the prime minister of the greatest of earthly kingdoms, was at the same time a prophet of God, receiving the light of heavenly inspiration. A man of like passions as ourselves, the pen of inspiration describes him as without fault. His business transactions, when subjected to the closest scrutiny of his enemies, were found to be without one flaw. He was an example of what every businessman may become when his heart is converted and consecrated, and when his motives are right in the sight of God.

Strict compliance with the requirements of Heaven brings temporal as well as spiritual blessings. Unwavering in his allegiance to God, unyielding in his mastery of self, Daniel, by his noble dignity and unswerving integrity, while yet a young man, won the "favor and tender love" of the heathen officer in whose charge he had been placed (Daniel 1:9). The same characteristics marked his afterlife. (*Prophets and Kings*, 546)

REFLECTION: *If all who claim they are Christians would not complain at their work, be on time, go the extra mile, never cheat on their hours at work, etc., then all Christians would be the most sought-after people in the world. Let us be real Christians in all we do. When people see you as a true follower of Jesus, they will be inexplicably drawn to you. Let us all learn to walk the walk and not just talk the walk.*

JULY 5

THE JUDGMENT

A fiery stream issued and came forth from before him: thousand thousands ministered unto him, and ten thousand times ten thousand stood before him: the judgment was set, and the books were opened.
Daniel 7:10

Thus was presented to the prophet's vision the great and solemn day when the characters and the lives of men should pass in review before the Judge of all the earth, and to every man should be rendered "according to his works." The Ancient of Days is God the Father. Says the psalmist: "Before the mountains were brought forth, or ever Thou hadst formed the earth and the world, even from everlasting to everlasting, Thou art God" (Psalm 90:2). It is He, the source of all being, and the fountain of all law, that is to preside in the judgment. And holy angels as ministers and witnesses, in number "ten thousand times ten thousand, and thousands of thousands," attend this great tribunal.

The books of record in heaven, in which the names and the deeds of men are registered, are to determine the decisions of the judgment. Says the prophet Daniel: "The judgment was set, and the books were opened." The revelator, describing the same scene, adds: "Another book was opened, which is the book of life: and the dead were judged out of those things which were written in the books, according to their works" (Revelation 20:12). (*Great Controversy*, 479, 480)

REFLECTION: *What a glorious scene! The Father, the Ancient of Days, enters the Most Holy Place, and the judgment is set. Then angels escort Jesus to the Father, and the judgment begins. The Father presides over the judgment, but Jesus, the Son of man, executes the judgment.*

JULY 6

THE LITTLE HORN

And he shall speak great words against the most High, and shall wear out the saints of the most High, and think to change times and laws: and they shall be given into his hand until a time and times and the dividing of time.
Daniel 7:25

Says Daniel, of the little horn, the papacy: "He shall think to change times and the law" (Daniel 7:25, R.V.). And Paul styled the same power the "man of sin," who was to exalt himself above God. One prophecy is a complement of the other. Only by changing God's law could the papacy exalt itself above God; whoever should understandingly keep the law as thus changed would be giving supreme honor to that power by which the change was made. Such an act of obedience to papal laws would be a mark of allegiance to the pope in the place of God.

The papacy has attempted to change the law of God. The second commandment, forbidding image worship, has been dropped from the law, and the fourth commandment has been so changed as to authorize the observance of the first instead of the seventh day as the Sabbath. But papists urge, as a reason for omitting the second commandment, that it is unnecessary, being included in the first, and that they are giving the law exactly as God designed it to be understood. This cannot be the change foretold by the prophet. An intentional, deliberate change is presented: "He shall think to change the times and the law." The change in the fourth commandment exactly fulfills the prophecy. (*The Great Controversy*, 446)

REFLECTION: *By claiming the authority to change God's law, the papal power sets itself above God. God's Law stands firm. No organization or person has the right to change what God has put in order.*

JULY 7

CLEANSING OF THE SANCTUARY

And he said unto me, Unto two thousand and three hundred days; then shall the sanctuary be cleansed.
Daniel 8:14

But the most important question remains to be answered: What is the cleansing of the sanctuary? ...

The cleansing, both in the typical and in the real service, must be accomplished with blood: in the former, with the blood of animals; in the latter, with the blood of Christ. Paul states, as the reason why this cleansing must be performed with blood, that without shedding of blood is no remission. ...

The ministration of the earthly sanctuary consisted of two divisions; the priests ministered daily in the holy place, while once a year the high priest performed a special work of atonement in the most holy, for the cleansing of the sanctuary. Day by day the repentant sinner brought his offering to the door of the tabernacle and, placing his hand upon the victim's head, confessed his sins, thus in figure transferring them from himself to the innocent sacrifice. ...

Such was the work that went on, day by day, throughout the year. The sins of Israel were thus transferred to the sanctuary, and a special work became necessary for their removal. God commanded that an atonement be made for each of the sacred apartments. ...

Once a year, on the great Day of Atonement, the priest entered the most holy place for the cleansing of the sanctuary. The work there performed completed the yearly round of ministration. (*The Great Controversy*, 417–419)

REFLECTION: *The Day of Atonement was a very solemn day; each Israelite was to make himself right with God and his fellow man. Both the individual and the sanctuary were to be cleansed from sin. We are living in the very last days of this earth's history. Let's get serious about our walk with God.*

DANIEL'S PRAYER

And I set my face unto the Lord God, to seek by prayer and
supplications, with fasting, and sackcloth, and ashes.
Daniel 9:3

"Lord, hear; O Lord, forgive; O Lord, hearken and do; defer not, for Thine own sake, O my God: for Thy city and Thy people are called by Thy name" (Verses 4–9, 16–19).

Heaven was bending low to hear the earnest supplication of the prophet. Even before he had finished his plea for pardon and restoration, the mighty Gabriel again appeared to him, and called his attention to the vision he had seen prior to the fall of Babylon and the death of Belshazzar. And then the angel outlined before him in detail the period of the seventy weeks, which was to begin at the time of "the going forth of the commandment to restore and to build Jerusalem" (Verse 25).

Daniel's prayer had been offered "'in the first year of Darius" (verse 1), the Median monarch whose general, Cyrus, had wrested from Babylonia the scepter of universal rule. The reign of Darius was honored of God. To him was sent the angel Gabriel, "to confirm and to strengthen him" (Daniel 11:1). Upon his death, within about two years of the fall of Babylon, Cyrus succeeded to the throne, and the beginning of his reign marked the completion of the seventy years since the first company of Hebrews had been taken by Nebuchadnezzar from their Judean home to Babylon. (*Prophets and Kings,* 556)

REFLECTION: *The prayer of Daniel, found in chapter nine, is the longest prayer recorded in the Old Testament. We generally think of Daniel as the prophet of prophecy, but Daniel was also very much the prophet of prayer. Each one of us has the privilege, as did Daniel, of a prayer life. There is a fountain of life in earnest and honest prayer.*

A Sanctified Life

O Lord, hear; O Lord, forgive; O Lord, hearken and do; defer not, for Thine own sake, O my God: for thy city and thy people are called by thy name.
Daniel 9:19

Those who experience the sanctification of the Bible will manifest a spirit of humility. Like Moses, they have had a view of the awful majesty of holiness, and they see their own unworthiness in contrast with the purity and exalted perfection of the Infinite One.

The prophet Daniel was an example of true sanctification. His long life was filled up with noble service for his Master. He was a man "greatly beloved" (Daniel 10:11) of Heaven. Yet instead of claiming to be pure and holy, this honored prophet identified himself with the really sinful of Israel as he pleaded before God in behalf of his people: "We do not present our supplications before Thee for our righteousness, but for Thy great mercies." "We have sinned, we have done wickedly." He declares: "I was speaking, and praying, and confessing my sin and the sin of my people." And when at a later time the Son of God appeared, to give him instruction, Daniel says: "My comeliness was turned in me into corruption, and I retained no strength" (Daniel 9:18, 15, 20; 10:8). (*The Great Controversy*, 470)

REFLECTION: *There can be no self-exaltation, no boastful claim to freedom from sin, on the part of those who walk in the shadow of Calvary's cross. They feel that it was their sin which caused the agony that broke the heart of the Son of God, and this thought will lead them to self-abasement. Those who live nearest to Jesus discern most clearly the frailty and sinfulness of humanity, and their only hope is in the merit of a crucified and risen Saviour. (The Great Controversy, 471)*

JULY 10

$\mathcal{S}$EVENTY $\mathcal{W}$EEKS

Seventy weeks are determined upon thy people and upon thy holy city,
to finish the transgression, and to make an end of sins, and to make
reconciliation for iniquity, and to bring in everlasting righteousness,
and to seal up the vision and prophecy, and to anoint the most Holy.
Daniel 9:24

Seventy weeks, representing 490 years, are declared by the angel to be cut off, as specially pertaining to the Jews. ...

"From the going forth of the commandment to restore and to build Jerusalem unto the Messiah the Prince shall be seven weeks, and threescore and two weeks"—namely, sixty-nine weeks, or 483 years. The decree of Artaxerxes went into effect in the autumn of 457 B.C. From this date, 483 years extend to the autumn of A.D. 27. At that time this prophecy was fulfilled. ... In the autumn of A.D. 27 Christ was baptized by John and received the anointing of the Spirit. ...

"And He shall confirm the covenant with many for one week." The "week" here brought to view is the last one of the seventy; it is the last seven years of the period allotted especially to the Jews. During this time, extending from A.D. 27 to A.D. 34.

"In the midst of the week He shall cause the sacrifice and the oblation to cease." In A.D. 31, three and a half years after His baptism, our Lord was crucified. With the great sacrifice offered upon Calvary, ended that system of offerings which for four thousand years had pointed forward to the Lamb of God. (*The Great Controversy*, 326, 327)

REFLECTION: *Nearly six hundred years before the crucifixion of Christ, Daniel was given a time prophecy that pinpointed to the exact year Jesus would die for our sins. What wisdom there is in being connected with God!*

JULY 11

REFORMS NEEDED

*Blow ye the trumpet in Zion, and sound an alarm in my
holy mountain: let all the inhabitants of the land tremble:
for the day of the LORD cometh, for it is nigh at hand.*
Joel 2:1

*I*n view of that great day the word of God, in the most solemn and impressive language, calls upon His people to
arouse from their spiritual lethargy and to seek His face
with repentance and humiliation: "Blow ye the trumpet in Zion,
and sound an alarm in My holy mountain: let all the inhabitants
of the land tremble: for the day of the Lord cometh, for it is nigh
at hand." "Sanctify a fast, call a solemn assembly: gather the people, sanctify the congregation, assemble the elders, gather the
children:…let the bridegroom go forth of his chamber, and the
bride out of her closet. Let the priests, the ministers of the Lord,
weep between the porch and the altar" (Joel 2:1, 15–17).…

To prepare a people to stand in the day of God, a great work
of reform was to be accomplished. God saw that many of His
professed people were not building for eternity, and in His mercy
He was about to send a message of warning to arouse them from
their stupor and lead them to make ready for the coming of the
Lord. (*The Great Controversy*, 311)

REFLECTION: *What a caring God we serve! Even when we have gone
astray and don't deserve another chance, God will still send a message
to each one of us. Are you listening?*

The Latter Rain

*Be glad then, ye children of Zion, and rejoice in the LORD your God: for he
hath given you the former rain moderately, and he will cause to come down
for you the rain, the former rain, and the latter rain in the first month.*

Joel 2:23

The work will be similar to that of the Day of Pentecost.
As the "former rain" was given, in the outpouring of the
Holy Spirit at the opening of the gospel, to cause the up-
springing of the precious seed, so the "latter rain" will be given
at its close for the ripening of the harvest. "Then shall we know, if
we follow on to know the Lord: His going forth is prepared as the
morning; and He shall come unto us as the rain, as the latter and
former rain unto the earth" (Hosea 6:3). "Be glad then, ye children of Zion, and rejoice in the Lord your God: for He hath given
you the former rain moderately, and He will cause to come down
for you the rain, the former rain, and the latter rain" (Joel 2:23).
"In the last days, saith God, I will pour out of My Spirit upon all
flesh. … And it shall come to pass, that whosoever shall call on
the name of the Lord shall be saved" (Acts 2:17, 21).

The great work of the gospel is not to close with less manifestation of the power of God than marked its opening. The prophecies which were fulfilled in the outpouring of the former rain at
the opening of the gospel are again to be fulfilled in the latter rain
at its close. (*The Great Controversy*, 611)

REFLECTION: *In the end, thousands of voices around the world will give
the last gospel call with power.*

JULY 13

$\mathcal{U}$NBELIEVING $\mathcal{C}$OMPANIONS

Can two walk together, except they be agreed?
Amos 3:3

he wife of Lot was a selfish, irreligious woman, and her
influence was exerted to separate her husband from
Abraham. But for her, Lot would not have remained in
Sodom, deprived of the counsel of the wise, God-fearing patriarch. The influence of his wife and the associations of that wicked
city would have led him to apostatize from God had it not been
for the faithful instruction he had early received from Abraham.
The marriage of Lot and his choice of Sodom for a home were the
first links in a chain of events fraught with evil to the world for
many generations.

No one who fears God can without danger connect himself
with one who fears Him not. "Can two walk together, except
they be agreed?"(Amos 3:3). The happiness and prosperity of
the marriage relation depends upon the unity of the parties; but
between the believer and the unbeliever there is a radical difference of tastes, inclinations, and purposes. They are serving two
masters, between whom there can be no concord. However pure
and correct one's principles may be, the influence of an unbelieving companion will have a tendency to lead away from God.
(*Patriarchs and Prophets*, 174)

REFLECTION: *This verse applies to all of our relationships. Do you have
an unbelieving spouse or friend? Pray for him or her to accept Jesus and
experience the beautiful life that only He can give. Another point that is
vital to our safety is that we don't get involved with others in a personal
relationship when we are not on the same foundation. They will always
tend to draw us away from Christ instead of us drawing them to Christ.*

JULY 14

CHRIST'S FIRST ADVENT

But thou, Bethlehem Ephratah, though thou be little among the thousands of Judah, yet out of thee shall he come forth unto me that is to be ruler in Israel; whose goings forth have been from of old, from everlasting.
Micah 5:2

At the time of Christ's first advent the priests and scribes of the Holy City, to whom were entrusted the oracles of God, might have discerned the signs of the times and proclaimed the coming of the Promised One. The prophecy of Micah designated His birthplace; Daniel specified the time of His advent (Micah 5:2; Daniel 9:25). God committed these prophecies to the Jewish leaders; they were without excuse if they did not know and declare to the people that the Messiah's coming was at hand. Their ignorance was the result of sinful neglect. The Jews were building monuments for the slain prophets of God, while by their deference to the great men of earth they were paying homage to the servants of Satan. Absorbed in their ambitious strife for place and power among men, they lost sight of the divine honors proffered them by the King of heaven. (*The Great Controversy*, 313)

REFLECTION: *How careful we need to be to not allow wrong influences to affect our discernment of truth and our commitment to God. Let's make sure that we are discerning the times in which we are living and not be like the leaders of old.*

JULY 15

*G*OD'S *S*TRANGE *A*CT

*The LORD is slow to anger, and great in power, and will not at
all acquit the wicked: the LORD hath his way in the whirlwind
and in the storm, and the clouds are the dust of his feet.*
Nahum 1:3

God's judgments will be visited upon those who are seeking to oppress and destroy His people. His long forbearance with the wicked emboldens men in transgression, but their punishment is nonetheless certain and terrible because it is long delayed. "The Lord shall rise up as in Mount Perazim, He shall be wroth as in the valley of Gibeon, that He may do His work, His strange work; and bring to pass His act, His strange act" (Isaiah 28:21). To our merciful God the act of punishment is a strange act. "As I live, saith the Lord God, I have no pleasure in the death of the wicked" (Ezekiel 33:11). The Lord is "merciful and gracious, long-suffering, and abundant in goodness and truth, ... forgiving iniquity and transgression and sin." Yet He will "by no means clear the guilty." "The Lord is slow to anger, and great in power, and will not at all acquit the wicked" (Exodus 34:6, 7; Nahum 1:3). By terrible things in righteousness He will vindicate the authority of His downtrodden law. The severity of the retribution awaiting the transgressor may be judged by the Lord's reluctance to execute justice. The nation with which He bears long, and which He will not smite until it has filled up the measure of its iniquity in God's account, will finally drink the cup of wrath unmixed with mercy. (*The Great Controversy*, 627)

REFLECTION: *To be with Christ forever will be more amazing than we can ever imagine. Why would we do anything to miss that? When Christ comes there will be only two classes: the saved and the lost. Let's make the right choice. Eternal life is at stake.*

FINALLY DESTRUCTION OF EVIL

For, behold, the day cometh, that shall burn as an oven; and
all the proud, yea, and all that do wickedly, shall be stubble:
and the day that cometh shall burn them up, saith the LORD of
hosts, that it shall leave them neither root nor branch.
Malachi 4:1

Satan, the root of every sin, and all evil workers, who are his branches, shall be utterly cut off. An end will be made of sin, with all the woe and ruin that have resulted from it. Says the psalmist, "Thou hast destroyed the wicked, thou hast put out their name forever and ever. O thou enemy, destructions are come to a perpetual end" (Psalm 9:5, 6).

But amid the tempest of divine judgment the children of God will have no cause for fear. "The Lord will be the hope of His people, and the strength of the children of Israel" (Joel 3:16). The day that brings terror and destruction to the transgressors of God's law will bring to the obedient "joy unspeakable and full of glory" "Gather My saints together unto Me," saith the Lord, "those that have made a covenant with Me by sacrifice. And the heavens shall declare His righteousness: for God is Judge Himself." (*Patriarchs and Prophets*, 341)

REFLECTION: *Be sure that you are on the Lord's side by making a full surrender of every area of your life to Him today.*

THE SPIRIT AND POWER OF ELIJAH

Behold, I will send you Elijah the prophet before the
coming of the great and dreadful day of the LORD.
Malachi 4:5

Today, in the spirit and power of Elias and of John the Baptist, messengers of God's appointment are calling the attention of a judgment-bound world to the solemn events soon to take place in connection with the closing hours of probation and the appearance of Christ Jesus as King of kings and Lord of lords. Soon every man is to be judged for the deeds done in the body. The hour of God's judgment has come, and upon the members of His church on earth rests the solemn responsibility of giving warning to those who are standing as it were on the very brink of eternal ruin. To every human being in the wide world who will give heed must be made plain the principles at stake in the great controversy being waged, principles upon which hang the destinies of all mankind.

In these final hours of probation for the sons of men, when the fate of every soul is so soon to be decided forever, the Lord of heaven and earth expects His church to arouse to action as never before. Those who have been made free in Christ through a knowledge of precious truth, are regarded by the Lord Jesus as His chosen ones, favored above all other people on the face of the earth; and He is counting on them to show forth the praises of Him who hath called them out of darkness into marvelous light. (*Prophets and Kings*, 716)

REFLECTION: *Don't delay in making your decision for Christ and salvation. Time is running out and we have a great work to do. That work is to lead as many as we can to Christ.*

JULY 18

SAVED FROM SIN

And she shall bring forth a son, and thou shalt call his name
JESUS: for he shall save his people from their sins.
Matthew 1:21

But instead of destroying the world, God sent His Son to save it. Though corruption and defiance might be seen in every part of the alien province, a way for its recovery was provided. At the very crisis, when Satan seemed about to triumph, the Son of God came with the embassage of divine grace. Through every age, through every hour, the love of God had been exercised toward the fallen race. Notwithstanding the perversity of men, the signals of mercy had been continually exhibited. And when the fullness of the time had come, the Deity was glorified by pouring upon the world a flood of healing grace that was never to be obstructed or withdrawn till the plan of salvation should be fulfilled.

Satan was exulting that he had succeeded in debasing the image of God in humanity. Then Jesus came to restore in man the image of his Maker. None but Christ can fashion anew the character that has been ruined by sin. He came to expel the demons that had controlled the will. He came to lift us up from the dust, to reshape the marred character after the pattern of His divine character, and to make it beautiful with His own glory. (*Desire of Ages*, 37)

REFLECTION: *God's gift of His Son proves He wanted to save the inhabitants of our world, not destroy them.*

God With Us

Behold, a virgin shall be with child, and shall bring forth a son, and they shall call his name Emmanuel, which being interpreted is, God with us.
Matthew 1:23

God commanded Moses for Israel, "Let them make Me a sanctuary; that I may dwell among them" (Exodus 25:8), and He abode in the sanctuary, in the midst of His people. Through all their weary wandering in the desert, the symbol of His presence was with them. So Christ set up His tabernacle in the midst of our human encampment. He pitched His tent by the side of the tents of men, that He might dwell among us, and make us familiar with His divine character and life. "The Word became flesh, and tabernacled among us (and we beheld His glory, glory as of the Only Begotten from the Father), full of grace and truth" (John 1:14, R. V., margin).

Since Jesus came to dwell with us, we know that God is acquainted with our trials, and sympathizes with our griefs. Every son and daughter of Adam may understand that our Creator is the friend of sinners. For in every doctrine of grace, every promise of joy, every deed of love, every divine attraction presented in the Saviour's life on earth, we see "God with us." (*The Desire of Ages*, 23, 24)

REFLECTION: *God makes it plain He wants to be with us for eternity. In all we do and all we go through God gives us a special promise that He will always be with us. We never need to feel alone, and we can always claim His promise.*

212 | JULY

JULY 20

OUR PERFECT EXAMPLE

*And Jesus answering said unto him, Suffer it to be so now: for thus
it becometh us to fulfill all righteousness. Then he suffered him.*
Matthew 3:15

As Jesus asked for baptism, John drew back, exclaiming, "I have need to be baptized of Thee, and comest Thou to me?" With firm yet gentle authority, Jesus answered, "Suffer it to be so now: for thus it becometh us to fulfill all righteousness." And John, yielding, led the Saviour down into the Jordan, and buried Him beneath the water. "And straightway coming up out of the water," Jesus "saw the heavens opened, and the Spirit like a dove descending upon Him."

Jesus did not receive baptism as a confession of guilt on His own account. He identified Himself with sinners, taking the steps that we are to take, and doing the work that we must do. His life of suffering and patient endurance after His baptism was also an example to us.

Upon coming up out of the water, Jesus bowed in prayer on the river bank. A new and important era was opening before Him. He was now, upon a wider stage, entering on the conflict of His life." (*The Desire of Ages*, 111)

REFLECTION: *Immediately after baptism Jesus was led into the wilderness and temped by Satan. This is another illustration of the Christian walk. When we make the decision to follow Christ, the devil will work even harder on us; but if God is for us, who can be against us? (See Romans 8:31.)*

$\mathcal{T}$HE $\mathcal{P}$OOR IN $\mathcal{S}$PIRIT

Blessed are the poor in spirit: for theirs is the kingdom of heaven.
Matthew 5:3

As something strange and new, these words fall upon the ears of the wondering multitude. Such teaching is contrary to all they have ever heard from priest or rabbi. They see in it nothing to flatter their pride or to feed their ambitious hopes. But there is about this new Teacher a power that holds them spellbound. The sweetness of divine love flows from His very presence as the fragrance from a flower. His words fall like "rain upon the mown grass: as showers that water the earth" (Psalm 72:6). All feel instinctively that here is One who reads the secrets of the soul, yet who comes near to them with tender compassion. Their hearts open to Him, and, as they listen, the Holy Spirit unfolds to them something of the meaning of that lesson which humanity in all ages so needs to learn. (*Thoughts of the Mount of Blessing, 6*)

REFLECTION: *Christ has not changed. He still reads the secrets of the soul. If we will let Him, Jesus still comes near with tender and compassionate entreaties, longing for us to give our sinful burdens to Him, the One who saves to the uttermost. Let us read His Word like it was directed to us personally.*

Those Who Hunger and Thirst

*Blessed are they which do hunger and thirst after
righteousness: for they shall be filled.*
Matthew 5:6

Righteousness is holiness, likeness to God, and "God is love" (1 John 4:16). It is conformity to the law of God, for "all Thy commandments are righteousness" (Psalm 119:172), and "love is the fulfilling of the law" (Romans 13:10). Righteousness is love, and love is the light and the life of God. The righteousness of God is embodied in Christ. We receive righteousness by receiving Him.

Not by painful struggles or wearisome toil, not by gift or sacrifice, is righteousness obtained; but it is freely given to every soul who hungers and thirsts to receive it. "Ho, every one that thirsteth, come ye to the waters, and he that hath no money; come ye, buy, and eat, … without money and without price." "Their righteousness is of Me, saith the Lord," and, "This is His name whereby He shall be called, The Lord Our Righteousness" (Isaiah 55:1; 54:17; Jeremiah 23:6).

No human agent can supply that which will satisfy the hunger and thirst of the soul. But Jesus says, "Behold, I stand at the door, and knock: if any man hear My voice, and open the door, I will come in to him, and will sup with him, and he with Me." "I am the bread of life: he that cometh to Me shall never hunger; and he that believeth on Me shall never thirst" (Revelation 3:20; John 6:35). (*Thoughts from the Mount of Blessing*, 18)

REFLECTION: *This world will never satisfy us. We may find temporary happiness and think we are filled. Soon, however, we will find we aren't satisfied. Only Christ can offer complete satisfaction.*

JULY 23

THE MERCIFUL

Blessed are the merciful: for they shall obtain mercy.
Matthew 5:7

The heart of man is by nature cold and dark and unloving; whenever one manifests a spirit of mercy and forgiveness, he does it not of himself, but through the influence of the divine Spirit moving upon his heart. "We love, because He first loved us" (1 John 4:19, R.V.).

God is Himself the source of all mercy. His name is "merciful and gracious" (Exodus 34:6). He does not treat us according to our desert. He does not ask if we are worthy of His love, but He pours upon us the riches of His love, to make us worthy. He is not vindictive. He seeks not to punish, but to redeem. Even the severity which He manifests through His providences is manifested for the salvation of the wayward. He yearns with intense desire to relieve the woes of men and to apply His balsam to their wounds. It is true that God "will by no means clear the guilty" (Exodus 34:7), but He would take away the guilt.

The merciful are "partakers of the divine nature," and in them the compassionate love of God finds expression. All whose hearts are in sympathy with the heart of Infinite Love will seek to reclaim and not to condemn. Christ dwelling in the soul is a spring that never runs dry. Where He abides, there will be an overflowing of beneficence. (*Thoughts from the Mount of Blessing*, 21, 22)

REFLECTION: *Ask the Lord to bring someone into your life today to show them God's love and mercy by being merciful and kind, even if you think they don't deserve it.*

THE PEACEMAKERS

Blessed are the peacemakers: for they shall be called the children of God.
Matthew 5:9

hrist is "the Prince of Peace" (Isaiah 9:6), and it is His mission to restore to earth and heaven the peace that sin has broken. "Being justified by faith, we have peace with God through our Lord Jesus Christ" (Romans 5:1). Whoever consents to renounce sin and open his heart to the love of Christ, becomes a partaker of this heavenly peace.

There is no other ground of peace than this. The grace of Christ received into the heart, subdues enmity; it allays strife and fills the soul with love. He who is at peace with God and his fellow men cannot be made miserable. Envy will not be in his heart; evil surmisings will find no room there; hatred cannot exist. The heart that is in harmony with God is a partaker of the peace of heaven and will diffuse its blessed influence on all around. The spirit of peace will rest like dew upon hearts weary and troubled with worldly strife.

Christ's followers are sent to the world with the message of peace. Whoever, by the quiet, unconscious influence of a holy life, shall reveal the love of Christ; whoever, by word or deed, shall lead another to renounce sin and yield his heart to God, is a peacemaker. (*Thoughts from the Mount of Blessing,* 27, 28)

REFLECTION: *When we're pushed, it's human nature to push back. Sometimes when we're wronged, we want to get even. Christ explains that there is no peace in revenge. Today, if someone crosses you, remember to be a peacemaker. You will be blessed.*

JULY 25

PERSECUTED FOR RIGHTEOUSNESS SAKE

Blessed are they which are persecuted for righteousness' sake: for theirs is the kingdom of heaven. Blessed are ye, when men shall revile you, and persecute you, and shall say all manner of evil against you falsely, for my sake.
Matthew 5:10, 11

In every age God's chosen messengers have been reviled and persecuted, yet through their affliction the knowledge of God has been spread abroad. Every disciple of Christ is to step into the ranks and carry forward the same work, knowing that its foes can do nothing against the truth, but for the truth. God means that truth shall be brought to the front and become the subject of examination and discussion, even through the contempt placed upon it. The minds of the people must be agitated; every controversy, every reproach, every effort to restrict liberty of conscience, is God's means of awakening minds that otherwise might slumber. (*Thoughts from the Mount of Blessing*, 33)

While the Lord has not promised His people exemption from trials, He has promised that which is far better. He has said, "As thy days, so shall thy strength be." "My grace is sufficient for thee: for My strength is made perfect in weakness" (Deuteronomy 33:25; 2 Corinthians 12:9). If you are called to go through the fiery furnace for His sake, Jesus will be by your side even as He was with the faithful three in Babylon. Those who love their Redeemer will rejoice at every opportunity of sharing with Him humiliation and reproach. The love they bear their Lord makes suffering for His sake sweet."(*Thoughts from the Mount of Blessing*, 30)

REFLECTION: *Character is mainly built by the little things. If we can't overcome the small things, when the large trials come, we will not be prepared. The faithful three had developed a strong character long before they were thrown in the furnace. Their character was revealed, not developed, in their hour of great trial.*

JULY 26

SALT OF THE EARTH

Ye are the salt of the earth: but if the salt have lost his savour,
wherewith shall it be salted? It is thenceforth good for nothing,
but to be cast out, and to be trodden under foot of men.
Matthew 5:13

Salt is valued for its preservative properties; and when God calls His children salt, He would teach them that His purpose in making them the subjects of His grace is that they may become agents in saving others. The object of God in choosing a people before all the world was not only that He might adopt them as His sons and daughters, but that through them the world might receive the grace that bringeth salvation (Titus 2:11). When the Lord chose Abraham, it was not simply to be the special friend of God, but to be a medium of the peculiar privileges the Lord desired to bestow upon the nations. Jesus, in that last prayer with His disciples before His crucifixion, said, "For their sakes I sanctify Myself, that they also might be sanctified through the truth" (John 17:19). In like manner Christians who are purified through the truth will possess saving qualities that preserve the world from utter moral corruption.

Salt must be mingled with the substance to which it is added; it must penetrate and infuse in order to preserve. So it is through personal contact and association that men are reached by the saving power of the gospel. ... Personal influence is a power. We must come close to those whom we desire to benefit.

The savor of the salt represents the vital power of the Christian—the love of Jesus in the heart, the righteousness of Christ pervading the life. (*Thoughts from the Mount of Blessing*, 35, 36)

REFLECTION: *Whether you have too little or too much salt, the taste is not good. This is an object lesson we all can understand. Allowing Christ to live through us keeps the salt content just right, we will be a blessing for those around us.*

JULY 27

LET YOUR LIGHT SHINE

Let your light so shine before men, that they may see your
good works, and glorify your Father which is in heaven.
Matthew 5:16

As the sun goes forth on its errand of love, dispelling the shades of night and awakening the world to life, so the followers of Christ are to go forth on their mission, diffusing the light of heaven upon those who are in the darkness of error and sin.

In the brilliant light of the morning, the towns and villages upon the surrounding hills stood forth clearly, making an attractive feature of the scene. Pointing to them, Jesus said, "A city set on a hill cannot be hid." And he added, "Neither do men light a lamp, and put it under the bushel, but on the stand; and it shineth unto all that are in the house" (R.V.). Most of those who listened to the words of Jesus were peasants and fishermen whose lowly dwellings contained but one room, in which the single lamp on its stand shone to all in the house. Even so, said Jesus, "Let your light so shine before men, that they may see your good works, and glorify your Father which is in heaven." (*Thoughts from the Mount of Blessing*, 38, 39)

REFLECTION: *When self is crucified and, in its place, we allow Jesus to enter our hearts, we will — by good works — be shining lights. This will be the greatest testimony that we can give. Let us set our sights high today, and every day, so others will see Jesus in us.*

FULFILL THE LAW

*Think not that I am come to destroy the law, or the
prophets: I am not come to destroy, but to fulfill.*
Matthew 5:17

The law given upon Sinai was the enunciation of the principle of love, a revelation to earth of the law of heaven. ... God had revealed the purpose of the law when He declared to Israel, "Ye shall be holy men unto Me" (Exodus 22:31). ...

It is the Creator of men, the Giver of the law, who declares that it is not His purpose to set aside its precepts. Everything in nature, from the mote in the sunbeam to the worlds on high, is under law. And upon obedience to these laws the order and harmony of the natural world depend. So there are great principles of righteousness to control the life of all intelligent beings, and upon conformity to these principles the well-being of the universe depends. Before this earth was called into being, God's law existed. Angels are governed by its principles, and in order for earth to be in harmony with heaven, man also must obey the divine statutes. To man in Eden Christ made known the precepts of the law "when the morning stars sang together, and all the sons of God shouted for joy" (Job 38:7). The mission of Christ on earth was not to destroy the law, but by His grace to bring man back to obedience to its precepts."(*Thoughts from the Mount Blessing*, 46–48)

REFLECTION: *True happiness and harmony in life is only to be found in following God's ways. Rebellion always brings discord and strife.*

JULY 29

$\mathcal{A}$NGER

But I say unto you, That whosoever is angry with his brother
without a cause shall be in danger of the judgment: and whosoever
shall say to his brother, Raca, shall be in danger of the council: but
whosoever shall say, Thou fool, shall be in danger of hell fire.
Matthew 5:22

Through Moses the Lord had said, "Thou shalt not hate thy brother in thine heart... Thou shalt not avenge, nor bear any grudge against the children of thy people, but thou shalt love thy neighbor as thyself" (Leviticus 19:17,18). The truths which Christ presented were the same that had been taught by the prophets, but they had become obscured through hardness of heart and love of sin. ...

The spirit of hatred and revenge originated with Satan, and it led him to put to death the Son of God. Whoever cherishes malice or unkindness is cherishing the same spirit, and its fruit will be unto death. In the revengeful thought the evil deed lies enfolded, as the plant in the seed. "Whosoever hateth his brother is a murderer: and ye know that no murderer hath eternal life abiding in him" (1 John 3:15). (*Thoughts from the Mount of Blessing*, 55, 56)

REFLECTION: *His example is for us. When we are brought in conflict with the enemies of Christ, we should say nothing in a spirit of retaliation or that would bear even the appearance of a railing accusation. He who stands as a mouthpiece for God should not utter words which even the Majesty of heaven would not use when contending with Satan. We are to leave with God the work of judging and condemning (Thoughts from the Mount of Blessing, 57). Today, let's ask God to help us surrender our feelings of hatred or revenge, and to give us His love for our neighbor.*

LOVE YOUR ENEMIES

But I say unto you, Love your enemies, bless them that
curse you, do good to them that hate you, and pray for them
which despitefully use you, and persecute you.
Matthew 5:44

While we were yet unloving and unlovely in character, "hateful, and hating one another," our heavenly Father had mercy on us. "After that the kindness and love of God our Saviour toward man appeared, not by works of righteousness which we have done, but according to His mercy He saved us" (Titus 3:3–5). His love received, will make us, in like manner, kind and tender, not merely toward those who please us, but to the most faulty and erring and sinful.

The children of God are those who are partakers of His nature. It is not earthly rank, nor birth, nor nationality, nor religious privilege, which proves that we are members of the family of God; it is love, a love that embraces all humanity. Even sinners whose hearts are not utterly closed to God's Spirit, will respond to kindness; while they may give hate for hate, they will also give love for love. But it is only the Spirit of God that gives love for hatred. To be kind to the unthankful and to the evil, to do good hoping for nothing again, is the insignia of the royalty of heaven, the sure token by which the children of the Highest reveal their high estate. (*Thoughts from the Mount of Blessing*, 75)

REFLECTION: *There's too much evil surmising and back biting in the world today, even within our own families and churches. If we would be like Christ, we will learn to love the sinner but hate the sin.*

PRAYER CLOSET

But thou, when thou prayest, enter into thy closet, and when thou hast shut thy door, pray to thy Father which is in secret; and thy Father which seeth in secret shall reward thee openly.
Matthew 6:6

Have a place for secret prayer. Jesus had select places for communion with God, and so should we. We need often to retire to some spot, however humble, where we can be alone with God.

"Pray to thy Father which is in secret." In the name of Jesus we may come into God's presence with the confidence of a child. No man is needed to act as a mediator. Through Jesus we may open our hearts to God as to one who knows and loves us.

In the secret place of prayer, where no eye but God's can see, no ear but His can hear, we may pour out our most hidden desires and longings to the Father of infinite pity, and in the hush and silence of the soul that voice which never fails to answer the cry of human need will speak to our hearts." (*Thoughts from the Mount of Blessing*, 55, 56)

REFLECTION: *In your quiet time with God, share with Him all of your worries and cares. He knows your problems, so in talk to Him about them. He will give you the needed answers and the courage and strength to follow through.*

AUGUST

AUGUST 1

ℱASTING

Moreover when ye fast, be not, as the hypocrites, of a sad countenance: for they disfigure their faces, that they may appear unto men to fast. Verily I say unto you, they have their reward. But thou, when thou fastest, anoint thine head, and wash thy face.
Matthew 6:16, 17

The fasting which the word of God enjoins is something more than a form. It does not consist merely in refusing food, in wearing sackcloth, in sprinkling ashes upon the head. He who fasts in real sorrow for sin will never court display.

The object of the fast which God calls upon us to keep is not to afflict the body for the sin of the soul, but to aid us in perceiving the grievous character of sin, in humbling the heart before God and receiving His pardoning grace. His command to Israel was, "Rend your heart, and not your garments, and turn unto the Lord your God" (Joel 2:13).

It will avail nothing for us to do penance or to flatter ourselves that by our own works we shall merit or purchase an inheritance among the saints. When the question was asked Christ, "What shall we do, that we might work the works of God?" He answered, "This is the work of God, that ye believe on Him whom He hath sent" (John 6:28, 29). Repentance is turning from self to Christ; and when we receive Christ so that through faith He can live His life in us, good works will be manifest. (*Thoughts from the Mount of Blessing*, 87)

REFLECTION: *We cannot live a long time without food. It's necessary to sustain life. When we fast, we are telling ourselves — for Christ already knows — that this specific issue is so important that we are willing to forgo food. Hunger pangs remind us over and over again how much we need the Lord in this particular situation.*

AUGUST 2

*T*REASURES IN *H*EAVEN

But lay up for yourselves treasures in heaven, where neither moth nor
rust doth corrupt, and where thieves do not break through nor steal.
Matthew 6:20

*T*reasure laid up on earth will not endure; thieves break through and steal; moth and rust corrupt; fire and storm sweep away your possessions. And "where your treasure is, there will your heart be also." Treasure laid up on the earth will engross the mind to the exclusion of heavenly things.

The love of money was the ruling passion in the Jewish age. Worldliness usurped the place of God and religion in the soul. So it is now. Avaricious greed for wealth exerts such a fascinating, bewitching influence over the life that it results in perverting the nobility and corrupting the humanity of men until they are drowned in perdition. The service of Satan is full of care, perplexity, and wearing labor, and the treasure men toil to accumulate on earth is only for a season.

Jesus said, "Lay up for yourselves treasures in heaven, where neither moth nor rust doth corrupt, and where thieves do not break through nor steal: for where your treasure is, there will your heart be also." (*Thoughts from the Mount of Blessing*, 88, 89)

REFLECTION: *This treasure that we lay up in heaven is nothing we have, or will have, on this earth — as far as material things go. The only thing we take to heaven with us is our character. Character is made of our thoughts and feelings. This character which takes our lifetime to build will in the end be a noble character or an evil one. Today, let's put some character treasure in the heavenly bank.*

AUGUST 3

CANNOT HAVE TWO MASTERS

*No man can serve two masters: for either he will hate the
one, and love the other; or else he will hold to the one, and
despise the other. Ye cannot serve God and mammon.*
Matthew 6:24

Christ does not say that man will not or shall not serve
two masters, but that he cannot. The interests of God
and the interests of mammon have no union or sympathy. Just where the conscience of the Christian warns him to
forbear, to deny himself, to stop, just there the worldling steps
over the line, to indulge his selfish propensities. On one side of
the line is the self-denying follower of Christ; on the other side is
the self-indulgent world lover, pandering to fashion, engaging in
frivolity, and pampering himself in forbidden pleasure. On that
side of the line the Christian cannot go.

No one can occupy a neutral position; there is no middle
class, who neither love God nor serve the enemy of righteousness. Christ is to live in His human agents and work through
their faculties and act through their capabilities. Their will must
be submitted to His will; they must act with His Spirit. Then it
is no more they that live, but Christ that lives in them. He who
does not give himself wholly to God is under the control of
another power, listening to another voice, whose suggestions
are of an entirely different character. (*Thoughts from the Mount
of Blessing*, 93, 94)

REFLECTION: *How often we want to be Christians but still live like the
world. This is impossible. We even have pastors today telling us it's
okay to sin. We must not be fooled by anyone who says we can do anything as long as we love Jesus. It's either all or nothing. Let's give all of
ourselves today to the Author and Finisher of our Faith — Jesus Christ.*

AUGUST 4

*K*INGDOM *F*IRST

But seek ye first the kingdom of God, and his righteousness;
and all these things shall be added unto you.
Matthew 6:33

The people who listened to the words of Christ were still anxiously watching for some announcement of the earthly kingdom. While Jesus was opening to them the treasures of heaven, the question uppermost in many minds was, How will a connection with Him advance our prospects in the world? Jesus shows that in making the things of the world their supreme anxiety they were like the heathen nations about them, living as if there were no God, whose tender care is over His creatures.

"All these things," said Jesus, "do the nations of the world seek after." "Your heavenly Father knoweth that ye have need of all these things. But seek ye first the kingdom of God, and His righteousness; and all these things shall be added unto you" (Luke 12:30; Matthew 6:32,33). I have come to open to you the kingdom of love and righteousness and peace. Open your hearts to receive this kingdom, and make its service your highest interest. Though it is a spiritual kingdom, fear not that your needs for this life will be uncared-for. If you give yourself to God's service, He who has all power in heaven and earth will provide for your needs. (*Thoughts from the Mount of Blessing*, 98, 99)

REFLECTION: *We all know that when we die we don't take anything with us. We need to take care of ourselves and families, but without Christ being the first, last, and best in everything, we will end up without a Savior.*

AUGUST 5

The Golden Rule

Therefore all things whatsoever ye would that men should do to you, do ye even so to them: for this is the law and the prophets.
Matthew 7:12

The golden rule is the principle of true courtesy, and its truest illustration is seen in the life and character of Jesus. Oh, what rays of softness and beauty shone forth in the daily life of our Saviour! What sweetness flowed from His very presence! The same spirit will be revealed in His children. Those with whom Christ dwells will be surrounded with a divine atmosphere. Their white robes of purity will be fragrant with perfume from the garden of the Lord. Their faces will reflect light from His, brightening the path for stumbling and weary feet.

But there is a yet deeper significance to the golden rule. Everyone who has been made a steward of the manifold grace of God is called upon to impart to souls in ignorance and darkness, even as, were he in their place, he would desire them to impart to him. The apostle Paul said, "I am debtor both to the Greeks, and to the barbarians; both to the wise, and to the unwise" (Romans 1:14). By all that you have known of the love of God, by all that you have received of the rich gifts of His grace above the most benighted and degraded soul upon the earth are you in debt to that soul to impart these gifts unto him. (*Thoughts from the Mount of Blessing*, 135)

REFLECTION: *We can't forget that when we take the name "Christian" it means much more than going to church. Our very presence will reflect Jesus. This is a serious responsibility, and not optional. But, oh, what an awesome privilege!*

AUGUST 6

CONFESS OR DENY CHRIST

*Whosoever therefore shall confess me before men, him will I confess
also before my Father which is in heaven. But whosoever shall deny me
before men, him will I also deny before my Father which is in heaven.*
Matthew 10:32, 33

He who would confess Christ must have Christ abiding in him. He cannot communicate that which he has not received. The disciples might speak fluently on doctrines, they might repeat the words of Christ Himself; but unless they possessed Christlike meekness and love, they were not confessing Him. A spirit contrary to the spirit of Christ would deny Him, whatever the profession. Men may deny Christ by evilspeaking, by foolish talking, by words that are untruthful or unkind. They may deny Him by shunning life's burdens, by the pursuit of sinful pleasure. They may deny Him by conforming to the world, by uncourteous behavior, by the love of their own opinions, by justifying self, by cherishing doubt, borrowing trouble, and dwelling in darkness. In all these ways they declare that Christ is not in them. And "whosoever shall deny Me before men," He says, "him will I also deny before My Father which is in heaven." (*The Desire of Ages*, 357)

REFLECTION: *Our only safety is to be like Jesus! We do this by reading His word — the Bible — which became flesh that we might have the perfect example to follow. Let's pray we will not deny Christ in whatever we do or say today.*

FIND REST

*Come unto me, all ye that labour and are heavy laden, and I
will give you rest. Take my yoke upon you, and learn of me;
for I am meek and lowly in heart: and ye shall find rest unto
your souls. For my yoke is easy, and my burden is light.*
Matthew 11:28–30

The yoke is an instrument of service. Cattle are yoked for
labor, and the yoke is essential that they may labor effectually. By this illustration Christ teaches us that we are
called to service as long as life shall last. We are to take upon us
His yoke, that we may be co-workers with Him. …

Our Lord desires them to lay aside this yoke of bondage. He
invites them to accept His yoke; He says, "My yoke is easy, and
My burden is light." He bids them seek first the kingdom of God
and His righteousness, and His promise is that all things needful
to them for this life shall be added. Worry is blind, and cannot
discern the future; but Jesus sees the end from the beginning.
In every difficulty He has His way prepared to bring relief. Our
heavenly Father has a thousand ways to provide for us, of which
we know nothing. Those who accept the one principle of making
the service and honor of God supreme will find perplexities vanish, and a plain path before their feet. (*The Desire of Ages*, 329, 330)

REFLECTION: *Oh, to know that with Jesus all things are possible! Christ
loves us so much He will yoke up with us to help with anything we
need. He is knocking today at your heart's door. Will you let Him come
into your heart? Let's be yoked today with Him and see our perplexities
vanish to reveal a plain path before our feet.*

AUGUST 8

BURIED TREASURE

Again, the kingdom of heaven is like unto treasure hid in a field;
the which when a man hath found, he hideth, and for joy thereof
goeth and selleth all that he hath, and buyeth that field.
Matthew 13:44

A man hires land to cultivate, and as the oxen plow the soil, buried treasure is unearthed. As the man discovers this treasure, he sees that a fortune is within his reach. Restoring the gold to its hiding place, he returns to his home and sells all that he has, in order to purchase the field containing the treasure. His family and his neighbors think that he is acting like a madman. Looking on the field, they see no value in the neglected soil. But the man knows what he is doing; and when he has a title to the field, he searches every part of it to find the treasure that he has secured.

This parable illustrates the value of the heavenly treasure, and the effort that should be made to secure it. The finder of the treasure in the field was ready to part with all that he had, ready to put forth untiring labor, in order to secure the hidden riches. So the finder of heavenly treasure will count no labor too great and no sacrifice too dear, in order to gain the treasures of truth.

In the parable the field containing the treasure represents the Holy Scriptures. And the gospel is the treasure. The earth itself is not so interlaced with golden veins and filled with precious things as is the word of God. (*Christ's Object Lessons*, 103, 104)

REFLECTION: *This single text in the Bible has so much meaning. Have you found the treasure yet? Will you search with all your heart? When you do, others might think you are a little crazy, but once you find Jesus, our Treasure, your happiness will have no bounds.*

AUGUST 9

Mustard Seed

*And Jesus said unto them, Because of your unbelief: for verily I
say unto you, If ye have faith as a grain of mustard seed, ye shall
say unto this mountain, Remove hence to yonder place; and it
shall remove; and nothing shall be impossible unto you.*
Matthew 17:20

The nine disciples were yet pondering upon the bitter
fact of their own failure; and when Jesus was once more
alone with them, they questioned, "Why could not we
cast him out?" Jesus answered them, "Because of your unbelief:
for verily I say unto you, If ye have faith as a grain of mustard
seed, ye shall say unto this mountain, Remove hence to yonder
place; and it shall remove; and nothing shall be impossible unto
you. Howbeit this kind goeth not out but by prayer and fasting."
Their unbelief, that shut them out from deeper sympathy with
Christ, and the carelessness with which they regarded the sacred
work committed to them, had caused their failure in the conflict
with the powers of darkness. ...

In order to succeed in such a conflict they must come to the
work in a different spirit. Their faith must be strengthened by
fervent prayer and fasting, and humiliation of heart. They must
be emptied of self, and be filled with the Spirit and power of
God. Earnest, persevering supplication to God in faith—faith
that leads to entire dependence upon God, and unreserved consecration to His work—can alone avail to bring men the Holy
Spirit's aid in the battle against principalities and powers, the
rulers of the darkness of this world, and wicked spirits in high
places. (*The Desire of Ages*, 429–431)

REFLECTION: *Do you have a "mountain" in your life today? Pray with
faith, knowing that God will do exactly as He says he will do, and then
act upon it.*

AUGUST 10

The Fig Tree

And when he saw a fig tree in the way, he came to it, and found nothing thereon, but leaves only, and said unto it, Let no fruit grow on thee henceforward for ever. And presently the fig tree withered away.
Matthew 21:19

*I*t was not the season for ripe figs, except in certain localities; and on the highlands about Jerusalem it might truly be said, "The time of figs was not yet." But in the orchard to which Jesus came, one tree appeared to be in advance of all the others. It was already covered with leaves. It is the nature of the fig tree that before the leaves open, the growing fruit appears. Therefore this tree in full leaf gave promise of well-developed fruit. But its appearance was deceptive. Upon searching its branches, from the lowest bough to the topmost twig, Jesus found "nothing but leaves." It was a mass of pretentious foliage, nothing more.

Christ uttered against it a withering curse. "No man eat fruit of thee hereafter forever," He said. The next morning, as the Saviour and His disciples were again on their way to the city, the blasted branches and drooping leaves attracted their attention. "Master," said Peter, "behold, the fig tree which Thou cursedst is withered away." …

That barren tree, flaunting its pretentious foliage in the very face of Christ, was a symbol of the Jewish nation. All the trees in the fig orchard were destitute of fruit; but the leafless trees raised no expectation, and caused no disappointment. By these trees the Gentiles were represented. *(The Desire of Ages, 581)*

REFLECTION: *Are we like the Jews back in Christ's day? Do we profess to be Christians when our actions are far from it? Today, let us live what we profess.*

AUGUST 11

$\mathcal{C}$LOUDS OF $\mathcal{H}$EAVEN

*And then shall appear the sign of the Son of man in heaven: and then
shall all the tribes of the earth mourn, and they shall see the Son of
man coming in the clouds of heaven with power and great glory.*
Matthew 24:30

$\mathcal{A}$nd He says, "Learn a parable of the fig tree; When
his branch is yet tender, and putteth forth leaves, ye
know that summer is nigh: so likewise ye, when ye
shall see all these things, know that He is near, even at the doors"
(Matthew 24:32, 33, margin).

Christ has given signs of His coming. He declares that we
may know when He is near, even at the doors. He says of those
who see these signs, "This generation shall not pass, till all these
things be fulfilled." These signs have appeared. Now we know
of a surety that the Lord's coming is at hand. "Heaven and earth
shall pass away," He says, "but My words shall not pass away."

Christ is coming with clouds and with great glory. A multitude of shining angels will attend Him. He will come to raise the
dead, and to change the living saints from glory to glory. He will
come to honor those who have loved Him, and kept His commandments, and to take them to Himself. He has not forgotten
them nor His promise. (*The Desire of Ages*, 632)

REFLECTION: *Many of us have heard since we were old enough to understand, that Jesus was coming soon. Today the signs are all around us.
This world is truly waxing old like a garment. We do not know the day
or hour, but we can and should know that it is near. Let's recommit our
lives today and be ready for His soon return.*

TEN VIRGINS

Then shall the kingdom of heaven be likened unto ten virgins,
which took their lamps, and went forth to meet the bridegroom.
And five of them were wise, and five were foolish.
Matthew 25:1, 2

The class represented by the foolish virgins are not hypocrites. They have a regard for the truth, they have advocated the truth, they are attracted to those who believe the truth; but they have not yielded themselves to the Holy Spirit's working. They have not fallen upon the Rock, Christ Jesus, and permitted their old nature to be broken up. This class are represented also by the stony-ground hearers. They receive the word with readiness, but they fail of assimilating its principles. Its influence is not abiding. The Spirit works upon man's heart, according to his desire and consent implanting in him a new nature; but the class represented by the foolish virgins have been content with a superficial work. They do not know God. They have not studied His character; they have not held communion with Him; therefore they do not know how to trust, how to look and live. Their service to God degenerates into a form. "They come unto thee as the people cometh, and they sit before thee as My people, and they hear thy words, but they will not do them; for with their mouth they show much love, but their heart goeth after their covetousness" (Ezekiel 33:31). (*Christ's Object Lessons*, 411)

REFLECTION: *It is so easy to get caught up in good things — even religious things. These good things are great to be a part of, but don't be distracted like the five foolish virgins; in the end they were not ready. We cannot fool ourselves into thinking that because we go to church and hold an office we are ready for Jesus. Let us be honest and make sure there is nothing between us and our Savior.*

AUGUST 13

THE TALENTS

*For the kingdom of heaven is as a man travelling into a far country, who
called his own servants, and delivered unto them his goods. And unto
one he gave five talents, to another two, and to another one; to every man
according to his several ability; and straightway took his journey.*
Matthew 25:14, 15

God gives the talents, the powers of the mind; we form
the character. It is formed by hard, stern battles with
self. Conflict after conflict must be waged against he-
reditary tendencies. We shall have to criticize ourselves closely,
and allow not one unfavorable trait to remain uncorrected.

Let no one say, I cannot remedy my defects of character. If
you come to this decision, you will certainly fail of obtaining everlasting life. The impossibility lies in your own will. If you will
not, then you can not overcome. The real difficulty arises from
the corruption of an unsanctified heart, and an unwillingness to
submit to the control of God.

Many whom God has qualified to do excellent work accomplish very little, because they attempt little. Thousands pass
through life as if they had no definite object for which to live,
no standard to reach. Such will obtain a reward proportionate to
their works. (*Christ Object Lessons*, 331)

REFLECTION: *The smallest trust is from God. With the blessing of God,
the one talent, through diligent use, will be doubled. The two used in
the service of Christ will be increased to four, and thus the humblest
instrument may grow in power and usefulness.*

August 14

*C*OMMUNION

And as they were eating, Jesus took bread, and blessed it, and brake it,
and gave it to the disciples, and said, Take, eat; this is my body.
Matthew 26:26

he Communion service points to Christ's second coming. It was designed to keep this hope vivid in the minds of the disciples. Whenever they met together to commemorate His death, they recounted how "He took the cup, and gave thanks, and gave it to them, saying, Drink ye all of it; for this is My blood of the new testament, which is shed for many for the remission of sins. But I say unto you, I will not drink henceforth of this fruit of the vine, until that day when I drink it new with you in My Father's kingdom." In their tribulation they found comfort in the hope of their Lord's return. Unspeakably precious to them was the thought, "As often as ye eat this bread, and drink this cup, ye do show the Lord's death till He come" (1 Corinthians 11:26).

These are the things we are never to forget.... And nothing less than the death of Christ could make His love efficacious for us. It is only because of His death that we can look with joy to His second coming. His sacrifice is the center of our hope. Upon this we must fix our faith. (*The Desire of Ages*, 659, 660)

REFLECTION: *Take some time to contemplate the beautiful symbolism in each part of the communion service representing Jesus' sacrifice for us.*

AUGUST 15

𝒯HE 𝒞UP

He went away again the second time, and prayed, saying, O my Father, if this cup may not pass away from me, except I drink it, thy will be done.
Matthew 26:42

Three times has He uttered that prayer. Three times has humanity shrunk from the last, crowning sacrifice. But now the history of the human race comes up before the world's Redeemer. He sees that the transgressors of the law, if left to themselves, must perish. He sees the helplessness of man. He sees the power of sin. The woes and lamentations of a doomed world rise before Him. He beholds its impending fate, and His decision is made. He will save man at any cost to Himself. He accepts His baptism of blood, that through Him perishing millions may gain everlasting life. He has left the courts of heaven, where all is purity, happiness, and glory, to save the one lost sheep, the one world that has fallen by transgression. And He will not turn from His mission. He will become the propitiation of a race that has willed to sin. His prayer now breathes only submission: "If this cup may not pass away from Me, except I drink it, Thy will be done." (*The Desire of Ages*, 690)

REFLECTION: *Oh, what a Savior we serve! Let us never complain about the little problems we face.*

AUGUST 16

THE BURDEN OF SIN

And about the ninth hour Jesus cried with a loud voice, saying, Eli, Eli, lama sabachthani? that is to say, My God, my God, why hast thou forsaken me? ... Jesus, when he had cried again with a loud voice, yielded up the ghost.
Matthew 27:46, 50

It was to redeem us that Jesus lived and suffered and died. He became "a Man of Sorrows," that we might be made partakers of everlasting joy. God permitted His beloved Son, full of grace and truth, to come from a world of indescribable glory, to a world marred and blighted with sin, darkened with the shadow of death and the curse. He permitted Him to leave the bosom of His love, the adoration of the angels, to suffer shame, insult, humiliation, hatred, and death. "The chastisement of our peace was upon Him; and with His stripes we are healed" (Isaiah 53:5). Behold Him in the wilderness, in Gethsemane, upon the cross! The spotless Son of God took upon Himself the burden of sin. He who had been one with God, felt in His soul the awful separation that sin makes between God and man. This wrung from His lips the anguished cry, "My God, My God, why hast Thou forsaken Me?" (Matthew 27:46). It was the burden of sin, the sense of its terrible enormity, of its separation of the soul from God—it was this that broke the heart of the Son of God. (*Steps to Christ*, 13)

REFLECTION: *Let no one tell us that we cannot be overcomers through Jesus Christ our Lord. That is a lie from Satan himself. It was sin that killed our Lord. Let us always keep that in mind when we are tempted to do wrong.*

AUGUST 17

*H*E IS *R*ISEN

And the angel answered and said unto the women, Fear not ye: for
I know that ye seek Jesus, which was crucified. He is not here: for
he is risen, as he said. Come, see the place where the Lord lay.
Matthew 28:5, 6

When the voice of the mighty angel was heard at Christ's tomb, saying, Thy Father calls Thee, the Saviour came forth from the grave by the life that was in Himself. Now was proved the truth of His words, "I lay down My life, that I might take it again. ... I have power to lay it down, and I have power to take it again." Now was fulfilled the prophecy He had spoken to the priests and rulers, "Destroy this temple, and in three days I will raise it up" (John 10:17, 18; 2:19).

Over the rent sepulcher of Joseph, Christ had proclaimed in triumph, "I am the resurrection, and the life." These words could be spoken only by the Deity. All created beings live by the will and power of God. They are dependent recipients of the life of God. From the highest seraph to the humblest animate being, all are replenished from the Source of life. Only He who is one with God could say, I have power to lay down My life, and I have power to take it again. In His divinity, Christ possessed the power to break the bonds of death. (*The Desire of Ages*, 786)

REFLECTION: *We should never despair when we get discouraged. Christ is God. His power is no less now than it was in the past. The very fact that He came forth should mean everything to us. He has faith in you and me to be eternally saved. Let's all be faithful to the end.*

THE LEPER

And there came a leper to him, beseeching him, and kneeling down to him, and saying unto him, If thou wilt, thou canst make me clean.
Mark 1:40

Away from his friends and his kindred, the leper must bear the curse of his malady. He was obliged to publish his own calamity, to rend his garments, and sound the alarm, warning all to flee from his contaminating presence. The cry, "Unclean! unclean!" coming in mournful tones from the lonely exile, was a signal heard with fear and abhorrence.

The leper is guided to the Saviour. Jesus is teaching beside the lake, and the people are gathered about Him. Standing afar off, the leper catches a few words from the Saviour's lips. He sees Him laying His hands upon the sick. He sees the lame, the blind, the paralytic, and those dying of various maladies rise up in health, praising God for their deliverance. Faith strengthens in his heart. …

He is a loathsome spectacle. The disease has made frightful inroads, and his decaying body is horrible to look upon. At sight of him the people fall back in terror. They crowd upon one another in their eagerness to escape from contact with him. Some try to prevent him from approaching Jesus, but in vain. He neither sees nor hears them. Their expressions of loathing are lost upon him. He sees only the Son of God. He hears only the voice that speaks life to the dying. Pressing to Jesus, he casts himself at His feet with the cry, "Lord, if Thou wilt, Thou canst make me clean." (*The Desire of Ages*, 262, 263)

REFLECTION: *Christ will make us clean today. Let us, as the leper did, see only the Life-Giver. No matter what the noise or confusion is, don't look to the left or the right. "Jesus only" is our watchword for the day.*

AUGUST 19

THE TOUCH OF FAITH

And he said unto her, Daughter, thy faith hath made thee
whole; go in peace, and be whole of thy plague.
Mark 5:34

"If I may but touch His garment, I shall be whole" (Matthew 9:21). It was a poor woman who spoke these words; a woman who for twelve years had suffered from a disease that made her life a burden. She had spent all her means upon physicians and remedies, only to be pronounced incurable. But as she heard of the Great Healer, her hopes revived. She thought, "If only I could get near enough to speak to Him, I might be healed." …

As He was passing, she reached forward and succeeded in barely touching the border of His garment. That moment she knew that she was healed. In that one touch was concentrated the faith of her life, and instantly her pain and feebleness disappeared. Instantly she felt the thrill as of an electric current passing through every fiber of her being. There came over her a sensation of perfect health. "She felt in her body that she was healed of that plague" (Verse 29). …

Many hold faith as an opinion. Saving faith is a transaction, by which those who receive Christ join themselves in covenant relation with God. A living faith means an increase of vigor, a confiding trust, by which, through the grace of Christ, the soul becomes a conquering power. (*The Ministry of Healing*, 59–62)

REFLECTION: *In the difficulties you face today, look to Jesus for answers, for healing, and for comfort. He is just as able today to bring relief as He was when He was here on earth. The words for today are "Look and Live."*

AUGUST 20

WHAT SHALL A MAN PROFIT?

*For what shall it profit a man, if he shall gain the
whole world, and lose his own soul?*
Mark 8:36

This is a question that demands consideration by every parent, every teacher, every student by every human being, young or old. No scheme of business or plan of life can be sound or complete that embraces only the brief years of this present life and makes no provision for the unending future. Let the youth be taught to take eternity into their reckoning. Let them be taught to choose the principles and seek the possessions that are enduring—to lay up for themselves that "treasure in the heavens that faileth not, where no thief approacheth, neither moth corrupteth;" to make to themselves friends "by means of the mammon of unrighteousness," that when it shall fail, these may receive them "into the eternal tabernacles" (Luke 12:33; 16:9, R.V.).

All who do this are making the best possible preparation for life in this world. No man can lay up treasure in heaven without finding his life on earth thereby enriched and ennobled.

"Godliness is profitable unto all things, having promise of the life that now is, and of that which is to come" (1 Timothy 4:8). (*Education*, 145)

REFLECTION: *We should live now as though we're living forever. Why center our lives around the things that will perish?*

AUGUST 21

The Rich Young Ruler

And he was sad at that saying, and went away
grieved: for he had great possessions.
Mark 10:22

His claim that he had kept the law of God was a deception. He showed that riches were his idol. He could not keep the commandments of God while the world was first in his affections. He loved the gifts of God more than he loved the Giver. Christ had offered the young man fellowship with Himself. "Follow Me," He said. But the Saviour was not so much to him as his own name among men or his possessions. To give up his earthly treasure, that was seen, for the heavenly treasure, that was unseen, was too great a risk. He refused the offer of eternal life, and went away, and ever after the world was to receive his worship. Thousands are passing through this ordeal, weighing Christ against the world; and many choose the world. Like the young ruler, they turn from the Saviour, saying in their hearts, I will not have this Man as my leader....

All should consider what it means to desire heaven, and yet to turn away because of the conditions laid down. Think of what it means to say "No" to Christ. The ruler said, No, I cannot give You all. Do we say the same? The Saviour offers to share with us the work God has given us to do. He offers to use the means God has given us, to carry forward His work in the world. Only in this way can He save us." (*The Desire of Ages*, 520–523)

REFLECTION: *A human lifetime is very short compared to eternity. The rich young ruler has been dead for two thousand years. I wonder if eternal life was worth forfeiting for a few measly years on this planet?*

AUGUST 22

PRAYER AND FAITH

Therefore I say unto you, What things soever ye desire, when ye pray, believe that ye receive them, and ye shall have them.
Mark 11:24

Prayer and faith are closely allied, and they need to be studied together. In the prayer of faith there is a divine science; it is a science that everyone who would make his lifework a success must understand. Christ says, "What things soever ye desire, when ye pray, believe that ye receive them, and ye shall have them" (Mark 11:24). He makes it plain that our asking must be according to God's will; we must ask for the things that He has promised, and whatever we receive must be used in doing His will. The conditions met, the promise is unequivocal.

For the pardon of sin, for the Holy Spirit, for a Christlike temper, for wisdom and strength to do His work, for any gift He has promised, we may ask; then we are to believe that we receive, and return thanks to God that we have received.

We need look for no outward evidence of the blessing. The gift is in the promise, and we may go about our work assured that what God has promised He is able to perform, and that the gift, which we already possess, will be realized when we need it most. (*Education*, 257, 258)

REFLECTION: *Prayer must become more than a form or ceremony. It must be like the air we breathe. When this takes place, then faith in the One who will save to the uttermost will not be just a saying. Mountains of difficulties will disappear. God is in the business of miracles.*

AUGUST 23

SUPERNATURAL SUFFERING

And he taketh with him Peter and James and John, and began to be
sore amazed, and to be very heavy; And saith unto them, My soul
is exceeding sorrowful unto death: tarry ye here, and watch.
Mark 14:33, 34

Behold Him contemplating the price to be paid for the human soul. In His agony He clings to the cold ground, as if to prevent Himself from being drawn farther from God. The chilling dew of night falls upon His prostrate form, but He heeds it not. From His pale lips comes the bitter cry, "O My Father, if it be possible, let this cup pass from Me." Yet even now He adds, "Nevertheless not as I will, but as Thou wilt."

The human heart longs for sympathy in suffering. This longing Christ felt to the very depths of His being. In the supreme agony of His soul He came to His disciples with a yearning desire to hear some words of comfort from those whom He had so often blessed and comforted, and shielded in sorrow and distress. The One who had always had words of sympathy for them was now suffering superhuman agony, and He longed to know that they were praying for Him and for themselves. How dark seemed the malignity of sin! Terrible was the temptation to let the human race bear the consequences of its own guilt, while He stood innocent before God. If He could only know that His disciples understood and appreciated this, He would be strengthened. (*The Desire of Ages*, 687)

REFLECTION: *A few words of encouragement might be just what is needed to make an eternal life difference for someone today.*

LORD OF THE SABBATH

And he said unto them, That the Son of man is Lord also of the Sabbath.
Luke 6:5

These words are full of instruction and comfort. Because the Sabbath was made for man, it is the Lord's day. It belongs to Christ. For "all things were made by Him; and without Him was not anything made that was made" (John 1:3). Since He made all things, He made the Sabbath. By Him it was set apart as a memorial of the work of creation. It points to Him as both the Creator and the Sanctifier. It declares that He who created all things in heaven and in earth, and by whom all things hold together, is the head of the church, and that by His power we are reconciled to God. For, speaking of Israel, He said, "I gave them My Sabbaths, to be a sign between Me and them, that they might know that I am the Lord that sanctify them," make them holy (Ezekiel 20:12). Then the Sabbath is a sign of Christ's power to make us holy. And it is given to all whom Christ makes holy. As a sign of His sanctifying power, the Sabbath is given to all who through Christ become a part of the Israel of God. (*The Desire of Ages*, 288)

REFLECTION: *The Sabbath shows us God's power in creation and redemption. What a beautiful gift He gave us in giving us the Sabbath.*

BORN AGAIN

Jesus answered and said unto him, Verily, verily, I say unto thee,
Except a man be born again, he cannot see the kingdom of God.
John 3:3

No human invention can find a remedy for the sinning soul. "The carnal mind is enmity against God: for it is not subject to the law of God, neither indeed can be" (Romans 8:7). "Out of the heart proceed evil thoughts, murders, adulteries, fornications, thefts, false witness, blasphemies" (Matthew 15:19). The fountain of the heart must be purified before the streams can become pure. He who is trying to reach heaven by his own works in keeping the law is attempting an impossibility.... This change can be brought about only by the effectual working of the Holy Spirit....

A person may not be able to tell the exact time or place, or to trace all the circumstances in the process of conversion; but this does not prove him to be unconverted. By an agency as unseen as the wind, Christ is constantly working upon the heart. Little by little, perhaps unconsciously to the receiver, impressions are made that tend to draw the soul to Christ. These may be received through meditating upon Him, through reading the Scriptures, or through hearing the word from the living preacher. Suddenly, as the Spirit comes with more direct appeal, the soul gladly surrenders itself to Jesus. By many this is called sudden conversion; but it is the result of long wooing by the Spirit of God,—a patient, protracted process." (*The Desire of Ages*, 172, 173)

REFLECTION: *When we allow the Holy Spirit into our heart, there is a change in us. Are you allowing Him to change you today?*

$\mathcal{S}$EARCH THE $\mathcal{S}$CRIPTURES

*Search the scriptures; for in them ye think ye have eternal
life: and they are they which testify of me.*
John 5:39

*I*n every age there is a new development of truth, a message of God to the people of that generation. The old truths are all essential; new truth is not independent of the old, but an unfolding of it. It is only as the old truths are understood that we can comprehend the new. When Christ desired to open to His disciples the truth of His resurrection, He began "at Moses and all the prophets" and "expounded unto them in all the scriptures the things concerning Himself" (Luke 24:27). But it is the light which shines in the fresh unfolding of truth that glorifies the old. He who rejects or neglects the new does not really possess the old. For him it loses its vital power and becomes but a lifeless form....

Many who claim to believe and to teach the gospel are in a similar error. They set aside the Old Testament Scriptures, of which Christ declared, "They are they which testify of Me" (John 5:39). In rejecting the Old, they virtually reject the New; for both are parts of an inseparable whole. No man can rightly present the law of God without the gospel, or the gospel without the law. The law is the gospel embodied, and the gospel is the law unfolded. The law is the root, the gospel is the fragrant blossom and fruit which it bears. (*Christ's Object Lessons*, 127, 128).

REFLECTION: *John 5:39 tells us to "Search the scriptures." 2 Timothy 3:16 says, "All scripture is given by inspiration of God." Jesus said that He did not come to change the law, but to fulfill it. These New Testament texts come from the Old Testament. The Old Testament is as important to our salvation today as it was when it was written. Old and New should be searched and studied together.*

THIEVES OF HOPE

*All that ever came before me are thieves and
robbers: but the sheep did not hear them.*
John 10:8

*J*esus told them plainly, "I am the door: by Me if any
man enter in, he shall be saved, and shall go in and out,
and find pasture. The thief cometh not, but for to steal,
and to kill, and to destroy: I am come that they might have life,
and that they might have it more abundantly."

Christ is the door to the fold of God. Through this door all
His children, from the earliest times, have found entrance. In
Jesus, as shown in types, as shadowed in symbols, as manifested
in the revelation of the prophets, as unveiled in the lessons given
to His disciples, and in the miracles wrought for the sons of men,
they have beheld "the Lamb of God, which taketh away the sin of
the world" (John 1:29), and through Him they are brought within
the fold of His grace. Many have come presenting other objects
for the faith of the world; ceremonies and systems have been devised by which men hope to receive justification and peace with
God, and thus find entrance to His fold. But the only door is
Christ, and all who have interposed something to take the place
of Christ, all who have tried to enter the fold in some other way,
are thieves and robbers. (*The Desire of Ages,* 477)

REFLECTION: *There is only one way to salvation, and that is Jesus.
Choose Him today!*

AUGUST 28

THE COMFORTER

And I will pray the Father, and he shall give you another
Comforter, that he may abide with you for ever.
John 14:16

O f the Spirit Jesus said, "He shall glorify Me." The Saviour came to glorify the Father by the demonstration of His love; so the Spirit was to glorify Christ by revealing His grace to the world. The very image of God is to be reproduced in humanity. The honor of God, the honor of Christ, is involved in the perfection of the character of His people.

"When He [the Spirit of truth] is come, He will reprove the world of sin, and of righteousness, and of judgment." The preaching of the word will be of no avail without the continual presence and aid of the Holy Spirit. This is the only effectual teacher of divine truth. Only when the truth is accompanied to the heart by the Spirit will it quicken the conscience or transform the life. One might be able to present the letter of the word of God, he might be familiar with all its commands and promises; but unless the Holy Spirit sets home the truth, no souls will fall on the Rock and be broken. No amount of education, no advantages, however great, can make one a channel of light without the co-operation of the Spirit of God. (*The Desire of Ages*, 671)

REFLECTION: *The words of a song come to mind when I read the passage above. "Come Holy Spirit I need you: Come sweet spirit I pray: Come in your own strength and your power: Come in your own special way." I believe that we should pray for the Holy Spirit to guide us every morning before we start the day.*

CONNECTED TO CHRIST

I am the vine, ye are the branches: He that abideth in me, and I in him,
the same bringeth forth much fruit: for without me ye can do nothing.
John 15:5

Though He was about to be removed from them, their spiritual union with Him was to be unchanged. The connection of the branch with the vine, He said, represents the relation you are to sustain to Me. The scion is engrafted into the living vine, and fiber by fiber, vein by vein, it grows into the vine stock. The life of the vine becomes the life of the branch. So the soul dead in trespasses and sins receives life through connection with Christ. By faith in Him as a personal Saviour the union is formed. The sinner unites his weakness to Christ's strength, his emptiness to Christ's fullness, his frailty to Christ's enduring might. Then he has the mind of Christ. The humanity of Christ has touched our humanity, and our humanity has touched divinity. Thus through the agency of the Holy Spirit man becomes a partaker of the divine nature. He is accepted in the Beloved....

This is no casual touch, no off-and-on connection. The branch becomes a part of the living vine. The communication of life, strength, and fruitfulness from the root to the branches is unobstructed and constant. Separated from the vine, the branch cannot live. No more, said Jesus, can you live apart from Me. The life you have received from Me can be preserved only by continual communion. Without Me you cannot overcome one sin, or resist one temptation.

Abiding in Christ means a constant receiving of His Spirit, a life of unreserved surrender to His service. (*The Desire of Ages*, 675, 676)

REFLECTION: *Have you chosen to abide in Christ, and to maintain that abiding relationship?*

*B*EARING *F*RUIT

Herein is my Father glorified, that ye bear much
fruit; so shall ye be my disciples.
John 15:8

*W*hen we live by faith on the Son of God, the fruits of the Spirit will be seen in our lives; not one will be missing.

A profession of religion places men in the church, but the character and conduct show whether they are in connection with Christ. If they bear no fruit, they are false branches. Their separation from Christ involves a ruin as complete as that represented by the dead branch. "If a man abide not in Me," said Christ, "he is cast forth as a branch, and is withered; and men gather them, and cast them into the fire, and they are burned."

"Herein is My Father glorified," said Jesus, "that ye bear much fruit." God desires to manifest through you the holiness, the benevolence, the compassion, of His own character. Yet the Saviour does not bid the disciples labor to bear fruit. He tells them to abide in Him. "If ye abide in Me," He says, "and My words abide in you, ye shall ask what ye will, and it shall be done unto you." It is through the word that Christ abides in His followers. This is the same vital union that is represented by eating His flesh and drinking His blood. The words of Christ are spirit and life. Receiving them, you receive the life of the Vine. (*The Desire of Ages*, 676, 677)

REFLECTION: *Only by this connection to Christ are we able to keep His command to love one another as He loves us. Can people see that we have a real connection with Christ? Do we produce fruit? Are we doing something that will lead others to Christ? Today would be a good day to be determined to be a fruit bearer.*

AUGUST 31

To Know God

*And this is life eternal, that they might know thee the only
true God, and Jesus Christ, whom thou hast sent.*
John 17:3

*I*n His prayer to the Father, Christ gave to the world a lesson which should be graven on mind and soul. "This is life eternal," He said, "that they might know Thee the only true God, and Jesus Christ, whom Thou hast sent" (John 17:3). This is true education. It imparts power. The experimental knowledge of God and of Jesus Christ whom He has sent, transforms man into the image of God. It gives to man the mastery of himself, bringing every impulse and passion of the lower nature under the control of the higher powers of the mind. It makes its possessor a son of God and an heir of heaven. It brings him into communion with the mind of the Infinite, and opens to him the rich treasures of the universe.

This is the knowledge which is obtained by searching the word of God. And this treasure may be found by every soul who will give all to obtain it.

"If thou criest after knowledge, and liftest up thy voice for understanding; if thou seekest her as silver, and searchest for her as for hid treasures; then shalt thou understand the fear of the Lord, and find the knowledge of God" (Proverbs 2:3–5). (*Christ's Object Lessons*, 114)

REFLECTION: *To know God is not merely to have a knowledge of Him, but to have received His forgiveness and righteousness.*

September

RECEIVE THE *Holy Spirit*

*And when he had said this, he breathed on them, and
saith unto them, Receive ye the Holy Ghost.*
John 20:22

efore He left His disciples, Christ "breathed on them,
and saith unto them, Receive ye the Holy Ghost"
(John 20:22). Again He said, "Behold, I send the promise of My Father upon you" (Luke 24:49). But not until after the
ascension was the gift received in its fullness. Not until through
faith and prayer the disciples had surrendered themselves fully
for His working was the outpouring of the Spirit received. Then
in a special sense the goods of heaven were committed to the
followers of Christ. "When He ascended up on high, He led captivity captive, and gave gifts unto men" (Ephesians 4:8). "Unto
every one of us is given grace, according to the measure of the
gift of Christ," the Spirit "dividing to every man severally as He
will" (Ephesians 4:7; 1 Corinthians 12:11). The gifts are already
ours in Christ, but their actual possession depends upon our re-
ception of the Spirit of God.

The promise of the Spirit is not appreciated as it should be.
Its fulfillment is not realized as it might be. It is the absence of the
Spirit that makes the gospel ministry so powerless. Learning, talents, eloquence, every natural or acquired endowment, may be
possessed; but without the presence of the Spirit of God, no heart
will be touched, no sinner be won to Christ. On the other hand, if
they are connected with Christ, if the gifts of the Spirit are theirs,
the poorest and most ignorant of His disciples will have a power
that will tell upon hearts. (*Christ's Object Lessons*, 327, 328)

REFLECTION: *Christ wants to give you the gift of the Holy Spirit; make
yourself available today.*

SEPTEMBER 2

Feed My Sheep

*He saith unto him the third time, Simon, son of Jonas, lovest thou
me? Peter was grieved because he said unto him the third time, Lovest
thou me? And he said unto him, Lord, thou knowest all things; thou
knowest that I love thee. Jesus saith unto him, Feed my sheep.*
John 21:17

The question that Christ had put to Peter was significant.
He mentioned only one condition of discipleship and
service. "Lovest thou Me?" He said. This is the essential
qualification. Though Peter might possess every other, yet without the love of Christ he could not be a faithful shepherd over
the Lord's flock.

Before His death, Jesus had said to him, "Whither I go, thou
canst not follow Me now; but thou shalt follow Me afterwards."
To this Peter had replied, "Lord, why cannot I follow Thee now?
I will lay down my life for Thy sake" (John 13:36,37). When he
said this, he little knew to what heights and depths Christ's feet
would lead the way. Peter had failed when the test came, but
again he was to have opportunity to prove his love for Christ. …
Jesus said, "When thou wast young, thou girdedst thyself, and
walkedst whither thou wouldest: but when thou shalt be old,
thou shalt stretch forth thy hands, and another shall gird thee, and
carry thee whither thou wouldest not. This spake He, signifying
by what death he should glorify God." (*The Desire of Ages*, 815)

REFLECTION: *Jesus was crucified and had risen when He went to Peter
and said "Feed My sheep." When these words were spoken Peter was
fishing. Peter went back to the work he had before he met the Savior.
Jesus was really saying, "I told you three and a half years ago to be fishers of men. Get out of the boat and feed my sheep." The same command
is given to us. Today find some way to feed His sheep.*

SEPTEMBER 3

THE GOSPEL COMMISSION

But ye shall receive power, after that the Holy Ghost is come upon you: and ye shall be witnesses unto me both in Jerusalem, and in all Judaea, and in Samaria, and unto the uttermost part of the earth.

Acts 1:8

Through the gift of the Holy Spirit the disciples were to receive a marvelous power. Their testimony was to be confirmed by signs and wonders. Miracles would be wrought, not only by the apostles, but by those who received their message. Jesus said, "In My name shall they cast out devils; they shall speak with new tongues; they shall take up serpents; and if they drink any deadly thing, it shall not hurt them; they shall lay hands on the sick, and they shall recover" (Mark 16:17, 18). ...

Thus Christ gave His disciples their commission. He made full provision for the prosecution of the work, and took upon Himself the responsibility for its success. So long as they obeyed His word, and worked in connection with Him, they could not fail. Go to all nations, He bade them. Go to the farthest part of the habitable globe, but know that My presence will be there. Labor in faith and confidence, for the time will never come when I will forsake you.

The Saviour's commission to the disciples included all the believers. It includes all believers in Christ to the end of time. It is a fatal mistake to suppose that the work of saving souls depends alone on the ordained minister. (*The Desire of Ages*, 821, 822)

REFLECTION: *What can you do today to bring someone to Jesus?*

CHRIST'S ASCENSION

And when he had spoken these things, while they beheld, he
was taken up; and a cloud received him out of their sight.
Acts 1:9

Christ had ascended to heaven in the form of humanity. The disciples had beheld the cloud receive Him. The same Jesus who had walked and talked and prayed with them; who had broken bread with them; who had been with them in their boats on the lake; and who had that very day toiled with them up the ascent of Olivet,—the same Jesus had now gone to share His Father's throne. And the angels had assured them that the very One whom they had seen go up into heaven, would come again even as He had ascended. He will come "with clouds; and every eye shall see Him." "The Lord Himself shall descend from heaven with a shout, with the voice of the Archangel, and with the trump of God: and the dead in Christ shall rise." "The Son of man shall come in His glory, and all the holy angels with Him, then shall He sit upon the throne of His glory" (Revelation 1:7; 1 Thessalonians 4:16; Matthew 25:31). Thus will be fulfilled the Lord's own promise to His disciples: "If I go and prepare a place for you, I will come again, and receive you unto Myself; that where I am, there ye may be also" (John 14:3). Well might the disciples rejoice in the hope of their Lord's return. (*The Desire of Ages*, 832)

REFLECTION: *We may also have the same joy the disciples had in the promise of their Savior's soon return. Today spend some time thinking of the preparation that is taking place. Christ himself is preparing heaven just for you. Your mansion is going to be handcrafted by our loving Savior.*

SEPTEMBER 5

ONE ACCORD

And when the day of Pentecost was fully come, they
were all with one accord in one place.
Acts 2:1

As the disciples waited for the fulfillment of the promise, they humbled their hearts in true repentance and confessed their unbelief. As they called to remembrance the words that Christ had spoken to them before His death they understood more fully their meaning. Truths which had passed from their memory were again brought to their minds, and these they repeated to one another. They reproached themselves for their misapprehension of the Saviour. Like a procession, scene after scene of His wonderful life passed before them. As they meditated upon His pure, holy life they felt that no toil would be too hard, no sacrifice too great, if only they could bear witness in their lives to the loveliness of Christ's character. Oh, if they could but have the past three years to live over, they thought, how differently they would act! If they could only see the Master again, how earnestly they would strive to show Him how deeply they loved Him, and how sincerely they sorrowed for having ever grieved Him by a word or an act of unbelief! But they were comforted by the thought that they were forgiven. And they determined that, so far as possible, they would atone for their unbelief by bravely confessing Him before the world. (*The Acts of the Apostles*, 36)

REFLECTION: *That same spirit of "one accord" has to be in place before we can be true witnesses for Christ. We have to stop the struggles among ourselves, even among our church family and be of one accord and finish the work.*

TONGUES OF FIRE

And there appeared unto them cloven tongues like as of fire, and it sat upon each of them. And they were all filled with the Holy Ghost, and began to speak with other tongues, as the Spirit gave them utterance.
Acts 2:3, 4

The Holy Spirit, assuming the form of tongues of fire, rested upon those assembled. This was an emblem of the gift then bestowed on the disciples, which enabled them to speak with fluency languages with which they had heretofore been unacquainted. The appearance of fire signified the fervent zeal with which the apostles would labor and the power that would attend their work.

There were dwelling at Jerusalem Jews, devout men, out of every nation under heaven." During the dispersion the Jews had been scattered to almost every part of the inhabited world, and in their exile they had learned to speak various languages. Many of these Jews were on this occasion in Jerusalem, attending the religious festivals then in progress. Every known tongue was represented by those assembled. This diversity of languages would have been a great hindrance to the proclamation of the gospel; God therefore in a miraculous manner supplied the deficiency of the apostles. The Holy Spirit did for them that which they could not have accomplished for themselves in a lifetime. They could now proclaim the truths of the gospel abroad, speaking with accuracy the languages of those for whom they were laboring. This miraculous gift was a strong evidence to the world that their commission bore the signet of Heaven. From this time forth the language of the disciples was pure, simple, and accurate, whether they spoke in their native tongue or in a foreign language. (*The Acts of the Apostles*, 39)

REFLECTION: *In your service for God, do you lack a necessary skill? Pray about it. Ask God about His will concerning this; ask Him to supply your deficiency.*

STEPHEN

*And Stephen, full of faith and power, did great
wonders and miracles among the people.*
Acts 6:8

Stephen, the foremost of the seven deacons, was a man of deep piety and broad faith.... He was very active in the cause of Christ and boldly proclaimed his faith.... Not only did he speak in the power of the Holy Spirit, but it was plain that he was a student of the prophecies and learned in all matters of the law. He ably defended the truths that he advocated and utterly defeated his opponents. To him was the promise fulfilled, "Settle it therefore in your hearts, not to meditate before what ye shall answer: for I will give you a mouth and wisdom, which all your adversaries shall not be able to gainsay nor resist" (Luke 21:14, 15).

As the priests and rulers saw the power that attended the preaching of Stephen, they were filled with bitter hatred. Instead of yielding to the evidence that he presented, they determined to silence his voice by putting him to death. On several occasions they had bribed the Roman authorities to pass over without comment instances where the Jews had taken the law into their own hands and had tried, condemned, and executed prisoners in accordance with their national custom. The enemies of Stephen did not doubt that they could again pursue such a course without danger to themselves. (*The Acts of the Apostles*, 97, 98)

REFLECTION: *What an example Stephen is to us today. He knew his Savior, and stood firmly for Him even though it cost him his life.*

SEPTEMBER 8

*L*IVE BY *F*AITH

For therein is the righteousness of God revealed from faith
to faith: as it is written, The just shall live by faith.
Romans 1:17

*I*n his epistle to the Romans, Paul set forth the great principles of the gospel. He stated his position on the questions which were agitating the Jewish and the Gentile churches, and showed that the hopes and promises which had once belonged especially to the Jews were now offered to the Gentiles also.

With great clearness and power the apostle presented the doctrine of justification by faith in Christ. He hoped that other churches also might be helped by the instruction sent to the Christians at Rome; but how dimly could he foresee the far-reaching influence of his words! Through all the ages the great truth of justification by faith has stood as a mighty beacon to guide repentant sinners into the way of life. It was this light that scattered the darkness which enveloped Luther's mind and revealed to him the power of the blood of Christ to cleanse from sin. The same light has guided thousands of sin-burdened souls to the true Source of pardon and peace. For the epistle to the church at Rome, every Christian has reason to thank God.

In this letter Paul gave free expression to his burden in behalf of the Jews. Ever since his conversion, he had longed to help his Jewish brethren to gain a clear understanding of the gospel message. "My heart's desire and prayer to God for Israel is," he declared, "that they might be saved." (*Acts of the Apostles,* 373, 374)

REFLECTION: *Faith is not a happy flight of feeling; it is simply taking God at His word — believing that He will fulfill His promises because He said He would.*

SEPTEMBER 9

*J*UDGE *O*THERS

Therefore thou art inexcusable, O man, whosoever thou art that
judget: for wherein thou judgest another, thou condemnest
thyself; for thou that judgest doest the same things.
Romans 2:1

The sin that leads to the most unhappy results is the cold, critical, unforgiving spirit that characterizes Pharisaism. When the religious experience is devoid of love, Jesus is not there; the sunshine of His presence is not there. No busy activity or Christless zeal can supply the lack. There may be a wonderful keenness of perception to discover the defects of others; but to everyone who indulges this spirit, Jesus says, "Thou hypocrite, first cast out the beam out of thine own eye; and then shalt thou see clearly to cast out the mote out of thy brother's eye." He who is guilty of wrong is the first to suspect wrong. By condemning another he is trying to conceal or excuse the evil of his own heart. It was through sin that men gained the knowledge of evil; no sooner had the first pair sinned than they began to accuse each other; and this is what human nature will inevitably do when uncontrolled by the grace of Christ.

When men indulge this accusing spirit, they are not satisfied with pointing out what they suppose to be a defect in their brother. If milder means fail of making him do what they think ought to be done, they will resort to compulsion. (*Thoughts from the Mount of Blessing*, 126)

REFLECTION: *Most people judge others to make themselves look better. Leave the judging to God, and allow Him to do the necessary work in your own life.*

SEPTEMBER 10

No Respecter of Persons

For there is no respect of persons with God.
Romans 2:11

No distinction on account of nationality, race, or caste, is recognized by God. He is the Maker of all mankind. All men are of one family by creation, and all are one through redemption. Christ came to demolish every wall of partition, to throw open every compartment of the temple courts, that every soul may have free access to God. His love is so broad, so deep, so full, that it penetrates everywhere. It lifts out of Satan's influence those who have been deluded by his deceptions, and places them within reach of the throne of God, the throne encircled by the rainbow of promise. In Christ there is neither Jew nor Greek, bond nor free.

In the years that followed the occupation of the Promised Land, the beneficent designs of Jehovah for the salvation of the heathen were almost wholly lost sight of, and it became necessary for Him to set forth His plan anew. "All the ends of the world," the psalmist was inspired to sing, "shall remember and turn unto the Lord: and all the kindreds of the nations shall worship before Thee." "Princes shall come out of Egypt; Ethiopia shall soon stretch out her hands unto God" (Psalm 22:27; 68:31). (*Prophets and Kings*, 369, 370)

REFLECTION: *Be sensitive to the needs of people, no matter what is their nationality or position in life. Reach them for Christ.*

SEPTEMBER 11

By the Law the Knowledge of Sin

Therefore by the deeds of the law there shall no flesh be justified in his sight: for by the law is the knowledge of sin.
Romans 3:20

The first step in reconciliation to God is the conviction of sin. "Sin is the transgression of the law." "By the law is the knowledge of sin" (1 John 3:4; Romans 3:20). In order to see his guilt, the sinner must test his character by God's great standard of righteousness. It is a mirror which shows the perfection of a righteous character and enables him to discern the defects in his own.

The law reveals to man his sins, but it provides no remedy. While it promises life to the obedient, it declares that death is the portion of the transgressor. The gospel of Christ alone can free him from the condemnation or the defilement of sin. He must exercise repentance toward God, whose law has been transgressed; and faith in Christ, his atoning sacrifice. Thus he obtains "remission of sins that are past" and becomes a partaker of the divine nature. He is a child of God, having received the spirit of adoption, whereby he cries: "Abba, Father!"

Is he now free to transgress God's law? Says Paul: "Do we then make void the law through faith? God forbid: yea, we establish the law." "How shall we, that are dead to sin, live any longer therein?" (Romans 3:31; 6:2). (*The Great Controversy*, 467, 468)

REFLECTION: *In Romans 7:12 God's Word describes His law as holy, just, and good. Some people say the law should be done away with. Why would you do away with something that is holy, just, and good? Paul says, "certainly not!"*

SEPTEMBER 12

THE PERFECT LAW

Do we then make void the law through faith?
God forbid: yea, we establish the law.
Romans 3:31

Because the law of the Lord is perfect, and therefore changeless, it is impossible for sinful men, in themselves, to meet the standard of its requirement. This was why Jesus came as our Redeemer. It was His mission, by making men partakers of the divine nature, to bring them into harmony with the principles of the law of heaven. When we forsake our sins and receive Christ as our Saviour, the law is exalted. The apostle Paul asks, "Do we then make void the law through faith? God forbid: yea, we establish the law" (Romans 3:31).

The new covenant promise is, "I will put My laws into their hearts, and in their minds will I write them" (Hebrews 10:16). While the system of types which pointed to Christ as the Lamb of God that should take away the sin of the world was to pass away at His death, the principles of righteousness embodied in the Decalogue are as immutable as the eternal throne. Not one command has been annulled, not a jot or tittle has been changed. Those principles that were made known to man in Paradise as the great law of life will exist unchanged in Paradise restored. When Eden shall bloom on earth again, God's law of love will be obeyed by all beneath the sun. (*Thoughts from the Mount of Blessing*, 50)

REFLECTION: *God's law from the beginning of time through the eternal ages will always be the same. It is the law of love. Allow God to write His laws in your heart today, and every day.*

ABRAHAM'S FAITH

What shall we say then that Abraham our father,
as pertaining to the flesh, hath found?
Romans 4:1

All boasting of merit in ourselves is out of place. "Let not the wise man glory in his wisdom, neither let the mighty man glory in his might, let not the rich man glory in his riches; but let him that glorieth, glory in this, that he understandeth and knoweth Me, that I am the Lord which exercise loving kindness, judgment, and righteousness in the earth; for in these things I delight, saith the Lord" (Jeremiah 9:23, 24).

The reward is not of works, lest any man should boast; but it is all of grace. "What shall we say then that Abraham our father, as pertaining to the flesh, hath found? For if Abraham were justified by works, he hath whereof to glory; but not before God. For what saith the scripture? Abraham believed God, and it was counted unto him for righteousness. Now to him that worketh is the reward not reckoned of grace, but of debt. But to him that worketh not, but believeth on Him that justifieth the ungodly, his faith is counted for righteousness" (Romans 4:1–5). Therefore there is no occasion for one to glory over another or to grudge against another. No one is privileged above another, nor can anyone claim the reward as a right. (*Christ's Object Lessons*, 401)

REFLECTION: *"He who grudges the reward to another forgets that he himself is saved by grace alone"* (Christ's Object Lessons, 402). *Our good works are a by-product of our love for Christ. A famous preacher of the gospel explained it this way. "A dog doesn't bark to become a dog, he barks because he is a dog." Christians have good works because they are Christians, not to become Christians.*

September 14

Peace with God

*Therefore being justified by faith, we have peace
with God through our Lord Jesus Christ.*
Romans 5:1

Christ is "the Prince of Peace" (Isaiah 9:6), and it is His mission to restore to earth and heaven the peace that sin has broken. "Being justified by faith, we have peace with God through our Lord Jesus Christ" (Romans 5:1). Whoever consents to renounce sin and open his heart to the love of Christ, becomes a partaker of this heavenly peace.

There is no other ground of peace than this. The grace of Christ received into the heart, subdues enmity; it allays strife and fills the soul with love. He who is at peace with God and his fellow men cannot be made miserable. Envy will not be in his heart; evil surmisings will find no room there; hatred cannot exist. The heart that is in harmony with God is a partaker of the peace of heaven and will diffuse its blessed influence on all around. The spirit of peace will rest like dew upon hearts weary and troubled with worldly strife.

Christ's followers are sent to the world with the message of peace. Whoever, by the quiet, unconscious influence of a holy life, shall reveal the love of Christ; whoever, by word or deed, shall lead another to renounce sin and yield his heart to God, is a peacemaker. (*Thoughts from the Mount of Blessing*, 27, 28)

REFLECTION: *A spirit of peace is evidence that we have a connection with heaven.*

SEPTEMBER 15

He Died for Sinners

But God commendeth his love toward us, in that, while
we were yet sinners, Christ died for us.
Romans 5:8

Not because we first loved Him did Christ love us; but "while we were yet sinners" He died for us. He does not treat us according to our desert. Although our sins have merited condemnation, He does not condemn us. Year after year He has borne with our weakness and ignorance, with our ingratitude and waywardness. Notwithstanding our wanderings, our hardness of heart, our neglect of His Holy Word, His hand is stretched out still.

Grace is an attribute of God exercised toward undeserving human beings. We did not seek for it, but it was sent in search of us. God rejoices to bestow His grace upon us, not because we are worthy, but because we are so utterly unworthy. Our only claim to His mercy is our great need.

The Lord God through Jesus Christ holds out His hand all the day long in invitation to the sinful and fallen. He will receive all. He welcomes all. It is His glory to pardon the chief of sinners. He will take the prey from the mighty, He will deliver the captive, He will pluck the brand from the burning. He will lower the golden chain of His mercy to the lowest depths of human wretchedness, and lift up the debased soul contaminated with sin. (*The Ministry of Healing*, 161)

REFLECTION: *Let's show the same love and kindness to others that Christ showed toward us.*

SEPTEMBER 16

RANSOMED AND EXALTED

*Moreover the law entered, that the offence might abound. But
where sin abounded, grace did much more abound.*
Romans 5:20

Through Christ's redeeming work the government of God
stands justified. The Omnipotent One is made known
as the God of love. Satan's charges are refuted, and his
character unveiled. Rebellion can never again arise. Sin can never again enter the universe. Through eternal ages all are secure
from apostasy. By love's self-sacrifice, the inhabitants of earth and
heaven are bound to their Creator in bonds of indissoluble union.

The work of redemption will be complete. In the place where
sin abounded, God's grace much more abounds. The earth itself,
the very field that Satan claims as his, is to be not only ransomed
but exalted. Our little world, under the curse of sin the one dark
blot in His glorious creation, will be honored above all other
worlds in the universe of God. Here, where the Son of God tabernacled in humanity; where the King of glory lived and suffered
and died, — here, when He shall make all things new, the tabernacle of God shall be with men, "and He will dwell with them, and
they shall be His people, and God Himself shall be with them,
and be their God." And through endless ages as the redeemed
walk in the light of the Lord, they will praise Him for His unspeakable Gift, — Immanuel, "God with us." (*Desire of Ages*, 26)

REFLECTION: *Just the thought of not being in heaven is more than any
of us wants to think about. To think of the beauty and wonders we
will see! Most of all, think of what Jesus did and suffered so we could
all be there.*

SEPTEMBER 17

SERVANTS OF RIGHTEOUSNESS

But now being made free from sin, and become servants to God,
ye have your fruit unto holiness, and the end everlasting life.
Romans 6:22

here was in Him nothing that responded to Satan's sophistry. He did not consent to sin. Not even by a thought did He yield to temptation. So it may be with us. Christ's humanity was united with divinity; He was fitted for the conflict by the indwelling of the Holy Spirit. And He came to make us partakers of the divine nature. So long as we are united to Him by faith, sin has no more dominion over us. God reaches for the hand of faith in us to direct it to lay fast hold upon the divinity of Christ, that we may attain to perfection of character.

And how this is accomplished, Christ has shown us. By what means did He overcome in the conflict with Satan? By the word of God. Only by the word could He resist temptation. "It is written," He said. And unto us are given "exceeding great and precious promises: that by these ye might be partakers of the divine nature, having escaped the corruption that is in the world through lust" (2 Peter 1:4). Every promise in God's word is ours. "By every word that proceedeth out of the mouth of God" are we to live. When assailed by temptation, look not to circumstances or to the weakness of self, but to the power of the word. All its strength is yours. "Thy word," says the psalmist, "have I hid in mine heart, that I might not sin against Thee" (Psalm 119:11). (*Desire of Ages*, 123)

REFLECTION: *When, by faith, we trust completely in God's Word and ask for His power, we will be overcomers. Let's hide God's precious promises in our hearts. We do not have to let sin be in charge of us.*

WAGES OF SIN IS DEATH

*The wages of sin is death; but the gift of God is
eternal life through Jesus Christ our Lord.*
Romans 6:23

While life is the inheritance of the righteous, death is the portion of the wicked. Moses declared to Israel: "I have set before thee this day life and good, and death and evil" (Deuteronomy 30:15). The death referred to in these scriptures is not that pronounced upon Adam, for all mankind suffer the penalty of his transgression. It is "the second death" that is placed in contrast with everlasting life.

In consequence of Adam's sin, death passed upon the whole human race. All alike go down into the grave. And through the provisions of the plan of salvation, all are to be brought forth from their graves. "There shall be a resurrection of the dead, both of the just and unjust;" "for as in Adam all die, even so in Christ shall all be made alive" (Acts 24:15; 1 Corinthians 15:22). But a distinction is made between the two classes that are brought forth. "All that are in the graves shall hear His voice, and shall come forth; they that have done good, unto the resurrection of life; and they that have done evil, unto the resurrection of damnation" (John 5:28, 29). They who have been "accounted worthy" of the resurrection of life are "blessed and holy." "On such the second death hath no power" (Revelation 20:6). (*The Great Controversy*, 544)

REFLECTION: *Eternal life cannot be earned, it's a gift. "The gift of God is eternal life" (Romans 6:23). However, there is something we can earn that is opposite; that is eternal death. This is why in Romans 6:23, the result of un-confessed sin is referred to as wages. Wages are earned.*

SEPTEMBER 19

*C*ARNAL

For we know that the law is spiritual: but I am carnal, sold under sin.
Romans 7:14

*I*t is not enough to perceive the loving-kindness of God, to see the benevolence, the fatherly tenderness, of His character. It is not enough to discern the wisdom and justice of His law, to see that it is founded upon the eternal principle of love. Paul the apostle saw all this when he exclaimed, "I consent unto the law that it is good." "The law is holy, and the commandment holy, and just, and good." But he added, in the bitterness of his soul-anguish and despair, "I am carnal, sold under sin" (Romans 7:16, 12, 14). He longed for the purity, the righteousness, to which in himself he was powerless to attain, and cried out, "O wretched man that I am! who shall deliver me from the body of this death?" (Romans 7:24). Such is the cry that has gone up from burdened hearts in all lands and in all ages. To all, there is but one answer, "Behold the Lamb of God, which taketh away the sin of the world" (John 1:29). ...

But in vain are men's dreams of progress, in vain all efforts for the uplifting of humanity, if they neglect the one Source of hope and help for the fallen race. "Every good gift and every perfect gift" (James 1:17) is from God. There is no true excellence of character apart from Him. And the only way to God is Christ. He says, "I am the way, the truth, and the life: no man cometh unto the Father, but by Me" (John 14:6). (*Steps to Christ*, 19–21)

REFLECTION: *Left to ourselves, our situation is hopeless. But Jesus offers the hope and help we need. What a beautiful gift!*

SEPTEMBER 20

No Condemnation

There is therefore now no condemnation to them which are in Christ Jesus, who walk not after the flesh, but after the Spirit.
Romans 8:1

The Bible says that "the devils also believe, and tremble;" but this is not faith (James 2:19). Where there is not only a belief in God's word, but a submission of the will to Him; where the heart is yielded to Him, the affections fixed upon Him, there is faith—faith that works by love and purifies the soul. Through this faith the heart is renewed in the image of God. And the heart that in its unrenewed state is not subject to the law of God, neither indeed can be, now delights in its holy precepts, exclaiming with the psalmist, "O how love I Thy law! It is my meditation all the day" (Psalm 119:97). And the righteousness of the law is fulfilled in us, "who walk not after the flesh, but after the Spirit" (Romans 8:1).

There are those who have known the pardoning love of Christ and who really desire to be children of God, yet they realize that their character is imperfect, their life faulty, and they are ready to doubt whether their hearts have been renewed by the Holy Spirit. To such I would say, Do not draw back in despair. We shall often have to bow down and weep at the feet of Jesus because of our shortcomings and mistakes, but we are not to be discouraged. (*Steps to Christ*, 63)

REFLECTION: *Think of a toddler learning to walk. If the toddler falls, we pick them up and they continue on towards their goal, which is to walk. When we are in Christ, our goal is to always walk with Christ. We may stumble, but when we do, Christ will pick us up and say, "Continue towards your goal, I'm right here." As we do this we will learn to not stumble.*

ALL THINGS WORK TOGETHER FOR GOOD

*And we know that all things work together for good to them that
love God, to them who are the called according to his purpose.*
Romans 8:28

Study the history of Joseph and of Daniel. The Lord did
not prevent the plottings of men who sought to do them
harm; but He caused all these devices to work for good to
His servants who amidst trial and conflict preserved their faith
and loyalty.

So long as we are in the world, we shall meet with adverse
influences. There will be provocations to test the temper; and it is
by meeting these in a right spirit that the Christian graces are developed. If Christ dwells in us, we shall be patient, kind, and forbearing, cheerful amid frets and irritations. Day by day and year
by year we shall conquer self, and grow into a noble heroism.
This is our allotted task; but it cannot be accomplished without
help from Jesus, resolute decision, unwavering purpose, continual watchfulness, and unceasing prayer. Each one has a personal
battle to fight. Not even God can make our characters noble or
our lives useful, unless we become co-workers with Him. Those
who decline the struggle lose the strength and joy of victory.

God will not suffer one of His truehearted workers to be
left alone, to struggle against great odds and be overcome. He
preserves as a precious jewel everyone whose life is hid with
Christ in Him. Of every such one He says: "I...will make thee
as a signet: for I have chosen thee" (Haggai 2:23). (*The Ministry of
Healing*, 487, 488)

REFLECTION: *Are you facing challenges as did Joseph or Daniel? Face
them with "help from Jesus, resolute decision, unwavering purpose,
continual watchfulness, and unceasing prayer."*

The Faithful Remnant

Even so then at this present time also there is a
remnant according to the election of grace.
Romans 11:5

otwithstanding Israel's failure as a nation, there remained among them a goodly remnant of such as
should be saved. At the time of the Saviour's advent
there were faithful men and women who had received with gladness the message of John the Baptist, and had thus been led to
study anew the prophecies concerning the Messiah. When the
early Christian church was founded, it was composed of these
faithful Jews who recognized Jesus of Nazareth as the one for
whose advent they had been longing. It is to this remnant that
Paul refers when he writes, "If the first fruit be holy, the lump is
also holy: and if the root be holy, so are the branches."

Paul likens the remnant in Israel to a noble olive tree, some of
whose branches have been broken off. He compares the Gentiles
to branches from a wild olive tree, grafted into the parent stock.
If some of the branches be broken off, he writes to the Gentile believers, and thou, being a wild olive tree, wert grafted in among
them, and with them partakest of the root and fatness of the olive
tree; boast not against the branches. (*The Acts of the Apostles*, 376)

REFLECTION: *God has always had a faithful remnant. With the believing
Jews, the remnant, God was able to graft in the believing Gentiles.*

OVERCOME EVIL WITH GOOD

Be not overcome of evil, but overcome evil with good.
Romans 12:21

D
o not retaliate. So far as you can do so, remove all cause for misapprehension. Avoid the appearance of evil. Do all that lies in your power, without the sacrifice of principle, to conciliate others. "If thou bring thy gift to the altar, and there rememberest that thy brother hath aught against thee; leave there thy gift before the altar, and go thy way; first be reconciled to thy brother, and then come and offer thy gift" (Matthew 5:23, 24).

If impatient words are spoken to you, never reply in the same spirit. Remember that "a soft answer turneth away wrath" (Proverbs 15:1). And there is wonderful power in silence. Words spoken in reply to one who is angry sometimes serve only to exasperate. But anger met with silence, in a tender, forbearing spirit, quickly dies away.

Under a storm of stinging, faultfinding words, keep the mind stayed upon the word of God. Let mind and heart be stored with God's promises. If you are ill-treated or wrongfully accused, instead of returning an angry answer, repeat to yourself the precious promises: "Be not overcome of evil, but overcome evil with good (Romans 12:21). (*The Ministry of Healing*, 485, 486)

REFLECTION: *I have experienced first hand that it is hard to fight with someone that will not fight back. Try this out for yourself. Give a soft answer even if you are wronged. Anger that has been vented against you will evaporate and the contention in most cases will cease. Then you can continue having a good day. Christ's council is to "Learn from me, for I am gentle and lowly in heart" (Matthew 11:29).*

How to Receive Righteousness

Love worketh no ill to his neighbour: therefore love is the fulfilling of the law.
Romans 13:10

Righteousness is holiness, likeness to God, and "God is love" (1 John 4:16). It is conformity to the law of God, for "all Thy commandments are righteousness" (Psalm 119:172), and "love is the fulfilling of the law" (Romans 13:10). Righteousness is love, and love is the light and the life of God. The righteousness of God is embodied in Christ. We receive righteousness by receiving Him.

Not by painful struggles or wearisome toil, not by gift or sacrifice, is righteousness obtained; but it is freely given to every soul who hungers and thirsts to receive it. "Ho, every one that thirsteth, come ye to the waters, and he that hath no money; come ye, buy, and eat, … without money and without price." "Their righteousness is of Me, saith the Lord," and, "This is His name whereby He shall be called, The Lord Our Righteousness" (Isaiah 55:1; 54:17; Jeremiah 23:6).

No human agent can supply that which will satisfy the hunger and thirst of the soul. But Jesus says, "Behold, I stand at the door, and knock: if any man hear My voice, and open the door, I will come in to him, and will sup with him, and he with Me." "I am the bread of life: he that cometh to Me shall never hunger; and he that believeth on Me shall never thirst" (Revelation 3:20; John 6:35). (*Thoughts from the Mount of Blessing,* 18)

REFLECTION: *We must hunger after His righteousness, not our own. Do we hunger like we do when we don't eat for a day? He is standing and knocking at your heart's door. Won't you let Him come in?*

SEPTEMBER 25

No Peace in Compromising

Let us therefore follow after the things which make for
peace, and things wherewith one may edify another.
Romans 14:19

*J*esus Himself never purchased peace by compromise.
His heart overflowed with love for the whole human
race, but He was never indulgent to their sins. He was
too much their friend to remain silent while they were pursuing a
course that would ruin their souls, — the souls He had purchased
with His own blood. He labored that man should be true to himself, true to his higher and eternal interest. The servants of Christ
are called to the same work, and they should beware lest, in seeking to prevent discord, they surrender the truth. They are to "follow after the things which make for peace" (Romans 14:19); but
real peace can never be secured by compromising principle. And
no man can be true to principle without exciting opposition. A
Christianity that is spiritual will be opposed by the children of
disobedience. But Jesus bade His disciples, "Fear not them which
kill the body, but are not able to kill the soul." Those who are true
to God need not fear the power of men nor the enmity of Satan.
In Christ their eternal life is secure. Their only fear should be lest
they surrender the truth, and thus betray the trust with which
God has honored them. (*The Desire of Ages*, 356)

REFLECTION: *We will never satisfy everyone, but we can edify or build*
up one another. Peace has always come with a price, but the path that
Christ asks us to travel will end with the words "well done, good and
faithful servant." Then we will have everlasting peace.

WRITTEN FOR US

For whatsoever things were written aforetime were written for our learning,
that we through patience and comfort of the scriptures might have hope.
Romans 15:4

Men whom God favored, and to whom He entrusted great responsibilities, were sometimes overcome by temptation and committed sin, even as we at the present day strive, waver, and frequently fall into error. Their lives, with all their faults and follies, are open before us, both for our encouragement and warning. If they had been represented as without fault, we, with our sinful nature, might despair at our own mistakes and failures. But seeing where others struggled through discouragements like our own, where they fell under temptations as we have done, and yet took heart again and conquered through the grace of God, we are encouraged in our striving after righteousness. As they, though sometimes beaten back, recovered their ground, and were blessed of God, so we too may be overcomers in the strength of Jesus. On the other hand, the record of their lives may serve as a warning to us. It shows that God will by no means clear the guilty. He sees sin in His most favored ones, and He deals with it in them even more strictly than in those who have less light and responsibility. (*Patriarchs and Prophets*, 238)

REFLECTION: *Here we have another principle. Not only are we to learn from Christ's perfect example, but we can and are admonished to learn from those who made bad choices and reaped hard results. That is a path that we do not have to travel. Those stories were written so we could avoid repeating the same mistakes.*

CHRIST ALL AND ALL

For I determined not to know any thing among you,
save Jesus Christ, and him crucified.
1 Corinthians 2:2

Paul well knew how his message would be regarded by both the Jews and the Greeks of Corinth. "We preach Christ crucified," he admitted, "unto the Jews a stumbling block, and unto the Greeks foolishness" (1 Corinthians 1:23). Among his Jewish hearers there were many who would be angered by the message he was about to proclaim. In the estimation of the Greeks his words would be absurd folly. He would be looked upon as weak-minded for attempting to show how the cross could have any connection with the elevation of the race or the salvation of mankind.

But to Paul the cross was the one object of supreme interest. Ever since he had been arrested in his career of persecution against the followers of the crucified Nazarene he had never ceased to glory in the cross. At that time there had been given him a revelation of the infinite love of God, as revealed in the death of Christ; and a marvelous transformation had been wrought in his life, bringing all his plans and purposes into harmony with heaven. From that hour he had been a new man in Christ. He knew by personal experience that when a sinner once beholds the love of the Father, as seen in the sacrifice of His Son, and yields to the divine influence, a change of heart takes place, and henceforth Christ is all and in all. (*The Acts of the Apostles*, 245)

REFLECTION: *Sometimes we make the Scriptures more complicated than they are. When you study, take time to make the principles in the Bible simple and practical, so they can work in your everyday life.*

THE TEMPLE OF GOD

Know ye not that ye are the temple of God, and
that the Spirit of God dwelleth in you?
1 Corinthians 3:16

From eternal ages it was God's purpose that every created being, from the bright and holy seraph to man, should be a temple for the indwelling of the Creator. Because of sin, humanity ceased to be a temple for God. Darkened and defiled by evil, the heart of man no longer revealed the glory of the Divine One. But by the incarnation of the Son of God, the purpose of Heaven is fulfilled. God dwells in humanity, and through saving grace the heart of man becomes again His temple. God designed that the temple at Jerusalem should be a continual witness to the high destiny open to every soul. But the Jews had not understood the significance of the building they regarded with so much pride. They did not yield themselves as holy temples for the Divine Spirit. The courts of the temple at Jerusalem, filled with the tumult of unholy traffic, represented all too truly the temple of the heart, defiled by the presence of sensual passion and unholy thoughts. In cleansing the temple from the world's buyers and sellers, Jesus announced His mission to cleanse the heart from the defilement of sin, — from the earthly desires, the selfish lusts, the evil habits, that corrupt the soul. (*The Desire of the Ages*, 161)

REFLECTION: *Only Christ can cleanse the soul temple. But He will not force an entrance. He comes not into the heart as to the temple of old; but He says, "Behold, I stand at the door, and knock: if any man hear My voice, and open the door, I will come in to him" (Revelation 3:20).* (*The Desire of the Ages*, 161)

SEPTEMBER 29

RUN THE RACE

And every man that striveth for the mastery is temperate in all things.
Now they do it to obtain a corruptible crown; but we an incorruptible.
1 Corinthians 9:25

The life of the apostle Paul was a constant conflict with self. He said, "I die daily" (1 Corinthians 15:31). His will and his desires every day conflicted with duty and the will of God. Instead of following inclination, he did God's will, however crucifying to his nature.

At the close of his life of conflict, looking back over its struggles and triumphs, he could say, "I have fought a good fight, I have finished my course, I have kept the faith: henceforth there is laid up for me a crown of righteousness, which the Lord, the righteous Judge, shall give me at that day" (2 Timothy 4:7, 8).

The Christian life is a battle and a march. In this warfare there is no release; the effort must be continuous and persevering. It is by unceasing endeavor that we maintain the victory over the temptations of Satan. Christian integrity must be sought with resistless energy and maintained with a resolute fixedness of purpose.

No one will be borne upward without stern, persevering effort in his own behalf. All must engage in this warfare for themselves; no one else can fight our battles. Individually we are responsible for the issues of the struggle; though Noah, Job, and Daniel were in the land they could deliver neither son nor daughter by their righteousness. (*The Ministry of Healing*, 452, 453)

REFLECTION: *In this battle against our sinful nature we must never give up. We may fall, but we must get up and move forward by God's grace.*

SEPTEMBER 30

CHRIST THE HEAD

But I would have you know, that the head of every man is Christ; and
the head of the woman is the man; and the head of Christ is God.
1 Corinthians 11:3

The Saviour did not commit the work of the gospel to Peter individually. At a later time, repeating the words that were spoken to Peter, He applied them directly to the church. And the same in substance was spoken also to the twelve as representatives of the body of believers. If Jesus had delegated any special authority to one of the disciples above the others, we should not find them so often contending as to who should be the greatest. They would have submitted to the wish of their Master, and honored the one whom He had chosen.

Instead of appointing one to be their head, Christ said to the disciples, "Be not ye called Rabbi;" "neither be ye called masters: for one is your Master, even Christ" (Matthew 23:8, 10).

"The head of every man is Christ." God, who put all things under the Saviour's feet, "gave Him to be the head over all things to the church, which is His body, the fullness of Him that filleth all in all" (1 Corinthians 11:3; Ephesians 1:22, 23). The church is built upon Christ as its foundation; it is to obey Christ as its head. It is not to depend upon man, or be controlled by man. Many claim that a position of trust in the church gives them authority to dictate what other men shall believe and what they shall do. This claim God does not sanction. The Saviour declares, "All ye are brethren." (*The Desire of the Ages*, 414)

REFLECTION: *God has given us the Holy Spirit to lead us into all truth, if we are open to receive it. The pastors and other church leaders are there to guide us, not dictate what we believe.*

OCTOBER

October 1

THE BODY OF CHRIST

Now ye are the body of Christ, and members in particular.
1 Corinthians 12:27

By a comparison of the church with the human body, the apostle aptly illustrated the close and harmonious relationship that should exist among all members of the church of Christ. "By one Spirit," he wrote, "are we all baptized into one body, whether we be Jews or Gentiles, whether we be bond or free; and have been all made to drink into one Spirit. For the body is not one member, but many. If the foot shall say, Because I am not the hand, I am not of the body; is it therefore not of the body? And if the ear shall say, Because I am not the eye, I am not of the body; is it therefore not of the body? If the whole body were an eye, where were the hearing? If the whole were hearing, where were the smelling? But now hath God set the members every one of them in the body, as it hath pleased Him. And if they were all one member, where were the body? But now are they many members, yet but one body. And the eye cannot say unto the hand, I have no need of thee. ... God hath tempered the body together, having given more abundant honor to that part which lacked: that there should be no schism in the body; but that the members should have the same care one for another. ... Now ye are the body of Christ, and members in particular. (*The Acts of the Apostles*, 317)

REFLECTION: *God has designed us well. We all are given different talents and abilities. All God asks of us is to use what He has given us to glorify Him and help our fellow brothers and sisters in Christ.*

OCTOBER 2

GIFT OF LOVE

Charity suffereth long, and is kind; charity envieth not;
charity vaunteth not itself, is not puffed up.
1 Corinthians 13:4

No matter how high the profession, he whose heart is not filled with love for God and his fellow men is not a true disciple of Christ. Though he should possess great faith and have power even to work miracles, yet without love his faith would be worthless. He might display great liberality; but should he, from some other motive than genuine love, bestow all his goods to feed the poor, the act would not commend him to the favor of God. In his zeal he might even meet a martyr's death, yet if not actuated by love, he would be regarded by God as a deluded enthusiast or an ambitious hypocrite.

"Charity suffereth long, and is kind; charity envieth not; charity vaunteth not itself, is not puffed up." The purest joy springs from the deepest humiliation. The strongest and noblest characters are built on the foundation of patience, love, and submission to God's will.

"Charity doth not behave itself unseemly, seeketh not her own, is not easily provoked, thinketh no evil." Christ-like love places the most favorable construction on the motives and acts of others. It does not needlessly expose their faults; it does not listen eagerly to unfavorable reports, but seeks rather to bring to mind the good qualities of others. (*The Acts of the Apostles*, 318, 319)

REFLECTION: *This chapter is so important that I believe we should read it every day. When we work with others to lead them to Christ, if the principles of this chapter are not conveyed, our efforts will most likely fail. All the knowledge and experience that heaven and earth has will fall short if our messages don't reflect the love of Christ. "Love never fails" (1 Corinthians 13:8).*

OCTOBER 3

A GOD OF ORDER

For God is not the author of confusion, but of
peace, as in all churches of the saints.
1 Corinthians 14:33

The order that was maintained in the early Christian church made it possible for them to move forward solidly as a well-disciplined army clad with the armor of God. The companies of believers, though scattered over a large territory, were all members of one body; all moved in concert and in harmony with one another. When dissension arose in a local church, as later it did arise in Antioch and elsewhere, and the believers were unable to come to an agreement among themselves, such matters were not permitted to create a division in the church, but were referred to a general council of the entire body of believers, made up of appointed delegates from the various local churches, with the apostles and elders in positions of leading responsibility. Thus the efforts of Satan to attack the church in isolated places were met by concerted action on the part of all, and the plans of the enemy to disrupt and destroy were thwarted.

"God is not the author of confusion, but of peace, as in all churches of the saints" (1 Corinthians 14:33). He requires that order and system be observed in the conduct of church affairs today no less than in the days of old. He desires His work to be carried forward with thoroughness and exactness so that He may place upon it the seal of His approval.

REFLECTION: *Christian is to be united with Christian, church with church, the human instrumentality co-operating with the divine, every agency subordinate to the Holy Spirit, and all combined in giving to the world the good tidings of the grace of God. (The Acts of the Apostles, 96)*

$\mathcal{N}$ew $\mathcal{B}$odies

For this corruptible must put on incorruption, and
this mortal must put on immortality.
1 Corinthians 15:53

With convincing power the apostle set forth the great truth of the resurrection. "If there be no resurrection of the dead," he argued, "then is Christ not risen: and if Christ be not risen, then is our preaching vain, and your faith is also vain.... Then they also which are fallen asleep in Christ are perished. If in this life only we have hope in Christ, we are of all men most miserable. But now is Christ risen from the dead, and become the first fruits of them that slept."

The apostle carried the minds of the Corinthian brethren forward to the triumphs of the resurrection morn, when all the sleeping saints are to be raised, henceforth to live forever with their Lord. "Behold," the apostle declared, "I show you a mystery: We shall not all sleep, but we shall all be changed, in a moment, in the twinkling of an eye, at the last trump: for the trumpet shall sound, and the dead shall be raised incorruptible, and we shall be changed. For this corruptible must put on incorruption, and this mortal must put on immortality. So when this corruptible shall have put on incorruption, and this mortal shall have put on immortality, then shall be brought to pass the saying that is written, Death is swallowed up in victory. O death, where is thy sting? O grave, where is thy victory? ... Thanks be to God, which giveth us the victory through our Lord Jesus Christ." (*The Acts of the Apostles*, 320)

REFLECTION: *Eye has not seen nor ear heard what God has in store for us. What an awesome thought!*

OCTOBER 5

THE CONSTRAINING POWER OF LOVE

For the love of Christ constraineth us; because we thus
judge, that if one died for all, then were all dead.
2 Corinthians 5:14

Christ gave no stinted service. He did not measure His work by hours. His time, His heart, His soul and strength, were given to labor for the benefit of humanity. Through weary days He toiled, and through long nights He bent in prayer for grace and endurance that He might do a larger work. With strong crying and tears He sent His petitions to heaven, that His human nature might be strengthened, that He might be braced to meet the wily foe in all his deceptive workings, and fortified to fulfill His missions of uplifting humanity. To His workers He says, "I have given you an example, that ye should do as I have done" (John 13:15).

"The love of Christ," said Paul, "constraineth us" (2 Corinthians 5:14). This was the actuating principle of his conduct; it was his motive power. If ever his ardor in the path of duty flagged for a moment, one glance at the cross caused him to gird up anew the loins of his mind and press forward in the way of self-denial. In his labors for his brethren he relied much upon the manifestation of infinite love in the sacrifice of Christ, with its subduing, constraining power. (*The Ministry of Healing*, 500)

REFLECTION: *Had Christ complained that the work was too hard or that He wasn't getting paid enough to work hard, where would we be? LOST! Paul followed Christ's example of hard work without complaining. What was the common thread? If you said "love" you are right. Let us ask the Lord to give us His love so we might not give stinted service.*

OCTOBER 6

*N*EW *C*REATURE

Therefore if any man be in Christ, he is a new creature: old
things are passed away; behold, all things are become new.
2 Corinthians 5:17

To the heart that has become purified, all is changed. Transformation of character is the testimony to the world of an indwelling Christ. The Spirit of God produces a new life in the soul, bringing the thoughts and desires into obedience to the will of Christ; and the inward man is renewed in the image of God. Weak and erring men and women show to the world that the redeeming power of grace can cause the faulty character to develop into symmetry and abundant fruitfulness.

The heart that receives the word of God is not as a pool that evaporates, not like a broken cistern that loses its treasure. It is like the mountain stream, fed by unfailing springs, whose cool, sparkling waters leap from rock to rock, refreshing the weary, the thirsty, the heavy-laden. It is like a river constantly flowing and, as it advances, becoming deeper and wider, until its life-giving waters are spread over all the earth. The stream that goes singing on its way leaves behind its gift of verdure and fruitfulness. The grass on its banks is a fresher green, the trees have a richer verdure, the flowers are more abundant. When the earth lies bare and brown under the summer's scorching heat, a line of verdure marks the river's course. (*Prophets and Kings*, 233)

REFLECTION: *Did you get that? Transformation of character is the testimony to the world of an indwelling Christ. Let's receive His word —*
100% of it — today, and be the testimony that is so rare to find.

OCTOBER 7

BE NOT UNEVENLY YOKED

*Be ye not unequally yoked together with unbelievers: for
what fellowship hath righteousness with unrighteousness?
and what communion hath light with darkness?*
2 Corinthians 6:14

When Christians consented to unite with those who were but half converted from paganism, they entered upon a path which led further and further from the truth. Satan exulted that he had succeeded in deceiving so large a number of the followers of Christ. He then brought his power to bear more fully upon these, and inspired them to persecute those who remained true to God. None understood so well how to oppose the true Christian faith as did those who had once been its defenders; and these apostate Christians, uniting with their half-pagan companions, directed their warfare against the most essential features of the doctrines of Christ.

It required a desperate struggle for those who would be faithful to stand firm against the deceptions and abominations which were disguised in sacerdotal garments and introduced into the church. The Bible was not accepted as the standard of faith. The doctrine of religious freedom was termed heresy, and its upholders were hated and proscribed.

After a long and severe conflict, the faithful few decided to dissolve all union with the apostate church if she still refused to free herself from falsehood and idolatry. ... They dared not tolerate errors fatal to their own souls, and set an example which would imperil the faith of their children and children's children." (*The Great Controversy*, 45)

REFLECTION: *Doesn't that sound like what is going on today? The Bible is laid aside for what feels good. Let our prayer be more earnest than ever, that we would not deviate from the Scriptures.*

OCTOBER 8

REMAIN UNDEFILED

Having therefore these promises, dearly beloved, let us cleanse ourselves from all filthiness of the flesh and spirit, perfecting holiness in the fear of God.
2 Corinthians 7:1

Every practice that weakens physical or mental strength unfits man for the service of his Creator. And will God be pleased with anything less than the best we can offer? Said Christ: "Thou shalt love the Lord thy God with all thy heart." Those who do love God with all the heart will desire to give Him the best service of their life, and they will be constantly seeking to bring every power of their being into harmony with the laws that will promote their ability to do His will. They will not, by the indulgence of appetite or passion, enfeeble or defile the offering which they present to their heavenly Father.

Peter says: "Abstain from fleshly lusts, which war against the soul (1 Peter 2:11). Every sinful gratification tends to benumb the faculties and deaden the mental and spiritual perceptions, and the word or the Spirit of God can make but a feeble impression upon the heart. Paul writes to the Corinthians: "Let us cleanse ourselves from all filthiness of the flesh and spirit, perfecting holiness in the fear of God (2 Corinthians 7:1). And with the fruits of the Spirit—"love, joy, peace, long-suffering, gentleness, goodness, faith, meekness"—he classes "temperance" (Galatians 5:22, 23). (*The Great Controversy*, 473, 474)

REFLECTION: *All through the Bible diet played in integral part of the followers of God. It was so important that Christ's first temptation was on appetite. Let us be more diligent in this area.*

*G*ODLY *S*ORROW

For godly sorrow worketh repentance to salvation not to be
repented of: but the sorrow of the world worketh death.
2 Corinthians 7:10

*T*rue confession is always of a specific character, and acknowledges particular sins. They may be of such a nature as to be brought before God only; they may be wrongs that should be confessed to individuals who have suffered injury through them; or they may be of a public character, and should then be as publicly confessed. But all confession should be definite and to the point, acknowledging the very sins of which you are guilty.

In the days of Samuel the Israelites wandered from God. They were suffering the consequences of sin; for they had lost their faith in God, lost their discernment of His power and wisdom to rule the nation, lost their confidence in His ability to defend and vindicate His cause. They turned from the great Ruler of the universe and desired to be governed as were the nations around them. Before they found peace they made this definite confession: "We have added unto all our sins this evil, to ask us a king" (1 Samuel 12:19). The very sin of which they were convicted had to be confessed. Their ingratitude oppressed their souls and severed them from God.

Confession will not be acceptable to God without sincere repentance and reformation. There must be decided changes in the life; everything offensive to God must be put away. This will be the result of genuine sorrow for sin." (*Steps to Christ*, 38, 39)

REFLECTION: *Many times we hang on to sins that keep us feeling guilty and full of pain. God is the answer. Christ is the sin bearer. Are there sins in your life today that you have been keeping? Give them to your only hope — Jesus. He will set you free.*

CASTING DOWN IMAGINATIONS

*Casting down imaginations, and every high thing that
exalteth itself against the knowledge of God, and bringing
into captivity every thought to the obedience of Christ.*
2 Corinthians 10:5

God wishes us to have the mastery over ourselves. But He cannot help us without our consent and co-operation. The divine Spirit works through the powers and faculties given to man. Of ourselves, we are not able to bring the purposes and desires and inclinations into harmony with the will of God; but if we are "willing to be made willing," the Saviour will accomplish this for us. ...

He who would build up a strong, symmetrical character, he who would be a well-balanced Christian, must give all and do all for Christ; for the Redeemer will not accept divided service. Daily he must learn the meaning of self-surrender. He must study the word of God, learning its meaning and obeying its precepts. Thus he may reach the standard of Christian excellence. Day by day God works with him, perfecting the character that is to stand in the time of final test. And day by day the believer is working out before men and angels a sublime experiment, showing what the gospel can do for fallen human beings. (*The Acts of the Apostles*, 482, 483)

REFLECTION: *So often we want to fight the Lord and play with the devil. In the end we find out that the devil was not playing, but is and has always tried to keep us from what is best for us. He wants us to lose the battle for eternal life. God only wants what is best and is there to help build a character fit for eternal life. Let us ever keep that in mind.*

OCTOBER 11

FAITH AND WORKS

Examine yourselves, whether ye be in the faith; prove
your own selves. Know ye not your own selves, how that
Jesus Christ is in you, except ye be reprobates?
2 Corinthians 13:5

The good tree will produce good fruit. If the fruit is unpalatable and worthless, the tree is evil. So the fruit borne in the life testifies as to the condition of the heart and the excellence of the character. Good works can never purchase salvation, but they are an evidence of the faith that acts by love and purifies the soul. And though the eternal reward is not bestowed because of our merit, yet it will be in proportion to the work that has been done through the grace of Christ.

Thus Christ set forth the principles of His kingdom, and showed them to be the great rule of life. To impress the lesson He adds an illustration. It is not enough, He says, for you to hear My words. By obedience you must make them the foundation of your character. Self is but shifting sand. If you build upon human theories and inventions, your house will fall. By the winds of temptation, the tempests of trial, it will be swept away. But these principles that I have given will endure. Receive Me; build on My words. (*Desire of Ages*, 314)

REFLECTION: *The more we love, the more good works will come out. It can't be helped. As that born from above, love grows and you do more and more; you don't even look at it as hard work. Let us pray today for that love from above that only our Savior can and will give.*

OCTOBER 12

REAL AND FALSE GOSPEL

O foolish Galatians, who hath bewitched you, that ye should not obey the truth, before whose eyes Jesus Christ hath been evidently set forth, crucified among you?
Galatians 3:1

The apostle urged the Galatians to leave the false guides by whom they had been misled, and to return to the faith that had been accompanied by unmistakable evidences of divine approval. The men who had attempted to lead them from their belief in the gospel were hypocrites, unholy in heart and corrupt in life. Their religion was made up of a round of ceremonies, through the performance of which they expected to gain the favor of God. They had no desire for a gospel that called for obedience to the word, "Except a man be born again, he cannot see the kingdom of God" (John 3:3). They felt that a religion based on such a doctrine, required too great a sacrifice, and they clung to their errors, deceiving themselves and others.

To substitute external forms of religion for holiness of heart and life is still as pleasing to the unrenewed nature as it was in the days of these Jewish teachers. Today, as then, there are false spiritual guides, to whose doctrines many listen eagerly. It is Satan's studied effort to divert minds from the hope of salvation through faith in Christ and obedience to the law of God. (*Acts of the Apostles*, 386, 387)

REFLECTION: *Self will justify anything and everything to get its own way. For self—you and me—to get our way, we will put the proverbial "frosting" over the bad to make it look good. Oh foolish us! Let's look only to Jesus today and obey His truth.*

OCTOBER 13

*F*RUIT OF THE *S*PIRIT

But the fruit of the Spirit is love, joy, peace, longsuffering, gentleness,
goodness, faith, meekness, temperance: against such there is no law.
Galatians 5:22, 23

*T*he plant does not germinate, grow, or bring forth fruit for itself, but to "give seed to the sower, and bread to the eater" (Isaiah 55:10). So no man is to live unto himself. The Christian is in the world as a representative of Christ, for the salvation of other souls.

There can be no growth or fruitfulness in the life that is centered in self. If you have accepted Christ as a personal Saviour, you are to forget yourself, and try to help others. Talk of the love of Christ, tell of His goodness. Do every duty that presents itself. Carry the burden of souls upon your heart, and by every means in your power seek to save the lost. As you receive the Spirit of Christ — the Spirit of unselfish love and labor for others — you will grow and bring forth fruit. The graces of the Spirit will ripen in your character. Your faith will increase, your convictions deepen, your love be made perfect. More and more you will reflect the likeness of Christ in all that is pure, noble, and lovely.

"The fruit of the Spirit is love, joy, peace, longsuffering, gentleness, goodness, faith, meekness, temperance" (Galatians 5:22, 23). This fruit can never perish, but will produce after its kind a harvest unto eternal life. (*Christ's Object Lessons*, 67, 68)

REFLECTION: *We need to pray every day to grow our fruit. This fruit, fruit of the Spirit, if nurtured, will grow and become sweeter; we will be like Jesus. As this takes place, people around us will be able to taste and see that God is good. Souls will be won.*

OCTOBER 14

Sowing and Reaping

*Be not deceived; God is not mocked: for whatsoever
a man soweth, that shall he also reap.*
Galatians 6:7

In the laws of God in nature, effect follows cause with unerring certainty. The reaping will testify as to what the sowing has been. The slothful worker is condemned by his work. The harvest bears witness against him. So in spiritual things: the faithfulness of every worker is measured by the results of his work. The character of his work, whether diligent or slothful, is revealed by the harvest. It is thus that his destiny for eternity is decided.

Every seed sown produces a harvest of its kind. So it is in human life. We all need to sow the seeds of compassion, sympathy, and love; for we shall reap what we sow. Every characteristic of selfishness, self-love, self-esteem, every act of self-indulgence, will bring forth a like harvest. He who lives for self is sowing to the flesh, and of the flesh he will reap corruption.

God destroys no man. Everyone who is destroyed will have destroyed himself. Everyone who stifles the admonitions of conscience is sowing the seeds of unbelief, and these will produce a sure harvest. (*Christ's Object Lessons*, 84, 85)

REFLECTION: *This is a principle that we should never forget. What we say and do produces fruit either for good or evil. Every day we are leaving a "paper trail" for others to see where our heart is. Let's leave a God "trail" today and every day.*

OCTOBER 15

*G*LORY IN THE *C*ROSS

But God forbid that I should glory, save in the cross of our Lord Jesus Christ, by whom the world is crucified unto me, and I unto the world.
Galatians 6:14

*I*f those who today are teaching the word of God, would uplift the cross of Christ higher and still higher, their ministry would be far more successful. If sinners can be led to give one earnest look at the cross, if they can obtain a full view of the crucified Saviour, they will realize the depth of God's compassion and the sinfulness of sin.

Christ's death proves God's great love for man. It is our pledge of salvation. To remove the cross from the Christian would be like blotting the sun from the sky. The cross brings us near to God, reconciling us to Him. With the relenting compassion of a father's love, Jehovah looks upon the suffering that His Son endured in order to save the race from eternal death, and accepts us in the Beloved.

Without the cross, man could have no union with the Father. On it depends our every hope. From it shines the light of the Saviour's love, and when at the foot of the cross the sinner looks up to the One who died to save him, he may rejoice with fullness of joy, for his sins are pardoned. Kneeling in faith at the cross, he has reached the highest place to which man can attain. (*The Acts of the Apostles*, 209)

REFLECTION: *It is our privilege also to glory in the cross. Jesus said, "if I be lifted up I will draw all men to me." It could also be said If I (put your name here) be lifted up (put your name here) will draw all men to Christ. Let us pick up our cross today and be lifted out of self and into Jesus Christ.*

OCTOBER 16

God's Free Grace

*To the praise of the glory of his grace, wherein he
hath made us accepted in the beloved.*
Ephesians 1:6

We ourselves owe everything to God's free grace. Grace in the covenant ordained our adoption. Grace in the Saviour effected our redemption, our regeneration, and our exaltation to heirship with Christ. Let this grace be revealed to others.

Give the erring one no occasion for discouragement. Suffer not a Pharisaical hardness to come in and hurt your brother. Let no bitter sneer rise in mind or heart. Let no tinge of scorn be manifest in the voice. If you speak a word of your own, if you take an attitude of indifference, or show suspicion or distrust, it may prove the ruin of a soul. He needs a brother with the Elder Brother's heart of sympathy to touch his heart of humanity. Let him feel the strong clasp of a sympathizing hand, and hear the whisper, Let us pray. God will give a rich experience to you both. Prayer unites us with one another and with God. Prayer brings Jesus to our side, and gives to the fainting, perplexed soul new strength to overcome the world, the flesh, and the devil. Prayer turns aside the attacks of Satan.

When one turns away from human imperfections to behold Jesus, a divine transformation takes place in the character. The Spirit of Christ working upon the heart conforms it to His image. Then let it be your effort to lift up Jesus. (*Christ Object Lessons*, 250)

REFLECTION: *Although there are times to rebuke and censure, we need to be more loving. We need to have the love of Christ, not enabling love. Today let's talk to someone that is suffering under the burden of sin, and pray with and for them. It may change their life.*

October 17

When Christ Dwells in the Heart

For by grace are ye saved through faith; and that not of yourselves:
it is the gift of God: Not of works, lest any man should boast.
Ephesians 2:8, 9

There are those who profess to serve God, while they rely upon their own efforts to obey His law, to form a right character, and secure salvation. Their hearts are not moved by any deep sense of the love of Christ, but they seek to perform the duties of the Christian life as that which God requires of them in order to gain heaven. Such religion is worth nothing. When Christ dwells in the heart, the soul will be so filled with His love, with the joy of communion with Him, that it will cleave to Him; and in the contemplation of Him, self will be forgotten. Love to Christ will be the spring of action. Those who feel the constraining love of God, do not ask how little may be given to meet the requirements of God; they do not ask for the lowest standard, but aim at perfect conformity to the will of their Redeemer. With earnest desire they yield all and manifest an interest proportionate to the value of the object which they seek. A profession of Christ without this deep love is mere talk, dry formality, and heavy drudgery. (*Steps to Christ*, 44, 45)

REFLECTION: *Let us never even allow our minds to think that it is boring or a pain to follow our Lord Jesus Christ. Let our love produce works, which can happen only by the grace of God.*

OCTOBER 18

WORKS THAT ARE PLEASING TO GOD

For we are his workmanship, created in Christ Jesus unto good works,
which God hath before ordained that we should walk in them.
Ephesians 2:10

It is not the length of time we labor but our willingness and fidelity in the work that makes it acceptable to God.

In all our service a full surrender of self is demanded. The smallest duty done in sincerity and self-forgetfulness is more pleasing to God than the greatest work when marred with self-seeking. He looks to see how much of the spirit of Christ we cherish, and how much of the likeness of Christ our work reveals. He regards more the love and faithfulness with which we work than the amount we do.

Only when selfishness is dead, when strife for supremacy is banished, when gratitude fills the heart, and love makes fragrant the life — it is only then that Christ is abiding in the soul, and we are recognized as laborers together with God.

However trying their labor, the true workers do not regard it as drudgery. They are ready to spend and to be spent; but it is a cheerful work, done with a glad heart. Joy in God is expressed through Jesus Christ. Their joy is the joy set before Christ — "to do the will of Him that sent Me, and to finish His work" (John 4:34). They are in co-operation with the Lord of glory. (*Christ Object Lessons*, 402, 403)

REFLECTION: *Today is a very simple thought, but profound. When we do things for our own reward, the reward ends up being cheap. But when we do things to please God, the reward is priceless.*

OCTOBER 19

Heaven Born Love

Now therefore ye are no more strangers and foreigners, but fellowcitizens with the saints, and of the household of God; And are built upon the foundation of the apostles and prophets, Jesus Christ himself being the chief corner stone.
Ephesians 2:19, 20

The word of God is to have a sanctifying effect on our association with every member of the human family. The leaven of truth will not produce the spirit of rivalry, the love of ambition, the desire to be first. True, heaven-born love is not selfish and changeable. It is not dependent on human praise. The heart of him who receives the grace of God overflows with love for God and for those for whom Christ died. Self is not struggling for recognition. He does not love others because they love and please him, because they appreciate his merits, but because they are Christ's purchased possession. If his motives, words, or actions are misunderstood or misrepresented, he takes no offense, but pursues the even tenor of his way. He is kind and thoughtful, humble in his opinion of himself, yet full of hope, always trusting in the mercy and love of God. ...

The countenance is changed. Christ abiding in the heart shines out in the faces of those who love Him and keep His commandments. Truth is written there. The sweet peace of heaven is revealed. There is expressed a habitual gentleness, a more than human love. (*Christ Object Lessons*, 101, 102)

REFLECTION: *If we love the Lord, we will love others and esteem them better than ourselves. We will not do good deeds to get recognition. We will begin to see that they have been purchased and are just as important to Christ as you and I. Today, by our actions let's show our sincere love for our friends and neighbors.*

OCTOBER 20

*G*ROWING BY *R*ECIEVING

From whom the whole body fitly joined together and compacted by that which every joint supplieth, according to the effectual working in the measure of every part, maketh increase of the body unto the edifying of itself in love.
Ephesians 4:16

The plants and flowers grow not by their own care or anxiety or effort, but by receiving that which God has furnished to minister to their life. The child cannot, by any anxiety or power of its own, add to its stature. No more can you, by anxiety or effort of yourself, secure spiritual growth. The plant, the child, grows by receiving from its surroundings that which ministers to its life—air, sunshine, and food. What these gifts of nature are to animal and plant, such is Christ to those who trust in Him. He is their "everlasting light," "a sun and shield" (Isaiah 60:19; Psalm 84:11)....

In the matchless gift of His Son, God has encircled the whole world with an atmosphere of grace as real as the air which circulates around the globe. All who choose to breathe this life-giving atmosphere will live and grow up to the stature of men and women in Christ Jesus.

As the flower turns to the sun, that the bright beams may aid in perfecting its beauty and symmetry, so should we turn to the Sun of Righteousness, that heaven's light may shine upon us, that our character may be developed into the likeness of Christ. (*Steps to Christ*, 68)

REFLECTION: *We all have had the sun shine on our faces and have said, "That feels so good." Today let's allow Christ the Sun of Righteousness to shine upon our hearts.*

OCTOBER 21

THE TRUE CHRISTIAN

Be ye therefore followers of God, as dear children; And walk in love, as Christ also hath loved us, and hath given himself for us an offering and a sacrifice to God for a sweetsmelling savour.
Ephesians 5:1, 2

God's ideal for His children is higher than the highest human thought can reach. "Be ye therefore perfect, even as your Father which is in heaven is perfect." This command is a promise. The plan of redemption contemplates our complete recovery from the power of Satan. Christ always separates the contrite soul from sin. He came to destroy the works of the devil, and He has made provision that the Holy Spirit shall be imparted to every repentant soul, to keep him from sinning.

The tempter's agency is not to be accounted an excuse for one wrong act. Satan is jubilant when he hears the professed followers of Christ making excuses for their deformity of character. It is these excuses that lead to sin. There is no excuse for sinning. A holy temper, a Christlike life, is accessible to every repenting, believing child of God.

The ideal of Christian character is Christlikeness. As the Son of man was perfect in His life, so His followers are to be perfect in their life. Jesus was in all things made like unto His brethren. He became flesh, even as we are. He was hungry and thirsty and weary. He was sustained by food and refreshed by sleep. He shared the lot of man; yet He was the blameless Son of God. He was God in the flesh. His character is to be ours. (*Desire of Ages*, 311)

REFLECTION: *These words are so vital for our eternal salvation. Let's contemplate these words more than once: The true Christian.*

MARRIAGE A FORETASTE OF HEAVEN

Submitting yourselves one to another in the fear of God. Wives, submit yourselves unto your own husbands, as unto the Lord. For the husband is the head of the wife, even as Christ is the head of the church: and he is the saviour of the body. Therefore as the church is subject unto Christ, so [let] the wives [be] to their own husbands in every thing. Husbands, love your wives, even as Christ also loved the church, and gave himself for it.

Ephesians 5:21–25

Though difficulties, perplexities, and discouragements may arise, let neither husband nor wife harbor the thought that their union is a mistake or a disappointment. Determine to be all that it is possible to be to each other. Continue the early attentions. In every way encourage each other in fighting the battles of life. Study to advance the happiness of each other. Let there be mutual love, mutual forbearance. Then marriage, instead of being the end of love, will be as it were the very beginning of love. The warmth of true friendship, the love that binds heart to heart, is a foretaste of the joys of heaven. ...

Let each give love rather than exact it. Cultivate that which is noblest in yourselves, and be quick to recognize the good qualities in each other. The consciousness of being appreciated is a wonderful stimulus and satisfaction. (*Ministry of Healing*, 360, 361)

REFLECTION: *God instituted family, not man, and He designed that husband and wife work as a team. If you want to grow in your marriage, you need to grow as an individual. Get your spouse something special like flowers or a card, but don't wait until it is a known special day like a birthday. Call it a "just because" day, "just because I love you." As you do this consistently you will see a difference.*

We Fight Against Principalities in High Places

For we wrestle not against flesh and blood, but against
principalities, against powers, against the rulers of the darkness
of this world, against spiritual wickedness in high places.
Ephesians 6:12

A noble character is not the result of accident; it is not due to special favors or endowments of Providence. It is the result of self-discipline, of subjection of the lower to the higher nature, of the surrender of self to the service of God and man. ...

The body is a most important medium through which the mind and the soul are developed for the upbuilding of character. Hence it is that the adversary of souls directs his temptations to the enfeebling and degrading of the physical powers. His success here often means the surrender of the whole being to evil. The tendencies of the physical nature, unless under the dominion of a higher power, will surely work ruin and death. The body is to be brought into subjection to the higher powers of the being. The passions are to be controlled by the will, which is itself to be under the control of God. The kingly power of reason, sanctified by divine grace, is to bear sway in the life. Intellectual power, physical stamina, and the length of life depend upon immutable laws. Through obedience to these laws, man may stand conqueror of himself, conqueror of his own inclinations, conqueror of principalities and powers, of "the rulers of the darkness of this world," and of "spiritual wickedness in high places" (Ephesians 6:12). (*Prophets and Kings*, 488)

REFLECTION: *Whatever we do, let's do it to the glory of God. Good things hardly ever come easy; Satan will make sure of that. But with God all things are possible. The watchword for today is, "Get thee behind me Satan!" Don't take your eyes off the Lord.*

October 24

THE MIND OF CHRIST

Let this mind be in you, which was also in Christ Jesus.
Philippians 2:5

"Learn of Me," says Jesus; "for I am meek and low-ly in heart: and ye shall find rest." We are to enter the school of Christ, to learn from Him meekness and lowliness. Redemption is that process by which the soul is trained for heaven. This training means a knowledge of Christ. It means emancipation from ideas, habits, and practices that have been gained in the school of the prince of darkness. The soul must be delivered from all that is opposed to loyalty to God.

In the heart of Christ, where reigned perfect harmony with God, there was perfect peace. He was never elated by applause, nor dejected by censure or disappointment. Amid the greatest op-position and the most cruel treatment, He was still of good cour-age. But many who profess to be His followers have an anxious, troubled heart, because they are afraid to trust themselves with God. They do not make a complete surrender to Him; for they shrink from the consequences that such a surrender may involve. Unless they do make this surrender, they cannot find peace.

It is the love of self that brings unrest. When we are born from above, the same mind will be in us that was in Jesus, the mind that led Him to humble Himself that we might be saved (*Desire of Ages*, 330)

REFLECTION: *What a thought! Christ was never elated by applause, nor dejected by censure or disappointment. As we draw closer to Christ and continue to develop our character, we will realize more and more that it is not about us, but Christ.*

October 25

Understanding the True Force of the Will

Wherefore, my beloved, as ye have always obeyed, not as in my presence only, but now much more in my absence, work out your own salvation with fear and trembling. For it is God which worketh in you both to will and to do of his good pleasure. Do all things without murmurings and disputings: That ye may be blameless and harmless, the sons of God, without rebuke, in the midst of a crooked and perverse nation, among whom ye shine as lights in the world.
Philippians 2:12–15

Everything depends on the right action of the will. Desires for goodness and purity are right, so far as they go; but if we stop here, they avail nothing. Many will go down to ruin while hoping and desiring to overcome their evil propensities. They do not yield the will to God. They do not choose to serve Him.

God has given us the power of choice; it is ours to exercise. We cannot change our hearts, we cannot control our thoughts, our impulses, our affections. We cannot make ourselves pure, fit for God's service. But we can choose to serve God, we can give Him our will; then He will work in us to will and to do according to His good pleasure. Thus our whole nature will be brought under the control of Christ.

Through the right exercise of the will, an entire change may be made in the life. By yielding up the will to Christ, we ally ourselves with divine power. We receive strength from above to hold us steadfast. A pure and noble life, a life of victory over appetite and lust, is possible to everyone who will unite his weak, wavering human will to the omnipotent, unwavering will of God. (*Ministry of Healing*, 176)

REFLECTION: *Building that noble character is ours to choose and to have. In fact, it is essential for our salvation. Let's make the right choices today.*

No Need for Sadness and Darkness

Rejoice in the lord always: and again I say, Rejoice.
Philippians 4:4

While the Christian's life will be characterized by humility, it should not be marked with sadness and self-depreciation. It is the privilege of everyone so to live that God will approve and bless him. It is not the will of our heavenly Father that we should be ever under condemnation and darkness. There is no evidence of true humility in going with the head bowed down and the heart filled with thoughts of self. We may go to Jesus and be cleansed, and stand before the law without shame and remorse.…The Christian's life should be one of faith, of victory, and joy in God. "Whatsoever is born of God overcometh the world: and this is the victory that overcometh the world, even our faith" (1 John 5:4). Truly spoke God's servant Nehemiah: "The joy of the Lord is your strength" (Nehemiah 8:10). And Paul says: "Rejoice in the Lord alway: and again I say, Rejoice." "Rejoice evermore. Pray without ceasing. In everything give thanks: for this is the will of God in Christ Jesus concerning you" (Philippians 4:4; 1 Thessalonians 5:16–18). (*Great Controversy*, 477)

REFLECTION: *As we continue to build a noble character, which consists of thoughts and feelings, we will rejoice in the Lord. We will have learned to put more trust in the One who saves. It will give us joy to think about others more than ourselves. We will begin to see things in such a different way.*

OCTOBER 27

OUR CREATOR

For by him were all things created, that are in heaven, and that are in earth, visible and invisible, whether they be thrones, or dominions, or principalities, or powers: all things were created by him, and for him.
Colossians 1:16

Before the entrance of evil there was peace and joy throughout the universe. All was in perfect harmony with the Creator's will. Love for God was supreme, love for one another impartial. Christ the Word, the Only Begotten of God, was one with the eternal Father,—one in nature, in character, and in purpose,—the only being in all the universe that could enter into all the counsels and purposes of God. By Christ the Father wrought in the creation of all heavenly beings. "By Him were all things created, that are in heaven,… whether they be thrones, or dominions, or principalities, or powers" (Colossians 1:16); and to Christ, equally with the Father, all heaven gave allegiance.

The law of love being the foundation of the government of God, the happiness of all created beings depended upon their perfect accord with its great principles of righteousness. God desires from all His creatures the service of love—homage that springs from an intelligent appreciation of His character. He takes no pleasure in a forced allegiance, and to all He grants freedom of will, that they may render Him voluntary service. (*The Great Controversy*, 493)

REFLECTION: *As we grow from faith to faith, and love Christ with a voluntary love, we will be saved. And then we will see Jesus create a new heavens and new earth. Can you imagine standing there watching Him? Lets make a commitment today to be there.*

*C*EREMONIAL *V*ERSUS *M*ORAL *L*AW

*Blotting out the handwriting of ordinances that was against us, which
was contrary to us, and took it out of the way, nailing it to his cross.*
Colossians 2:14

*T*he ceremonial law was thus given to Moses, and by him written in a book. But the law of Ten Commandments spoken from Sinai had been written by God Himself on the tables of stone, and was sacredly preserved in the ark. ...

The ceremonial system was made up of symbols pointing to Christ, to His sacrifice and His priesthood. This ritual law, with its sacrifices and ordinances, was to be performed by the Hebrews until type met antitype in the death of Christ, the Lamb of God that taketh away the sin of the world. Then all the sacrificial offerings were to cease. It is this law that Christ "took ... out of the way, nailing it to His cross" (Colossians 2:14). But concerning the law of Ten Commandments the psalmist declares, "Forever, O Lord, Thy word is settled in heaven" (Psalm 119:89). ...The law of God is as immutable as His throne. It will maintain its claims upon mankind in all ages. ...

While the Saviour's death brought to an end the law of types and shadows, it did not in the least detract from the obligation of the moral law. On the contrary, the very fact that it was necessary for Christ to die in order to atone for the transgression of that law, proves it to be immutable. (*Patriarchs and Prophets*, 364, 365)

REFLECTION: *It should make us so happy that we no longer need to perform the ceremonial law. Christ took that place after His resurrection. It should make us just as happy that God's Law, the Ten Commandments, will never cease to exist. What would it be like if there was no law? Utter chaos would be the result. God is so good!*

Watch and Be Sober

Therefore let us not sleep, as do others; but let us watch and be sober.
1 Thessalonians 5:6

There are in the world today many who close their eyes to the evidences that Christ has given to warn men of His coming. They seek to quiet all apprehension, while at the same time the signs of the end are rapidly fulfilling, and the world is hastening to the time when the Son of man shall be revealed in the clouds of heaven. Paul teaches that it is sinful to be indifferent to the signs which are to precede the second coming of Christ. Those guilty of this neglect he calls children of the night and of darkness. He encourages the vigilant and watchful with these words: "But ye, brethren, are not in darkness, that that day should overtake you as a thief. Ye are all the children of light, and the children of the day: we are not of the night, nor of darkness. Therefore let us not sleep, as do others; but let us watch and be sober."

Especially important to the church in our time are the teachings of the apostle upon this point. To those living so near the great consummation, the words of Paul should come with telling force: "Let us, who are of the day, be sober, putting on the breastplate of faith and love; and for a helmet, the hope of salvation. For God hath not appointed us to wrath, but to obtain salvation by our Lord Jesus Christ, who died for us, that, whether we wake or sleep, we should live together with Him." (*The Acts of the Apostles*, 260)

Reflection: *The watchful Christian is a working Christian, seeking zealously to do all in his power for the advancement of the gospel. (The Acts of the Apostles, 260)*

OCTOBER 30

REJECTION LEADS TO WITHDRAWAL

And for this cause God shall send them strong
delusion, that they should believe a lie.
2 Thessalonians 2:11

Terrible were the trials that were to beset the true church. Even at the time when the apostle was writing, the "mystery of iniquity" had already begun to work. The developments that were to take place in the future were to be "after the working of Satan with all power and signs and lying wonders, and with all deceivableness of unrighteousness in them that perish."

Especially solemn is the apostle's statement regarding those who should refuse to receive "the love of the truth." "For this cause," he declared of all who should deliberately reject the messages of truth, "God shall send them strong delusion, that they should believe a lie: that they all might be damned who believed not the truth, but had pleasure in unrighteousness." Men cannot with impunity reject the warnings that God in mercy sends them. From those who persist in turning from these warnings, God withdraws His Spirit, leaving them to the deceptions that they love.

Thus Paul outlined the baleful work of that power of evil which was to continue through long centuries of darkness and persecution before the second coming of Christ. (*Acts of Apostles*, 266)

REFLECTION: *As the Bible says, we should study to show ourselves approved to our Lord and we will not need to be ashamed when we rightly divide the Word of truth. So often we want to believe something because that is what we have been told since we can remember. We want to defend what the Bible does not defend. God wants us to study for ourselves and not allow teachers, preachers, friends or family to study for us. Let's not defend tradition, but defend the whole truth and nothing but the truth.*

BEING DECEIVED

*Now the Spirit speaketh expressly, that in the latter times some shall depart
from the faith, giving heed to seducing spirits, and doctrines of devils;
Speaking lies in hypocrisy; having their conscience seared with a hot iron.*
1 Timothy 4:1, 2

Now the Spirit speaketh expressly, that in the latter times some shall depart from the faith, giving heed to seducing spirits, and doctrines of devils; Speaking lies in hypocrisy; having their conscience seared with a hot iron" (1 Timothy 4:1, 2).

Satan uses the listless, sleepy indolence of professed Christians to strengthen his forces and win souls to his side. Many, who think that though they are doing no actual work for Christ, they are yet on His side, are enabling the enemy to pre-occupy ground and gain advantages. By their failure to be diligent workers for the Master, by leaving duties undone and words unspoken, they have allowed Satan to gain control of souls who might have been won for Christ.

We can never be saved in indolence and inactivity. There is no such thing as a truly converted person living a helpless, useless life. It is not possible for us to drift into heaven. No sluggard can enter there. If we do not strive to gain an entrance into the kingdom, if we do not seek earnestly to learn what constitutes its laws, we are not fitted for a part in it. Those who refuse to co-operate with God on earth would not co-operate with Him in heaven. It would not be safe to take them to heaven.

There is more hope for publicans and sinners than for those who know the word of God but refuse to obey it. (*Christ Object Lessons*, 279, 280)

REFLECTION: *The only safety for us is in trusting implicitly and following faithfully the instruction of the Word of God. We will never enter into heaven calling ourselves Christians but never being like Jesus. Let's make a decided effort to work and be more like the Lord today.*

November

November 1

*W*E ARE *S*TEWARDS

For we brought nothing into this world, and it
is certain we can carry nothing out.
1 Timothy 6:7

*T*he rich man had all that money could procure, but he did not possess the riches that would have kept his account right with God. He had lived as if all that he possessed were his own. He had neglected the call of God and the claims of the suffering poor. But at length there comes a call which he cannot neglect. By a power which he cannot question or resist he is commanded to quit the premises of which he is no longer steward. The once-rich man is reduced to hopeless poverty. The robe of Christ's righteousness, woven in the loom of heaven, can never cover him. He who once wore the richest purple, the finest linen, is reduced to nakedness. His probation is ended. He brought nothing into the world, and he can take nothing out of it.

Christ lifted the curtain and presented this picture before priests and rulers, scribes and Pharisees. Look at it, you who are rich in this world's goods and are not rich toward God. Will you not contemplate this scene? That which is highly esteemed among men is abhorrent in the sight of God. Christ asks, "What shall it profit a man, if he shall gain the whole world, and lose his own soul? or what shall a man give in exchange for his soul?" (Mark 8:36, 37). (*Christ Object Lessons*, 267)

REFLECTION: *There are many today who are unconverted. They may take part in the church service, they may say they love God, but in their everyday lives they show how much they love the world. Let us have an account that is right with God.*

NOVEMBER 2

*G*REATEST *B*ATTLE *E*VER *F*OUGHT

*And that they may recover themselves out of the snare of
the devil, who are taken captive by him at his will.*
2 Timothy 2:26

The whole heart must be yielded to God, or the change can never be wrought in us by which we are to be restored to His likeness. By nature we are alienated from God. The Holy Spirit describes our condition in such words as these: "Dead in trespasses and sins;" "the whole head is sick, and the whole heart faint;" "no soundness in it." We are held fast in the snare of Satan, "taken captive by him at his will" (Ephesians 2:1; Isaiah 1:5, 6; 2 Timothy 2:26). God desires to heal us, to set us free. But since this requires an entire transformation, a renewing of our whole nature, we must yield ourselves wholly to Him.

The warfare against self is the greatest battle that was ever fought. The yielding of self, surrendering all to the will of God, requires a struggle; but the soul must submit to God before it can be renewed in holiness. …

God does not force the will of His creatures. He cannot accept an homage that is not willingly and intelligently given. A mere forced submission would prevent all real development of mind or character; it would make man a mere automaton. Such is not the purpose of the Creator. (*Steps to Christ*, 43)

REFLECTION: *It takes a love, which we as sinful human beings don't have or get on our own, a heaven-born love that only wants volunteer submission, not forced, to serve a God like that. This is what the Christian life is all about. Let's serve Him better today than ever.*

November 3

SHALL SUFFER PERSECUTION

Yea, and all that will live godly in Christ Jesus shall suffer persecution.
2 Timothy 3:12

S o it will be with all who will live godly in Christ Jesus. Persecution and reproach await all who are imbued with the Spirit of Christ. The character of the persecution changes with the times, but the principle — the spirit that under- lies it — is the same that has slain the chosen of the Lord ever since the days of Abel.

In all ages Satan has persecuted the people of God. He has tortured them and put them to death, but in dying they became conquerors. They bore witness to the power of One mightier than Satan. Wicked men may torture and kill the body, but they cannot touch the life that is hid with Christ in God. They can incarcerate men and women in prison walls, but they cannot bind the spirit.

Through trial and persecution the glory — the character — of God is revealed in His chosen ones. The believers in Christ, hated and persecuted by the world, are educated and disciplined in the school of Christ. On earth they walk in narrow paths; they are purified in the furnace of affliction. (*Acts of the Apostles,* 576)

REFLECTION: *Why is it that many churches are having the opposite ef- fect? So many churches today seem to be more of an entertainment center. When we take our stand and choose to glorify the Lord by living Godly lives, then make no mistake, we will suffer persecution.*

ᴀʟʟ Sᴄʀɪᴘᴛᴜʀᴇ ɪꜱ Pʀᴏꜰɪᴛᴀʙʟᴇ

*All scripture is given by inspiration of God, and is profitable for
doctrine, for reproof, for correction, for instruction in righteousness.*
2 Timothy 3:16

During the first twenty-five hundred years of human
history, there was no written revelation. Those who
had been taught of God, communicated their knowledge to others, and it was handed down from father to son,
through successive generations. The preparation of the written
word began in the time of Moses. Inspired revelations were then
embodied in an inspired book. This work continued during the
long period of sixteen hundred years--from Moses, the historian
of creation and the law, to John, the recorder of the most sublime
truths of the gospel.

The Bible points to God as its author; yet it was written by
human hands; and in the varied style of its different books it presents the characteristics of the several writers. The truths revealed
are all "given by inspiration of God" (2 Timothy 3:16); yet they
are expressed in the words of men. The Infinite One by His Holy
Spirit has shed light into the minds and hearts of His servants.
He has given dreams and visions, symbols and figures; and those
to whom the truth was thus revealed have themselves embodied
the thought in human language." (*The Great Controversy*, v)

REFLECTION: *The word "inspired" means "God-breathed." What
a God we serve that allows you and me to share the gospel in our
own personality.*

NOVEMBER 5

REWARD OF GOOD WORKS

Who gave himself for us, that he might redeem us from all iniquity,
and purify unto himself a peculiar people, zealous of good works.
Titus 2:14

In the trust given to the first disciples, believers in every age have shared. Everyone who has received the gospel has been given sacred truth to impart to the world. God's faithful people have always been aggressive missionaries, consecrating their resources to the honor of His name and wisely using their talents in His service.

The unselfish labor of Christians in the past should be to us an object lesson and an inspiration. The members of God's church are to be zealous of good works, separating from worldly ambition and walking in the footsteps of Him who went about doing good. With hearts filled with sympathy and compassion, they are to minister to those in need of help, bringing to sinners a knowledge of the Saviour's love. Such work calls for laborious effort, but it brings a rich reward. Those who engage in it with sincerity of purpose will see souls won to the Saviour, for the influence that attends the practical carrying out of the divine commission is irresistible. (*Acts of the Apostles*, 109, 110)

REFLECTION: *Our prayer should be that we would love more. As this becomes an action in our everyday lives, we will have more compassion towards others. There will be a burning desire to reach every one that is not saved. If faithful, in heaven we try to recall any hardships that we might have gone through, but we will only say, "Heaven was certainly cheap enough!"*

Jesus Pays the Debt

*If thou count me therefore a partner, receive him as myself. If he hath
wronged thee, or oweth thee ought, put that on mine account; I Paul
have written [it] with mine own hand, I will repay it: albeit I do not
say to thee how thou owest unto me even thine own self besides.*
Philemon 1:17–19

Paul voluntarily proposed to assume the debt of Onesimus
in order that the guilty one might be spared the disgrace
of punishment, and might again enjoy the privileges he
had forfeited. "If thou count me therefore a partner," he wrote
to Philemon, "receive him as myself. If he hath wronged thee, or
oweth thee aught, put that on mine account; I Paul have written
it with mine own hand, I will repay it."

How fitting an illustration of the love of Christ for the repentant sinner! The servant who had defrauded his master had nothing with which to make restitution. The sinner who has robbed
God of years of service has no means of canceling the debt. Jesus
interposes between the sinner and God, saying, I will pay the
debt. Let the sinner be spared; I will suffer in his stead. (*Acts of
the Apostles*, 458)

REFLECTION: *I am sure that if you are honest with yourself, it becomes
clear that we could never begin to pay the debt that we owe Jesus.
And yet He freely cancels our debts. When we have that kind of love
which only comes from above, we will forgive others that despise and
mistreat us.*

NOVEMBER 7

*M*INISTERING *A*NGELS

*Are they not all ministering spirits, sent forth to minister
for them who shall be heirs of salvation?*
Hebrews 1:14

The connection of the visible with the invisible world, the ministration of angels of God, and the agency of evil spirits, are plainly revealed in the Scriptures, and inseparably interwoven with human history. There is a growing tendency to disbelief in the existence of evil spirits, while the holy angels that "minister for them who shall be heirs of salvation" (Hebrews 1:14) are regarded by many as spirits of the dead. But the Scriptures not only teach the existence of angels, both good and evil, but present unquestionable proof that these are not disembodied spirits of dead men.

Before the creation of man, angels were in existence; for when the foundations of the earth were laid, "the morning stars sang together, and all the sons of God shouted for joy" (Job 38:7). After the fall of man, angels were sent to guard the tree of life, and this before a human being had died. Angels are in nature superior to men, for the psalmist says that man was made "a little lower than the angels (Psalm 8:5).

Angels are sent on missions of mercy to the children of God. To Abraham, with promises of blessing; ... to Daniel, while seeking divine wisdom in the court of a heathen king, or abandoned to become the lions' prey; ... to Paul and his companions in the night of tempest on the sea; — thus holy angels have, in all ages, ministered to God's people. (*The Great Controversy*, 511, 512)

REFLECTION: *Let's never forget that we do not fight alone, because every Christian has a guardian angel. These angels from heaven watch and will shield us from the power of Satan.*

CHRIST OUR BROTHER

*For both he that sanctifieth and they who are sanctified are all of
one: for which cause he is not ashamed to call them brethren.*
Hebrews 2:11

*J*esus teaches us to call *His* Father our Father. He is not
ashamed to call us brethren (Hebrews 2:11). So ready,
so eager, is the Saviour's heart to welcome us as members of the family of God, that in the very first words we are to
use in approaching God He places the assurance of our divine
relationship, "Our Father."

Here is the announcement of that wonderful truth, so full of
encouragement and comfort, that God loves us as He loves His
Son. This is what Jesus said in His last prayer for His disciples,
Thou "hast loved them, as Thou hast loved Me" (John 17:23)....

How can we ever be in doubt and uncertainty, and feel that
we are orphans? It was in behalf of those who had transgressed
the law that Jesus took upon Him human nature; He became like
unto us, that we might have everlasting peace and assurance. We
have an Advocate in the heavens, and whoever accepts Him as
a personal Saviour is not left an orphan to bear the burden of his
own sins. (*Thoughts from the Mount of Blessing*, 104)

REFLECTION: *Not one of us has to be left out. God's love knows no
bounds. No matter what we have done, when we are truly sorry for
that sin and turn away by His power, we become his sons and daughters — children of the heavenly King and a brother and sister to Jesus.
Amazing Grace!*

November 9

He Was Tempted

*For in that he himself hath suffered being tempted, he
is able to succour them that are tempted.*
Hebrews 2:18

Christ alone had experience in all the sorrows and temptations that befall human beings. Never another of woman born was so fiercely beset by temptation; never another bore so heavy a burden of the world's sin and pain. Never was there another whose sympathies were so broad or so tender. A sharer in all the experiences of humanity, He could feel not only for, but with, every burdened and tempted and struggling one.

What He taught, He lived. "I have given you an example," He said to His disciples; "that ye should do as I have done." "I have kept My Father's commandments" (John 13:15; 15:10). Thus in His life, Christ's words had perfect illustration and support. And more than this; what He taught, He was. His words were the expression, not only of His own life experience, but of His own character. Not only did He teach the truth, but He was the truth. It was this that gave His teaching, power. (*Education*, 78)

REFLECTION: *Because He became one of us and overcame, we can overcome by being one with Him. And just like Jesus we will have power like Him when our lips coincide with our actions. We will not only have the truth, but like Christ, we will be truth as it is in Jesus.*

PERSEVERING THROUGH DIFFICULTIES

But Christ as a son over his own house; whose house are we, if we hold
fast the confidence and the rejoicing of the hope firm unto the end.
Hebrews 3:6

Throughout the history of God's people great mountains of difficulty, apparently insurmountable, have loomed up before those who were trying to carry out the purposes of Heaven. Such obstacles are permitted by the Lord as a test of faith. When we are hedged about on every side, this is the time above all others to trust in God and in the power of His Spirit. The exercise of a living faith means an increase of spiritual strength and the development of an unfaltering trust. It is thus that the soul becomes a conquering power. Before the demand of faith, the obstacles placed by Satan across the pathway of the Christian will disappear; for the powers of heaven will come to his aid. "Nothing shall be impossible unto you" (Matthew 17:20).

The way of the world is to begin with pomp and boasting. God's way is to make the day of small things the beginning of the glorious triumph of truth and righteousness. Sometimes He trains His workers by bringing to them disappointment and apparent failure. It is His purpose that they shall learn to master difficulties.

Often men are tempted to falter before the perplexities and obstacles that confront them. But if they will hold the beginning of their confidence steadfast unto the end, God will make the way clear. Success will come to them as they struggle against difficulties. (*Prophets and Kings*, 594, 595)

REFLECTION: *So often it is the little things that make such a big impact. Remember when we are faithful in the small things in life we will be faithful in the larger things. Let's take one day at a time.*

NOVEMBER 11

*L*ET THE *S*UN *S*HINE INTO *Y*OUR *H*EART

*Wherefore (as the Holy Ghost saith, To day if ye will hear
his voice, Harden not your hearts, as in the provocation,
in the day of temptation in the wilderness).*
Hebrews 3:7, 8

*I*t is not God that blinds the eyes of men or hardens their
hearts. He sends them light to correct their errors, and to
lead them in safe paths; it is by the rejection of this light
that the eyes are blinded and the heart hardened. Often the process is gradual, and almost imperceptible. Light comes to the
soul through God's word, through His servants, or by the direct
agency of His Spirit; but when one ray of light is disregarded,
there is a partial benumbing of the spiritual perceptions, and the
second revealing of light is less clearly discerned. So the darkness
increases, until it is night in the soul. Thus it had been with these
Jewish leaders. They were convinced that a divine power attended Christ, but in order to resist the truth, they attributed the work
of the Holy Spirit to Satan. In doing this they deliberately chose
deception; they yielded themselves to Satan, and henceforth they
were controlled by his power. (*Desire of Ages*, 322)

REFLECTION: *If we saw ourselves as servants of God we would be more
attentive in making the best choices in this conflict between good and
evil. It is often our sinful independence from God that makes us so
careless. Conscience is the voice of God, and when resisted, it grieves
the Holy Spirit. Many wait for more light while rejecting present light.
They wait for better opportunities and neglect present duties. If we
are not careful, the light we have will be withdrawn, and we will be
left in darkness.*

NOVEMBER 12

*T*RUST THE *L*ORD

Take heed, brethren, lest there be in any of you an evil
heart of unbelief, in departing from the living God.
Hebrews 3:12

W hy should we be ungrateful and distrustful? Jesus
is our friend; all heaven is interested in our welfare;
and our anxiety and fear grieve the Holy Spirit of
God. We should not indulge in a solicitude that only frets and
wears us, but does not help us to bear trials. No place should be
given to that distrust of God which leads us to make a preparation against future want the chief pursuit of life, as though our
happiness consisted in these earthly things. It is not the will of
God that His people should be weighed down with care. But
our Lord does not tell us that there are no dangers in our path.
He does not propose to take His people out of the world of sin
and evil, but He points us to a never-failing refuge. He invites
the weary and care-laden, "Come unto Me, all ye that labor and
are heavy-laden, and I will give you rest." Lay off the yoke of
anxiety and worldly care that you have placed on your own
neck, and "take My yoke upon you, and learn of Me; for I am
meek and lowly in heart: and ye shall find rest unto your souls"
(Matthew 11:28, 29). We may find rest and peace in God, casting all our care upon Him; for He careth for us. (See 1 Peter 5:7.)
(*Patriarchs and Prophets*, 294)

REFLECTION: *If we would remember all that the Lord has done for us,*
our faith would be strong. But too often we forget the goodness of the
Lord, and instead remember the evil others have done to us.

NOVEMBER 13

Steadfast Unto the End

For we are made partakers of Christ, if we hold the
beginning of our confidence stedfast unto the end.
Hebrews 3:14

Many of the greatest scholars and statesmen, the world's most eminent men, will in these last days turn from the light because the world by wisdom knows not God. Yet God's servants are to improve every opportunity to communicate the truth to these men. Some will acknowledge their ignorance of the things of God and will take their place as humble learners at the feet of Jesus, the Master Teacher.

In every effort to reach the higher classes, the worker for God needs strong faith. Appearances may seem forbidding, but in the darkest hour there is light above. The strength of those who love and serve God will be renewed day by day. The understanding of the Infinite is placed at their service, that in carrying out His purposes they may not err. Let these workers hold the beginning of their confidence firm unto the end, remembering that the light of God's truth is to shine amid the darkness that enshrouds our world. There is to be no despondency in connection with God's service. The faith of the consecrated worker is to stand every test brought to bear upon it. God is able and willing to bestow upon His servants all the strength they need and to give them the wisdom that their varied necessities demand. He will more than fulfill the highest expectations of those who put their trust in Him. (*Acts and the Apostles*, 241, 243)

REFLECTION: *We stand by going forward. We are to increase in strength that we may remain faithful unto Him. He is able and willing to give us the Holy Spirit, but we must have firmness and decision, maintaining under all circumstances a living faith in Jesus.*

Delay Not God's Plan

So we see that they could not enter in because of unbelief.
Hebrews 3:19

*I*t was not the will of God that Israel should wander forty years in the wilderness; He desired to lead them directly to the land of Canaan and establish them there, a holy, happy people. But "they could not enter in because of unbelief" (Hebrews 3:19). Because of their backsliding and apostasy they perished in the desert, and others were raised up to enter the Promised Land. In like manner, it was not the will of God that the coming of Christ should be so long delayed and His people should remain so many years in this world of sin and sorrow. But unbelief separated them from God. As they refused to do the work which He had appointed them, others were raised up to proclaim the message. In mercy to the world, Jesus delays His coming, that sinners may have an opportunity to hear the warning and find in Him a shelter before the wrath of God shall be poured out. (*The Great Controversy*, 458)

REFLECTION: *God wants so much to come again. The delay is not His fault, but ours. We can hasten that day, and are actually responsible to do this. Let's go forward today instead of backsliding.*

ENTER HIS REST

Let us therefore fear, lest, a promise being left us of entering into his rest, any of you should seem to come short of it.
Hebrews 4:1

A life in Christ is a life of restfulness. There may be no ecstasy of feeling, but there should be an abiding, peaceful trust. Your hope is not in yourself; it is in Christ. Your weakness is united to His strength, your ignorance to His wisdom, your frailty to His enduring might. So you are not to look to yourself, not to let the mind dwell upon self, but look to Christ. Let the mind dwell upon His love, upon the beauty, the perfection, of His character. Christ in His self-denial, Christ in His humiliation, Christ in His purity and holiness, Christ in His matchless love—this is the subject for the soul's contemplation. It is by loving Him, copying Him, depending wholly upon Him, that you are to be transformed into His likeness.

Jesus says, "Abide in Me." These words convey the idea of rest, stability, confidence. Again He invites, "Come unto Me, … and I will give you rest" (Matthew 11:28). The words of the psalmist express the same thought: "Rest in the Lord, and wait patiently for Him." And Isaiah gives the assurance, "In quietness and in confidence shall be your strength" (Psalm 37:7; Isaiah 30:15). This rest is not found in inactivity; for in the Saviour's invitation the promise of rest is united with the call to labor: "Take My yoke upon you: … and ye shall find rest" (Matthew 11:29). The heart that rests most fully upon Christ will be most earnest and active in labor for Him. (*Steps to Christ*, 70, 71)

REFLECTION: *When we are focused on self we have no rest. It is when we think and talk of Jesus and abide in Him that we have peace and rest.*

THE WORD IS QUICK AND POWERFUL

For the word of God is quick, and powerful, and sharper than any twoedged sword, piercing even to the dividing asunder of soul and spirit, and of the joints and marrow, and is a discerner of the thoughts and intents of the heart.
Hebrews 4:12

The Bible has little to say in praise of men. Little space is given to recounting the virtues of even the best men who have ever lived. This silence is not without purpose; it is not without a lesson. All the good qualities that men possess are the gift of God; their good deeds are performed by the grace of God through Christ. Since they owe all to God the glory of whatever they are or do belongs to Him alone; they are but instruments in His hands. More than this—as all the lessons of Bible history teach—it is a perilous thing to praise or exalt men; for if one comes to lose sight of his entire dependence on God, and to trust to his own strength, he is sure to fall. Man is contending with foes who are stronger than he. "We wrestle not against flesh and blood, but against principalities, against powers, against the rulers of the darkness of this world, against wicked spirits in high places" (Ephesians 6:12). It is impossible for us in our own strength to maintain the conflict; and whatever diverts the mind from God, whatever leads to self-exaltation or to self-dependence, is surely preparing the way for our overthrow. The tenor of the Bible is to inculcate distrust of human power and to encourage trust in divine power. (*Patriarchs and Prophets*, 717)

REFLECTION: *The truths of the Bible, treasured in the heart and mind and obeyed in the life, transforms the character. The Word is to be searched diligently with a teachable spirit.*

NOVEMBER 17

OUR GREAT HIGH PRIEST

Seeing then that we have a great high priest, that is passed into the heavens, Jesus the Son of God, let us hold fast our profession.
Hebrews 4:14

The sacrificial service that had pointed to Christ passed away; but the eyes of men were turned to the true sacrifice for the sins of the world. The earthly priesthood ceased; but we look to Jesus, the minister of the new covenant, and "to the blood of sprinkling, that speaketh better things than that of Abel." "The way into the holiest of all was not yet made manifest, while as the first tabernacle was yet standing: ... but Christ being come an high priest of good things to come, by a greater and more perfect tabernacle, not made with hands, ... by His own blood He entered in once into the holy place, having obtained eternal redemption for us" (Hebrews 12:24; 9:8–12).

"Wherefore He is able also to save them to the uttermost that come unto God by Him, seeing He ever liveth to make intercession for them" (Hebrews 7:25). Though the ministration was to be removed from the earthly to the heavenly temple; though the sanctuary and our great high priest would be invisible to human sight, yet the disciples were to suffer no loss thereby. They would realize no break in their communion, and no diminution of power because of the Saviour's absence. While Jesus ministers in the sanctuary above, He is still by His Spirit the minister of the church on earth. (*Desire of Ages*, 166)

REFLECTION: *Christ intercedes for us, not as a mere petitioner, but as a conqueror over sin. And He is able to deliver us from every temptation!*

WOUNDING CHRIST AGAIN

If they shall fall away, to renew them again unto repentance; seeing they crucify to themselves the Son of God afresh, and put him to an open shame.
Hebrews 6:6

We often sorrow because our evil deeds bring unpleasant consequences to ourselves; but this is not repentance. Real sorrow for sin is the result of the working of the Holy Spirit. The Spirit reveals the ingratitude of the heart that has slighted and grieved the Saviour, and brings us in contrition to the foot of the cross. By every sin Jesus is wounded afresh; and as we look upon Him whom we have pierced, we mourn for the sins that have brought anguish upon Him. Such mourning will lead to the renunciation of sin.

The worldling may pronounce this sorrow a weakness; but it is the strength which binds the penitent to the Infinite One with links that cannot be broken. It shows that the angels of God are bringing back to the soul the graces that were lost through hardness of heart and transgression. The tears of the penitent are only the raindrops that precede the sunshine of holiness. (*Desire of Ages*, 300)

REFLECTION: *As we pray for more understanding about the sin issue, and ask the Lord to give us the heart we need, it will become clearer that committing sin is like wounding our Savior afresh. Let's see sin as so terrible that we no longer want any part of it.*

NOVEMBER 19

CHRIST PRESENT THROUGH THE SPIRIT

Wherefore he is able also to save them to the uttermost that come unto God by him, seeing he ever liveth to make intercession for them.
Hebrews 7:25

Though the ministration was to be removed from the earthly to the heavenly temple; though the sanctuary and our great high priest would be invisible to human sight, yet the disciples were to suffer no loss thereby. They would realize no break in their communion, and no diminution of power because of the Saviour's absence. While Jesus ministers in the sanctuary above, He is still by His Spirit the minister of the church on earth. He is withdrawn from the eye of sense, but His parting promise is fulfilled, "Lo, I am with you alway, even unto the end of the world" (Matthew 28:20). While He delegates His power to inferior ministers, His energizing presence is still with His church.

Seeing then that we have a great high priest, ... Jesus, the Son of God, let us hold fast our profession. For we have not an high priest which cannot be touched with the feeling of our infirmities; but was in all points tempted like as we are, yet without sin. Let us therefore come boldly unto the throne of grace, that we may obtain mercy, and find grace to help in time of need" (Hebrews 4:14–16). (*Desire of Ages*, 166)

REFLECTION: *All through this devotional we have learned that God has spared nothing to save you and me! Even as sinners we can come boldly to the throne of Grace through our Lord, Jesus Christ. Today's thought is "No excuses."*

THE HEAVENLY SANCTUARY

Now of the things which we have spoken this is the sum: We have such an high priest, who is set on the right hand of the throne of the Majesty in the heavens; A minister of the sanctuary, and of the true tabernacle, which the Lord pitched, and not man.
Hebrews 8:1, 2

Thus those who were studying the subject found indisputable proof of the existence of a sanctuary in heaven. Moses made the earthly sanctuary after a pattern which was shown him. Paul teaches that that pattern was the true sanctuary which is in heaven. And John testifies that he saw it in heaven.

In the temple in heaven, the dwelling place of God, His throne is established in righteousness and judgment. In the most holy place is His law, the great rule of right by which all mankind are tested. The ark that enshrines the tables of the law is covered with the mercy seat, before which Christ pleads His blood in the sinner's behalf. Thus is represented the union of justice and mercy in the plan of human redemption. This union infinite wisdom alone could devise and infinite power accomplish; it is a union that fills all heaven with wonder and adoration. The cherubim of the earthly sanctuary, looking reverently down upon the mercy seat, represent the interest with which the heavenly host contemplate the work of redemption. This is the mystery of mercy into which angels desire to look--that God can be just while He justifies the repenting sinner and renews His intercourse with the fallen race." (*The Great Controversy*, 415)

REFLECTION: *The work in the earthly sanctuary was vitally important to mankind. God's work in behalf of you and me and all humanity is taking place by Christ Himself in the sanctuary in heaven. The work is almost done. Are you ready?*

THE NEW COVENANT

For this is the covenant that I will make with the house of Israel after those days, saith the Lord; I will put my laws into their mind, and write them in their hearts: and I will be to them a God, and they shall be to me a people.
Hebrews 8:10

He who becomes a partaker of the divine nature will be in harmony with God's great standard of righteousness, His holy law. This is the rule by which God measures the actions of men. This will be the test of character in the judgment.

There are many who claim that by the death of Christ the law was abrogated; but in this they contradict Christ's own words, "Think not that I am come to destroy the law, or the prophets. ... Till heaven and earth pass, one jot or one tittle shall in no wise pass from the law" (Matthew 5:17, 18). It was to atone for man's transgression of the law that Christ laid down His life. Could the law have been changed or set aside, then Christ need not have died. By His life on earth He honored the law of God. By His death He established it. He gave His life as a sacrifice, not to destroy God's law, not to create a lower standard, but that justice might be maintained, that the law might be shown to be immutable, that it might stand fast forever. (*Christ Object Lessons*, 314)

REFLECTION: *"As many as received Him, to them gave He power to become the sons of God, even to them that believe on His name" (John 1:12). Under the new covenant the conditions by which eternal life may be gained are the same as under the old — perfect obedience.*

FINALLY, FULLY CUT OFF FROM GOD

For if we sin wilfully after that we have received the knowledge of the truth, there remaineth no more sacrifice for sins, But a certain fearful looking for of judgment and fiery indignation, which shall devour the adversaries.
Hebrews 10:26, 27

"Whosoever speaketh a word against the Son of man," said Christ, "it shall be forgiven him: but whosoever speaketh against the Holy Ghost, it shall not be forgiven him" (Matthew 12:32). These words were spoken by our Saviour when the gracious works which He had performed through the power of God were attributed by the Jews to Beelzebub. It is through the agency of the Holy Spirit that God communicates with man; and those who deliberately reject this agency as satanic, have cut off the channel of communication between the soul and Heaven.

God works by the manifestation of His Spirit to reprove and convict the sinner; and if the Spirit's work is finally rejected, there is no more that God can do for the soul. The last resource of divine mercy has been employed. The transgressor has cut himself off from God, and sin has no remedy to cure itself. There is no reserved power by which God can work to convict and convert the sinner. "Let him alone" (Hosea 4:17) is the divine command. (*Patriarchs and Prophets*, 404, 405)

REFLECTION: *Oh the thought of committing the unpardonable sin. It is through our own course of action day after day after day that we ourselves cut off our communication with the only One who can save us. When the Holy Spirit convicts us of sin, let's make the decided effort to obey.*

NOVEMBER 23

*T*HROUGH *F*AITH

Through faith we understand that the worlds were framed by the word of God, so that things which are seen were not made of things which do appear.
Hebrews 11:3

The deepest students of science are constrained to recognize in nature the working of infinite power. But to man's unaided reason, nature's teaching cannot but be contradictory and disappointing. Only in the light of revelation can it be read aright. "Through faith we understand" (Hebrews 11:3).

In the beginning God" (Genesis 1:1). Here alone can the mind in its eager questioning, fleeing as the dove to the ark, find rest. Above, beneath, beyond, abides Infinite Love, working out all things to accomplish "the good pleasure of His goodness" (2 Thessalonians 1:11).

The invisible things of Him since the creation of the world are … perceived through the things that are made, even His everlasting power and divinity" (Romans 1:20, R.V.). But their testimony can be understood only through the aid of the divine Teacher. "What man knoweth the things of a man, save the spirit of man which is in him? even so the things of God knoweth no man, but the Spirit of God" (1 Corinthians 2:11).

"When He, the Spirit of truth, is come, He will guide you into all truth" (John 16:13). Only by the aid of that Spirit who in the beginning "was brooding upon the face of the waters;" of that Word by whom "all things were made;" of that "true Light, which lighteth every man that cometh into the world," can the testimony of science be rightly interpreted. Only by their guidance can its deepest truths be discerned. (*Education*, 134)

REFLECTION: *Nature points to an Intelligent Designer as the Author of all that is. Things didn't just happen, they had an eternal purpose.*

NOVEMBER 24

Seeing Heaven by Faith

For he looked for a city which hath foundations,
whose builder and maker is God.
Hebrews 11:10

The lesson is for God's messengers today, when the cities of the nations are as verily in need of a knowledge of the attributes and purposes of the true God as were the Ninevites of old. Christ's ambassadors are to point men to the nobler world, which has largely been lost sight of. According to the teaching of the Holy Scriptures, the only city that will endure is the city whose builder and maker is God. With the eye of faith man may behold the threshold of heaven, flushed with God's living glory. Through His ministering servants the Lord Jesus is calling upon men to strive with sanctified ambition to secure the immortal inheritance. He urges them to lay up treasure beside the throne of God. ...

Our God is a God of mercy. With long-sufferance and tender compassion He deals with the transgressors of His law. And yet, in this our day, when men and women have so many opportunities for becoming familiar with the divine law as revealed in Holy Writ, the great Ruler of the universe cannot behold with any satisfaction the wicked cities, where reign violence and crime. The end of God's forbearance with those who persist in disobedience is approaching rapidly. (*Prophets and Kings*, 275)

REFLECTION: *The world is in chaos; and the cities, especially the large ones, are becoming more wicked. It is past time for Christians to stand and share the everlasting gospel message. We are not all teachers or preachers, but we can all share with others what God has done in our lives.*

THE CROSS, OUR HOPE

Looking unto Jesus the author and finisher of our faith; who for the joy that was set before him endured the cross, despising the shame, and is set down at the right hand of the throne of God.

Hebrews 12:2

If those who today are teaching the word of God, would uplift the cross of Christ higher and still higher, their ministry would be far more successful. If sinners can be led to give one earnest look at the cross, if they can obtain a full view of the crucified Saviour, they will realize the depth of God's compassion and the sinfulness of sin.

Christ's death proves God's great love for man. It is our pledge of salvation. To remove the cross from the Christian would be like blotting the sun from the sky. The cross brings us near to God, reconciling us to Him. With the relenting compassion of a father's love, Jehovah looks upon the suffering that His Son endured in order to save the race from eternal death, and accepts us in the Beloved.

Without the cross, man could have no union with the Father. On it depends our every hope. From it shines the light of the Saviour's love, and when at the foot of the cross the sinner looks up to the One who died to save him, he may rejoice with fullness of joy, for his sins are pardoned. Kneeling in faith at the cross, he has reached the highest place to which man can attain. (*Acts of the Apostles*, 209, 210)

REFLECTION: *Look to the cross, and spend some time contemplating the story of our redemption. As we do, we will be drawn closer to Jesus. Let's try to understand what Christ has done for us. Do you see Him there? He is the Author and Finisher of our faith. The more we contemplate the cross, the more we realize that we can never fully comprehend what Jesus did for us. What can we do? We can express our gratitude with all our heart, mind and soul. As we do, our love for Him will grow.*

NOVEMBER 26

God Will Vindicate Us

Let brotherly love continue.
Hebrews 13:1

*E*ven under false accusation those who are in the right can afford to be calm and considerate. God is acquainted with all that is misunderstood and misinterpreted by men, and we can safely leave our case in His hands. He will as surely vindicate the cause of those who put their trust in Him as He searched out the guilt of Achan. Those who are actuated by the spirit of Christ will possess that charity which suffers long and is kind.

It is the will of God that union and brotherly love should exist among His people. The prayer of Christ just before His crucifixion was that His disciples might be one as He is one with the Father, that the world might believe that God had sent Him. This most touching and wonderful prayer reaches down the ages, even to our day; for His words were, "Neither pray I for these alone, but for them also which shall believe on Me through their word" (John 17:20). While we are not to sacrifice one principle of truth, it should be our constant aim to reach this state of unity. This is the evidence of our discipleship. Said Jesus, "By this shall all men know that ye are My disciples, if ye have love one to another." (*Patriarchs and Prophets*, 520)

REFLECTION: *At the end of time just before our Lord returns, there will be such a demarcation between the true followers of God and those who profess to be His followers. Today let us pray to love one another like Jesus loves us.*

NOVEMBER 27

DOERS OF GOD'S WORD

But be ye doers of the word, and not hearers only, deceiving your own selves.
James 1:22

John and Judas are representatives of those who profess to be Christ's followers. Both these disciples had the same opportunities to study and follow the divine Pattern. Both were closely associated with Jesus and were privileged to listen to His teaching. Each possessed serious defects of character; and each had access to the divine grace that transforms character. But while one in humility was learning of Jesus, the other revealed that he was not a doer of the word, but a hearer only. One, daily dying to self and overcoming sin, was sanctified through the truth; the other, resisting the transforming power of grace and indulging selfish desires, was brought into bondage to Satan.

Such transformation of character as is seen in the life of John is ever the result of communion with Christ. There may be marked defects in the character of an individual, yet when he becomes a true disciple of Christ, the power of divine grace transforms and sanctifies him. Beholding as in a glass the glory of the Lord, he is changed from glory to glory, until he is like Him whom he adores.

John was a teacher of holiness, and in his letters to the church he laid down unerring rules for the conduct of Christians. "Every man that hath this hope in him," he wrote, "purifieth himself, even as He is pure." "He that saith he abideth in Him ought himself also so to walk, even as He walked" (1 John 3:3; 2:6). (*Acts of the Apostles*, 558, 559)

REFLECTION: *The apostle Paul wrote, "This is the will of God, even your sanctification" (1 Thessalonians 4:3). And true sanctification comes by receiving the love of Christ, which is then exemplified in the life. Good works do not purchase the love of God, but they reveal that we possess that love.*

THE NOBLE CHARACTER | 347

CHRIST-LIKE TEMPER

But as he which hath called you is holy, so be ye holy in all manner
of conversation; Because it is written, Be ye holy; for I am holy.
1 Peter 1:15, 16

The apostle exhorts us, "As He which hath called you is holy, so be ye holy in all manner of conversation; because it is written, Be ye holy; for I am holy" (1 Peter 1:15, 16). The grace of Christ is to control the temper and the voice. Its working will be seen in politeness and tender regard shown by brother for brother, in kind, encouraging words. An angel presence is in the home. The life breathes a sweet perfume, which ascends to God as holy incense. Love is manifested in kindness, gentleness, forbearance, and long-suffering.

The countenance is changed. Christ abiding in the heart shines out in the faces of those who love Him and keep His commandments. Truth is written there. The sweet peace of heaven is revealed. There is expressed a habitual gentleness, a more than human love.

The leaven of truth works a change in the whole man, making the coarse refined, the rough gentle, the selfish generous. By it the impure are cleansed, washed in the blood of the Lamb. Through its life-giving power it brings all there is of mind and soul and strength into harmony with the divine life. Man with his human nature becomes a partaker of divinity. Christ is honored in excellence and perfection of character. As these changes are effected, angels break forth in rapturous song, and God and Christ rejoice over souls fashioned after the divine similitude. (*Christ's Object Lessons*, 102)

REFLECTION: *Peter went from being a rough-spoken fisherman to being a well-spoken New Testament author for Christ. When Christ abides in our hearts, He changes even our words and conversations. (See also James 1:26.)*

NOVEMBER 29

LIVELY STONES

Ye also, as lively stones, are built up a spiritual house, an holy priesthood,
to offer up spiritual sacrifices, acceptable to God by Jesus Christ.
1 Peter 2:5

Upon the foundation that Christ Himself had laid, the apostles built the church of God. In the Scriptures the figure of the erection of a temple is frequently used to illustrate the building of the church. Zechariah refers to Christ as the Branch that should build the temple of the Lord. He speaks of the Gentiles as helping in the work: "They that are far off shall come and build in the temple of the Lord;" and Isaiah declares, "The sons of strangers shall build up thy walls" (Zechariah 6:12, 15; Isaiah 60:10).

Writing of the building of this temple, Peter says, "To whom coming, as unto a living stone, disallowed indeed of men, but chosen of God, and precious, ye also, as lively stones, are built up a spiritual house, an holy priesthood, to offer up spiritual sacrifices, acceptable to God by Jesus Christ (1 Peter 2:4, 5).

In the quarry of the Jewish and the Gentile world the apostles labored, bringing out stones to lay upon the foundation. In his letter to the believers at Ephesus, Paul said, "Now therefore ye are no more strangers and foreigners, but fellow citizens with the saints, and of the household of God; and are built upon the foundation of the apostles and prophets, Jesus Christ Himself being the Chief Cornerstone; in whom all the building fitly framed together groweth unto an holy temple in the Lord: in whom ye also are builded together for an habitation of God through the Spirit" (Ephesians 2:19–22). (*The Acts of the Apostles*, 595, 596)

REFLECTION: *For other foundation can no man lay than that is laid, which is Jesus Christ. (The Acts of the Apostles, 596)*

NOVEMBER 30

CHRIST OUR EXAMPLE

For even hereunto were ye called: because Christ also suffered for us, leaving us an example, that ye should follow his steps.
1 Peter 2:21

*I*f we abide in Christ, if the love of God dwells in us, our feelings, our thoughts, our purposes, our actions, will be in harmony with the will of God as expressed in the precepts of His holy law. "Little children, let no man deceive you: he that doeth righteousness is righteous, even as He is righteous" (1 John 3:7). Righteousness is defined by the standard of God's holy law, as expressed in the ten precepts given on Sinai.

That so-called faith in Christ which professes to release men from the obligation of obedience to God, is not faith, but presumption. "By grace are ye saved through faith." But "faith, if it hath not works, is dead" (Ephesians 2:8; James 2:17). Jesus said of Himself before He came to earth, "I delight to do Thy will, O My God: yea, Thy law is within My heart" (Psalm 40:8). And just before He ascended again to heaven He declared, "I have kept My Father's commandments, and abide in His love" (John 15:10). The Scripture says, "Hereby we do know that we know Him, if we keep His commandments. . . . He that saith he abideth in Him ought himself also so to walk even as He walked" (1 John 2:3–6). "Because Christ also suffered for us, leaving us an example, that ye should follow His steps" (1 Peter 2:21). (*Steps to Christ*, 61)

REFLECTION: *In the life of Jesus we see Him drawing close to the most needy and the most hopeless. As we draw nearer to Christ, we will draw nearer to those who suffer the most.*

DECEMBER

ONE OF SATAN'S INVENTIONS

Whose adorning let it not be that outward adorning of plaiting the hair, and of wearing of gold, or of putting on of apparel; But let it be the hidden man of the heart, in that which is not corruptible, even the ornament of a meek and quiet spirit, which is in the sight of God of great price.
1 Peter 3:3, 4

The mother has no time to study the principles of physical development, that she may know how to care for the health of her children. She has no time for ministering to their mental or spiritual needs, no time to sympathize with them in their little disappointments and trials, or to share in their interests and pursuits.

Almost as soon as they come into the world the children are subjected to fashion's influence. They hear more of dress than of their Saviour. They see their mothers consulting the fashion plates more earnestly than the Bible. The display of dress is treated as of greater importance than the development of character. Parents and children are robbed of that which is best and sweetest and truest in life. For fashion's sake they are cheated out of a preparation for the life to come.

It was the adversary of all good who instigated the invention of the ever-changing fashions. He desires nothing so much as to bring grief and dishonor to God by working the misery and ruin of human beings. One of the means by which he most effectually accomplishes this is the devices of fashion that weaken the body as well as enfeeble the mind and belittle the soul. (*Ministry of Healing*, 291)

REFLECTION: *What a contrast between Christ and Satan. Christ works for our salvation and tells us the path to follow. Satan works for our destruction and tells us what we want to hear to please ourselves. Let's not allow fashion and materialism to keep us from Christ.*

DECEMBER 2

Judgment Begins at the House of God

For the time is come that judgment must begin at the house of God: and if it first begin at us, what shall the end be of them that obey not the gospel of God?
1 Peter 4:17

In the typical service only those who had come before God with confession and repentance, and whose sins, through the blood of the sin offering, were transferred to the sanctuary, had a part in the service of the Day of Atonement. So in the great day of final atonement and investigative judgment the only cases considered are those of the professed people of God. The judgment of the wicked is a distinct and separate work, and takes place at a later period. "Judgment must begin at the house of God: and if it first begin at us, what shall the end be of them that obey not the gospel?" (1 Peter 4:17).

The books of record in heaven, in which the names and the deeds of men are registered, are to determine the decisions of the judgment. Says the prophet Daniel: "The judgment was set, and the books were opened." The revelator, describing the same scene, adds: "Another book was opened, which is the book of life: and the dead were judged out of those things which were written in the books, according to their works" (Revelation 20:12). (*The Great Controversy*, 480)

REFLECTION: *Every one of us has a detailed record in heaven. It has all our deeds good or bad. Not one detail is missing. We will be judged by our everyday lives. Let's make sure today that Jesus is our Lord, not just our Savior.*

DECEMBER 3

The Christian Ladder

Giving all diligence, add to your faith virtue; and to virtue knowledge; and to knowledge temperance; and to temperance patience; and to patience godliness; and to godliness brotherly kindness; and to brotherly kindness charity. For if these things be in you, and abound, they make you that ye shall neither be barren nor unfruitful in the knowledge of our Lord Jesus Christ.

2 Peter 1:5–8

These words are full of instruction, and strike the keynote of victory. The apostle presents before the believers the ladder of Christian progress, every step of which represents advancement in the knowledge of God, and in the climbing of which there is to be no standstill. Faith, virtue, knowledge, temperance, patience, godliness, brotherly kindness, and charity are the rounds of the ladder. We are saved by climbing round after round, mounting step after step, to the height of Christ's ideal for us. Thus He is made unto us wisdom, and righteousness, and sanctification, and redemption.

God has called His people to glory and virtue, and these will be manifest in the lives of all who are truly connected with Him. Having become partakers of the heavenly gift, they are to go on unto perfection, being "kept by the power of God through faith" (1 Peter 1:5). It is the glory of God to give His virtue to His children. He desires to see men and women reaching the highest standard; and when by faith they lay hold of the power of Christ, when they plead His unfailing promises, and claim them as their own, when with an importunity that will not be denied they seek for the power of the Holy Spirit, they will be made complete in Him. (*Acts of the Apostles*, 530)

REFLECTION: *As you add to your faith every day, it is like climbing a ladder. Our goal as Christians is to reach higher and higher. It all begins with faith.*

DECEMBER 4

PROBATION EXTENDED

The Lord is not slack concerning his promise, as some men count
slackness; but is longsuffering to us-ward, not willing that any
should perish, but that all should come to repentance.

2 Peter 3:9

God permits the wicked to prosper and to reveal their enmity against Him, that when they shall have filled up the measure of their iniquity all may see His justice and mercy in their utter destruction. The day of His vengeance hastens, when all who have transgressed His law and oppressed His people will meet the just recompense of their deeds; when every act of cruelty or injustice toward God's faithful ones will be punished as though done to Christ Himself.

There is another and more important question that should engage the attention of the churches of today. The apostle Paul declares that "all that will live godly in Christ Jesus shall suffer persecution" (2 Timothy 3:12). Why is it, then, that persecution seems in a great degree to slumber? The only reason is that the church has conformed to the world's standard and therefore awakens no opposition. The religion which is current in our day is not of the pure and holy character that marked the Christian faith in the days of Christ and His apostles. It is only because of the spirit of compromise with sin, because the great truths of the word of God are so indifferently regarded, because there is so little vital godliness in the church, that Christianity is apparently so popular with the world. Let there be a revival of the faith and power of the early church, and the spirit of persecution will be revived, and the fires of persecution will be rekindled. (*Great Controversy*, 48)

REFLECTION: *There will come a day very soon when probation will close. Are you ready? The watch word for the day is, "Get ready!"*

DECEMBER 5

*F*ELLOWSHIP WITH *G*OD

That which we have seen and heard declare we unto you, that
ye also may have fellowship with us: and truly our fellowship
is with the Father, and with his Son Jesus Christ.
1 John 1:3

As a witness for Christ, John entered into no controversy, no wearisome contention. He declared what
he knew, what he had seen and heard. He had been
intimately associated with Christ, had listened to His teachings,
had witnessed His mighty miracles. Few could see the beauties
of Christ's character as John saw them. For him the darkness had
passed away; on him the true light was shining. His testimony
in regard to the Saviour's life and death was clear and forcible.
Out of the abundance of a heart overflowing with love for the
Saviour he spoke; and no power could stay his words.

"That which was from the beginning," he declared, "which
we have heard, which we have seen with our eyes, which we
have looked upon, and our hands have handled, of the Word of
life; ... that which we have seen and heard declare we unto you,
that ye also may have fellowship with us: and truly our fellowship is with the Father, and with His Son Jesus Christ."

So may every true believer be able, through his own experience, to "set to his seal that God is true" (John 3:33). He can bear
witness to that which he has seen and heard and felt of the power
of Christ. (*Acts of the Apostles*, 555)

REFLECTION: *A testimony is like a fingerprint, no two are the same, and*
no one can take it away. Do you have a testimony of your faith? Let
your friends hear about it!

DECEMBER 6

CONFESS THY SINS

*If we confess our sins, he is faithful and just to forgive us
our sins, and to cleanse us from all unrighteousness.*
1 John 1:9

The Lord says, "Only acknowledge thine iniquity, that thou hast transgressed against the Lord thy God." "Then will I sprinkle clean water upon you, and ye shall be clean; from all your filthiness and from all your idols will I cleanse you" (Jeremiah 3:13; Ezekiel 36:25).

But we must have a knowledge of ourselves, a knowledge that will result in contrition, before we can find pardon and peace. The Pharisee felt no conviction of sin. The Holy Spirit could not work with him. His soul was encased in a self-righteous armor which the arrows of God, barbed and true-aimed by angel hands, failed to penetrate. It is only he who knows himself to be a sinner that Christ can save. He came "to heal the brokenhearted, to preach deliverance to the captives, and recovering of sight to the blind, to set at liberty them that are bruised" (Luke 4:18). But "they that are whole need not a physician" (Luke 5:31). We must know our real condition, or we shall not feel our need of Christ's help. We must understand our danger, or we shall not flee to the refuge. We must feel the pain of our wounds, or we should not desire healing. (*Christ's Object Lessons*, 158)

REFLECTION: *If we behold His perfection, we will see our imperfection. We are then to give Him our sins that we might receive His righteousness.*

December 7

$\mathcal{H}$ERE IS THE $\mathcal{T}$EST

He that saith, I know him, and keepeth not his commandments, is a liar,
and the truth is not in him. But whoso keepeth his word, in him verily
is the love of God perfected: hereby know we that we are in him.
1 John 2:4, 5

Let none deceive themselves with the belief that they can become holy while willfully violating one of God's requirements. The commission of a known sin silences the witnessing voice of the Spirit and separates the soul from God. "Sin is the transgression of the law." And "whosoever sinneth transgresseth the law hath not seen Him, neither known Him (1 John 3:6). Though John in his epistles dwells so fully upon love, yet he does not hesitate to reveal the true character of that class who claim to be sanctified while living in transgression of the law of God. "He that saith, I know Him, and keepeth not His commandments, is a liar, and the truth is not in him. But whoso keepeth His word, in him verily is the love of God perfected" (1 John 2:4, 5). Here is the test of every man's profession. We cannot accord holiness to any man without bringing him to the measurement of God's only standard of holiness in heaven and in earth. If men feel no weight of the moral law, if they belittle and make light of God's precepts, if they break one of the least of these commandments, and teach men so, they shall be of no esteem in the sight of Heaven, and we may know that their claims are without foundation." (*The Great Controversy*, 472)

REFLECTION: *If we are not honest with ourselves, there is no way we can be honest with God. Lay your problems at the feet of Jesus and He will change your life.*

DECEMBER 8

WHAT CONSTITUTES TRUE LOVE FOR GOD

He that saith he is in the light, and hateth his
brother, is in darkness even until now.
1 John 2:9

*I*t is not the opposition of the world that most endangers the church of Christ. It is the evil cherished in the hearts of believers that works their most grievous disaster and most surely retards the progress of God's cause. There is no surer way of weakening spirituality than by cherishing envy, suspicion, faultfinding, and evil surmising. On the other hand, the strongest witness that God has sent His Son into the world is the existence of harmony and union among men of varied dispositions who form His church. ...

In the church of God today brotherly love is sadly lacking. Many who profess to love the Saviour do not love one another. Unbelievers are watching to see if the faith of professed Christians is exerting a sanctifying influence upon their lives; and they are quick to discern the defects in character, the inconsistencies in action. Let Christians not make it possible for the enemy to point to them and say, Behold how these people, standing under the banner of Christ, hate one another. ...

Those who have never experienced the tender, winning love of Christ cannot lead others to the fountain of life. His love in the heart is a constraining power, which leads men to reveal Him in the conversation, in the tender, pitiful spirit, in the uplifting of the lives of those with whom they associate. Christian workers who succeed in their efforts must know Christ; and in order to know Him, they must know His love. In heaven their fitness as workers is measured by their ability to love as Christ loved and to work as He worked. (*Acts of the Apostles, 549–551*)

REFLECTION: *To be like Jesus in every aspect should be our goal and passion. The world is watching to see if what we say matches with how we live. Let's pray for the love of Christ to permeate us fully.*

THE SONS OF GOD

Behold, what manner of love the Father hath bestowed upon us, that we should be called the sons of God: therefore the world knoweth us not, because it knew him not.

1 John 3:1

As the inspired apostle John beheld the height, the depth, the breadth of the Father's love toward the perishing race, he was filled with adoration and reverence; and, failing to find suitable language in which to express the greatness and tenderness of this love, he called upon the world to behold it. "Behold, what manner of love the Father hath bestowed upon us, that we should be called the sons of God" (1 John 3:1). What a value this places upon man! Through transgression the sons of man become subjects of Satan. Through faith in the atoning sacrifice of Christ the sons of Adam may become the sons of God. By assuming human nature, Christ elevates humanity. Fallen men are placed where, through connection with Christ, they may indeed become worthy of the name "sons of God."...

The matchless love of God for a world that did not love Him! The thought has a subduing power upon the soul and brings the mind into captivity to the will of God. The more we study the divine character in the light of the cross, the more we see mercy, tenderness, and forgiveness blended with equity and justice, and the more clearly we discern innumerable evidences of a love that is infinite and a tender pity surpassing a mother's yearning sympathy for her wayward child. (*Steps to Christ*, 15)

REFLECTION: *The Father not only gave His Son to bear our sins, but He gave Him to the human race; Jesus will forever bear the human form. More than this, Jesus will forever bear the scars of our redemption, the scars in His hands and side.*

PROSPER IN HEALTH

Beloved, I wish above all things that thou mayest prosper
and be in health, even as thy soul prospereth.
3 John 2

The Saviour in His miracles revealed the power that is continually at work in man's behalf, to sustain and to heal him. Through the agencies of nature, God is working, day by day, hour by hour, moment by moment, to keep us alive, to build up and restore us. When any part of the body sustains injury, a healing process is at once begun; nature's agencies are set at work to restore soundness. But the power working through these agencies is the power of God. All life-giving power is from Him. When one recovers from disease, it is God who restores him.

Sickness, suffering, and death are work of an antagonistic power. Satan is the destroyer; God is the restorer.

The words spoken to Israel are true today of those who recover health of body or health of soul. "I am the Lord that healeth thee" (Exodus 15:26).

The desire of God for every human being is expressed in the words, "Beloved, I wish above all things that thou mayest prosper and be in health, even as thy soul prospereth" (3 John 2).

He it is who "forgiveth all thine iniquities; who healeth all thy diseases; who redeemeth thy life from destruction; who crowneth thee with loving-kindness and tender mercies" (Psalm 103:3, 4). (*The Ministry of Healing*, 112, 113)

REFLECTION: *By restoring us physically, the Lord teaches us that we can be restored spiritually. Let us cooperate with God in the work of restoration.*

DECEMBER 11

A Satanic Weapon

*Yet Michael the archangel, when contending with the devil
he disputed about the body of Moses, durst not bring against
him a railing accusation, but said, The Lord rebuke thee.*
Jude 9

Christ Himself, when contending with Satan about the body of Moses, "durst not bring against him a railing accusation" (Jude 9). Had He done this, He would have placed Himself on Satan's ground, for accusation is the weapon of the evil one. He is called in Scripture, "the accuser of our brethren" (Revelation 12:10). Jesus would employ none of Satan's weapons. He met him with the words, "The Lord rebuke thee" (Jude 9).

His example is for us. When we are brought in conflict with the enemies of Christ, we should say nothing in a spirit of retaliation or that would bear even the appearance of a railing accusation. He who stands as a mouthpiece for God should not utter words which even the Majesty of heaven would not use when contending with Satan. We are to leave with God the work of judging and condemning. (*Thoughts from the Mount of Blessing*, 57)

REFLECTION: *Christ tells us to love our enemies, which is only possible with His grace. Without Him, we would be just like Satan, railing against one another. Today, let's receive the love of Christ for our enemies, and listen for the still, small voice, the Holy Spirit.*

THE LORD COMETH

And Enoch also, the seventh from Adam, prophesied of these, saying,
Behold, the Lord cometh with ten thousands of his saints.
Jude 14

The doctrine of the second advent is the very keynote of the Sacred Scriptures. From the day when the first pair turned their sorrowing steps from Eden, the children of faith have waited the coming of the Promised One to break the destroyer's power and bring them again to the lost Paradise. Holy men of old looked forward to the advent of the Messiah in glory, as the consummation of their hope. Enoch, only the seventh in descent from them that dwelt in Eden, he who for three centuries on earth walked with his God, was permitted to behold from afar the coming of the Deliverer. "Behold," he declared, "the Lord cometh with ten thousands of His saints, to execute judgment upon all" (Jude 14, 15). The patriarch Job in the night of his affliction exclaimed with unshaken trust: "I know that my Redeemer liveth, and that He shall stand at the latter day upon the earth: … in my flesh shall I see God: whom I shall see for myself, and mine eyes shall behold, and not another" (Job 19:25–27). (*The Great Controversy*, 299)

REFLECTION: *"Let the heavens rejoice, and let the earth be glad … before the Lord: for He cometh, for He cometh to judge the earth: He shall judge the world with righteousness, and the people with His truth"* (Psalm 96:11–13).

REVELATION—REVEALING THE PAST, PRESENT, AND THE FUTURE

The Revelation of Jesus Christ, which God gave unto him, to shew unto his servants things which must shortly come to pass; and he sent and signified it by his angel unto his servant John: Blessed is he that readeth, and they that hear the words of this prophecy, and keep those things which are written therein: for the time is at hand.
Revelation 1:1, 3

A revelation is something revealed. The Lord Himself revealed to His servant the mysteries contained in this book, and He designs that they shall be open to the study of all. Its truths are addressed to those living in the last days of this earth's history, as well as to those living in the days of John. Some of the scenes depicted in this prophecy are in the past, some are now taking place; some bring to view the close of the great conflict between the powers of darkness and the Prince of heaven, and some reveal the triumphs and joys of the redeemed in the earth made new.

Let none think, because they cannot explain the meaning of every symbol in the Revelation, that it is useless for them to search this book in an effort to know the meaning of the truth it contains. …

In the Revelation all the books of the Bible meet and end. Here is the complement of the book of Daniel. One is a prophecy; the other a revelation. (*Acts of the Apostles*, 584, 585)

REFLECTION: *This book reveals things that all should know right now. It is as important as water to the body. As you go through each chapter make sure you ask the Lord to give you wisdom to understand, and a contrite and open heart.*

The Number Seven

Saying, I am Alpha and Omega, the first and the last: and, What thou seest, write in a book, and send it unto the seven churches which are in Asia; unto Ephesus, and unto Smyrna, and unto Pergamos, and unto Thyatira, and unto Sardis, and unto Philadelphia, and unto Laodicea.

Revelation 1:11

The names of the seven churches are symbolic of the church in different periods of the Christian Era. The number seven indicates completeness, and is symbolic of the fact that the messages extend to the end of time, while the symbols used reveal the condition of the church at different periods in the history of the world.

Christ is spoken of as walking in the midst of the golden candlesticks. Thus is symbolized His relation to the churches. He is in constant communication with His people. He knows their true state. He observes their order, their piety, their devotion.... With untiring wakefulness and unremitting vigilance, He watches to see whether the light of any of His sentinels is burning dim or going out. If the candlesticks were left to mere human care, the flickering flame would languish and die; but He is the true watchman in the Lord's house, the true warden of the temple courts. His continued care and sustaining grace are the source of life and light.

Christ is represented as holding the seven stars in His right hand. This assures us that no church faithful to its trust need fear coming to nought, for not a star that has the protection of Omnipotence can be plucked out of the hand of Christ. Acts of the (*Apostles*, 585, 586)

REFLECTION: *Starting in Genesis and ending in Revelation, the number seven means completeness. The Bible is full of meaning, and we have the responsibility and the privilege to study and find out what God is telling us.*

DECEMBER 15

NEVER LET TIME MAKE US FORGET

Nevertheless I have somewhat against thee, because thou hast left thy first love. Remember therefore from whence thou art fallen, and repent, and do the first works; or else I will come unto thee quickly, and will remove thy candlestick out of his place, except thou repent.

Revelation 2:4, 5

At the first the experience of the church at Ephesus was marked with childlike simplicity and fervor. The believers sought earnestly to obey every word of God, and their lives revealed an earnest, sincere love for Christ. They rejoiced to do the will of God because the Saviour was in their hearts as an abiding presence. Filled with love for their Redeemer, their highest aim was to win souls to Him. ...

But after a time the zeal of the believers began to wane, and their love for God and for one another grew less. Coldness crept into the church. Some forgot the wonderful manner in which they had received the truth. One by one the old standard-bearers fell at their post. Some of the younger workers, who might have shared the burdens of these pioneers, and thus have been prepared for wise leadership, had become weary of oft-repeated truths. In their desire for something novel and startling they attempted to introduce new phases of doctrine, more pleasing to many minds, but not in harmony with the fundamental principles of the gospel. ...

As these false doctrines were urged, differences sprang up, and the eyes of many were turned from beholding Jesus as the Author and Finisher of their faith. The discussion of unimportant points of doctrine, and the contemplation of pleasing fables of man's invention, occupied time that should have been spent in proclaiming the gospel. (*Acts of the Apostles*, 578–580)

REFLECTION: *Many Christians start out with much zeal in their new-found faith. Then with time, many lose that zeal and start backsliding. Let's recommit ourselves and be faithful until the end. Jesus is coming soon.*

December 16

$\mathcal{H}$ope for $\mathcal{L}$aodicea

As many as I love, I rebuke and chasten: be zealous therefore, and repent.
Revelation 3:19

$\mathcal{B}$ut when tribulation comes upon us, how many of us are like Jacob! We think it the hand of an enemy; and in the darkness we wrestle blindly until our strength is spent, and we find no comfort or deliverance. To Jacob the divine touch at break of day revealed the One with whom he had been contending—the Angel of the covenant; and, weeping and helpless, he fell upon the breast of Infinite Love, to receive the blessing for which his soul longed. We also need to learn that trials mean benefit, and not to despise the chastening of the Lord nor faint when we are rebuked of Him.

"Happy is the man whom God correcteth: … He maketh sore, and bindeth up: He woundeth, and His hands make whole. He shall deliver thee in six troubles: yea, in seven there shall no evil touch thee" (Job 5:17–19). To every stricken one, Jesus comes with the ministry of healing. The life of bereavement, pain, and suffering may be brightened by precious revealings of His presence.

God would not have us remain pressed down by dumb sorrow, with sore and breaking hearts. He would have us look up and behold His dear face of love. The blessed Saviour stands by many whose eyes are so blinded by tears that they do not discern Him. He longs to clasp our hands, to have us look to Him in simple faith, permitting Him to guide us. (*Thoughts from the Mount of Blessing*, 12)

REFLECTION: *All of heaven is interested in the salvation of man. Only here on planet Earth do we find anyone indifferent and careless towards the human family. The message to the Laodiceans is that your case is not hopeless.*

DECEMBER 17

*W*ORTHY IS THE *L*AMB

And every creature which is in heaven, and on the earth, and under
the earth, and such as are in the sea, and all that are in them, heard
I saying, Blessing, and honour, and glory, and power, be unto him
that sitteth upon the throne, and unto the Lamb for ever and ever.

Revelation 5:13

With unutterable love, Jesus welcomes His faithful ones to the joy of their Lord. ... As they gather about the great white throne, gladness unspeakable will fill their hearts, when they behold those whom they have won for Christ, and see that one has gained others, and these still others, all brought into the haven of rest, there to lay their crowns at Jesus' feet and praise Him through the endless cycles of eternity.

As the ransomed ones are welcomed to the City of God, there rings out upon the air an exultant cry of adoration. The two Adams are about to meet. The Son of God is standing with outstretched arms to receive the father of our race—the being whom He created, who sinned against his Maker, and for whose sin the marks of the crucifixion are borne upon the Saviour's form. As Adam discerns the prints of the cruel nails, he does not fall upon the bosom of his Lord, but in humiliation casts himself at His feet, crying: "Worthy, worthy is the Lamb that was slain!" Tenderly the Saviour lifts him up and bids him look once more upon the Eden home from which he has so long been exiled. (*The Great Controversy*, 647)

REFLECTION: *It has been said that whatever we may have to endure or whatever the cost to get to heaven, all will say, "It was cheap enough." Any trial will seem trivial compared to the blessings waiting for Christ's faithful followers.*

THE FOUR WINDS

*And after these things I saw four angels standing on the four corners
of the earth, holding the four winds of the earth, that the wind
should not blow on the earth, nor on the sea, nor on any tree.*
Revelation 7:1

The present is a time of overwhelming interest to all living. Rulers and statesmen, men who occupy positions of trust and authority, thinking men and women of all classes, have their attention fixed upon the events taking place about us. They are watching the strained, restless relations that exist among the nations. They observe the intensity that is taking possession of every earthly element, and they recognize that something great and decisive is about to take place—that the world is on the verge of a stupendous crisis.

Angels are now restraining the winds of strife, that they may not blow until the world shall be warned of its coming doom; but a storm is gathering, ready to burst upon the earth; and when God shall bid His angels loose the winds, there will be such a scene of strife as no pen can picture.

The Bible, and the Bible only, gives a correct view of these things. Here are revealed the great final scenes in the history of our world, events that already are casting their shadows before, the sound of their approach causing the earth to tremble and men's hearts to fail them for fear. (*Education*, 179, 180)

REFLECTION: *God's restraining power is slowly being withdrawn from the world. When the servants of God are sealed, then will come the time of trouble spoken of in Scripture.*

DECEMBER 19

REWARD TO THOSE WHO HONOR HIM

After this I beheld, and, lo, a great multitude, which no man could number,
of all nations, and kindreds, and people, and tongues, stood before the throne,
and before the Lamb, clothed with white robes, and palms in their hands.
Revelation 7:9

Nearest the throne are those who were once zealous in the cause of Satan, but who, plucked as brands from the burning, have followed their Saviour with deep, intense devotion. Next are those who perfected Christian characters in the midst of falsehood and infidelity, those who honored the law of God when the Christian world declared it void, and the millions, of all ages, who were martyred for their faith. And beyond is the "great multitude, which no man could number, of all nations, and kindreds, and people, and tongues, … before the throne, and before the Lamb, clothed with white robes, and palms in their hands" (Revelation 7:9). Their warfare is ended, their victory won. They have run the race and reached the prize. The palm branch in their hands is a symbol of their triumph, the white robe an emblem of the spotless righteousness of Christ which now is theirs. (*The Great Controversy*, 665)

REFLECTION: *There is not one of us that Christ wants to let go of. No matter how bad we think we are, God sees good in us. Accept that love today.*

DECEMBER 20

It Will All Be Worth It

And I said unto him, Sir, thou knowest. And he said to me, These
are they which came out of great tribulation, and have washed
their robes, and made them white in the blood of the Lamb.
Revelation 7:14

In all ages the Saviour's chosen have been educated and disciplined in the school of trial. They walked in narrow paths on earth; they were purified in the furnace of affliction. For Jesus' sake they endured opposition, hatred, calumny. They followed Him through conflicts sore; they endured self-denial and experienced bitter disappointments. By their own painful experience they learned the evil of sin, its power, its guilt, its woe; and they look upon it with abhorrence. A sense of the infinite sacrifice made for its cure humbles them in their own sight and fills their hearts with gratitude and praise which those who have never fallen cannot appreciate. They love much because they have been forgiven much. Having been partakers of Christ's sufferings, they are fitted to be partakers with Him of His glory

The heirs of God have come from garrets, from hovels, from dungeons, from scaffolds, from mountains, from deserts, from the caves of the earth, from the caverns of the sea. On earth they were "destitute, afflicted, tormented." Millions went down to the grave loaded with infamy because they steadfastly refused to yield to the deceptive claims of Satan. By human tribunals they were adjudged the vilest of criminals. But now "God is judge Himself" (Psalm 50:6). Now the decisions of earth are reversed. (*The Great Controversy*, 649, 650)

REFLECTION: *God sees and hears everything! From the past to the present He knows what we all have or will go through. But as we accept His love more and more each day we will see that our trials are not in vain.*

THE FAITHFUL REMNANT

*And the dragon was wroth with the woman, and went to make
war with the remnant of her seed, which keep the commandments
of God, and have the testimony of Jesus Christ.*
Revelation 12:17

Zechariah's vision of Joshua and the Angel applies with peculiar force to the experience of God's people in the closing scenes of the great day of atonement. The remnant church will then be brought into great trial and distress. Those who keep the commandments of God and the faith of Jesus will feel the ire of the dragon and his hosts. Satan numbers the world as his subjects; he has gained control even of many professing Christians. But here is a little company who are resisting his supremacy. If he could blot them from the earth, his triumph would be complete. As he influenced the heathen nations to destroy Israel, so in the near future he will stir up the wicked powers of earth to destroy the people of God. Men will be required to render obedience to human edicts in violation of the divine law.

Those who are true to God will be menaced, denounced, proscribed. They will be "betrayed both by parents, and brethren, and kinsfolks, and friends," even unto death (Luke 21:16). Their only hope is in the mercy of God; their only defense will be prayer. As Joshua pleaded before the Angel, so the remnant church, with brokenness of heart and unfaltering faith, will plead for pardon and deliverance through Jesus, their Advocate. They are fully conscious of the sinfulness of their lives, they see their weakness and unworthiness; and they are ready to despair. (*Prophets and Kings*, 587, 588)

REFLECTION: *Satan makes war against them, but the remnant prevails because their Commander is Jesus. By His strength they keep the commandments of God against fierce opposition.*

DECEMBER 22

THE FIRST BEAST

And I stood upon the sand of the sea, and saw a beast rise up out of the sea, having seven heads and ten horns, and upon his horns ten crowns, and upon his heads the name of blasphemy.

Revelation 13:1

These records of the past clearly reveal the enmity of Rome toward the true Sabbath and its defenders, and the means which she employs to honor the institution of her creating. The word of God teaches that these scenes are to be repeated as Roman Catholics and Protestants shall unite for the exaltation of the Sunday.

The prophecy of Revelation 13 declares that the power represented by the beast with lamblike horns shall cause "the earth and them which dwell therein" to worship the papacy — there symbolized by the beast "like unto a leopard." The beast with two horns is also to say "to them that dwell on the earth, that they should make an image to the beast;" and, furthermore, it is to command all, "both small and great, rich and poor, free and bond," to receive the mark of the beast (Revelation 13:11–16). It has been shown that the United States is the power represented by the beast with lamblike horns, and that this prophecy will be fulfilled when the United States shall enforce Sunday observance, which Rome claims as the special acknowledgment of her supremacy. But in this homage to the papacy the United States will not be alone. The influence of Rome in the countries that once acknowledged her dominion is still far from being destroyed. And prophecy foretells a restoration of her power. "I saw one of his heads as it were wounded to death; and his deadly wound was healed: and all the world wondered after the beast" (Verse 3). (*The Great Controversy*, 578)

REFLECTION: *And the revelator declares, also referring to the papacy: "All that dwell upon the earth shall worship him, whose names are not written in the book of life" (Revelation 13:8).*

DECEMBER 23

144,000

And I looked, and, lo, a Lamb stood on the mount Sion,
and with him an hundred forty and four thousand, having
his Father's name written in their foreheads.
Revelation 14:1

*I*n this world their minds were consecrated to God; they served Him with the intellect and with the heart; and now He can place His name "in their foreheads." "And they shall reign for ever and ever" (Revelation 22:5). They do not go in and out as those who beg a place. They are of that number to whom Christ says, "Come, ye blessed of My Father, inherit the kingdom prepared for you from the foundation of the world." He welcomes them as His children, saying, "Enter thou into the joy of thy Lord" (Matthew 25:34, 21).

These are they which follow the Lamb withersoever He goeth. These were redeemed from among men, being the first fruits unto God and to the Lamb" (Revelation 14:4). The vision of the prophet pictures them as standing on Mount Zion, girt for holy service, clothed in white linen, which is the righteousness of the saints. But all who follow the Lamb in heaven must first have followed Him on earth, not fretfully or capriciously, but in trustful, loving, willing obedience, as the flock follows the shepherd

I heard the voice of harpers harping with their harps: and they sung as it were a new song before the throne:… and no man could learn that song but the hundred and forty and four thousand, which were redeemed from the earth. … In their mouth was found no guile: for they are without fault before the throne of God" (Verses 2–5). (*Acts of the Apostles*, 590, 591)

REFLECTION: *The 144,000 will pass through the great time of trouble, a time of trouble such never was since there was a nation; they have stood without an intercessor during the time of the seven last plagues.*

December 24

First Angel's Message

And I saw another angel fly in the midst of heaven, having the everlasting gospel to preach unto them that dwell on the earth, and to every nation, and kindred, and tongue, and people, saying with a loud voice, Fear God, and give glory to him; for the hour of his judgment is come: and worship him that made heaven, and earth, and the sea, and the fountains of waters.

Revelation 14:6, 7

To prepare a people to stand in the day of God, a great work of reform was to be accomplished. God saw that many of His professed people were not building for eternity, and in His mercy He was about to send a message of warning to arouse them from their stupor and lead them to make ready for the coming of the Lord.

This warning is brought to view in Revelation 14. Here is a threefold message represented as proclaimed by heavenly beings and immediately followed by the coming of the Son of man to reap "the harvest of the earth." The first of these warnings announces the approaching judgment. The prophet beheld an angel flying "in the midst of heaven, having the everlasting gospel to preach unto them that dwell on the earth, and to every nation, and kindred, and tongue, and people, saying with a loud voice, Fear God, and give glory to Him; for the hour of His judgment is come: and worship Him that made heaven, and earth, and the sea, and the fountains of waters" (Revelation 14:6, 7). (*The Great Controversy*, 311)

REFLECTION: *This first angel's message is part of the everlasting gospel. It is to go to the whole world. It calls upon all to worship God as their Creator. It points to the seventh-day Sabbath.*

The Second Angel's Message

There followed another angel, saying, Babylon is fallen,
is fallen, that great city, because she made all nations
drink of the wine of the wrath of her fornication.
Revelation 14:8

The term "Babylon" is derived from "Babel," and signifies confusion. It is employed in Scripture to designate the various forms of false or apostate religion. In Revelation 17 Babylon is represented as a woman — a figure which is used in the Bible as the symbol of a church, a virtuous woman representing a pure church, a vile woman an apostate church. …

The woman (Babylon) of Revelation 17 is described as "arrayed in purple and scarlet color, and decked with gold and precious stones and pearls, having a golden cup in her hand full of abominations and filthiness: … and upon her forehead was a name written, Mystery, Babylon the Great, the mother of harlots." Says the prophet: "I saw the woman drunk with the blood of the saints, and with the blood of the martyrs of Jesus." Babylon is further declared to be "that great city, which reigneth over the kings of the earth" (Revelation 17:4–6, 18). The power that for so many centuries maintained despotic sway over the monarchs of Christendom is Rome. …

Babylon is said to be "the mother of harlots." By her daughters must be symbolized churches that cling to her doctrines and traditions, and follow her example of sacrificing the truth and the approval of God, in order to form an unlawful alliance with the world. The message of Revelation 14, announcing the fall of Babylon must apply to religious bodies that were once pure and have become corrupt. (*The Great Controversy*, 382)

REFLECTION: *As the everlasting gospel and the Sabbath truth are proclaimed around the world, so too will be the message concerning the fall of these apostate religious institutions.*

THE THIRD ANGEL'S MESSAGE

If any man worship the beast and his image, and receive his mark in his forehead, or in his hand, the same shall drink of the wine of the wrath of God, which is poured out without mixture into the cup of his indignation; and he shall be tormented with fire and brimstone in the presence of the holy angels, and in the presence of the Lamb.

Revelation 14:9, 10

The powers of earth, uniting to war against the commandments of God, will decree that "all, both small and great, rich and poor, free and bond" (Revelation 13:16), shall conform to the customs of the church by the observance of the false sabbath. All who refuse compliance will be visited with civil penalties, and it will finally be declared that they are deserving of death. On the other hand, the law of God enjoining the Creator's rest day demands obedience and threatens wrath against all who transgress its precepts.

With the issue thus clearly brought before him, whoever shall trample upon God's law to obey a human enactment receives the mark of the beast; he accepts the sign of allegiance to the power which he chooses to obey instead of God. ...

But not one is made to suffer the wrath of God until the truth has been brought home to his mind and conscience, and has been rejected. There are many who have never had an opportunity to hear the special truths for this time. The obligation of the fourth commandment has never been set before them in its true light. ... Everyone is to have sufficient light to make his decision intelligently. (*The Great Controversy*, 604, 605)

REFLECTION: *The Sabbath will be the great test of loyalty.*

December 27

The Plagues

And I heard a great voice out of the temple saying to the seven angels, Go your ways, and pour out the vials of the wrath of God upon the earth.
Revelation 16:1

God's judgments will be visited upon those who are seeking to oppress and destroy His people. His long forbearance with the wicked emboldens men in transgression, but their punishment is nonetheless certain and terrible because it is long delayed.... To our merciful God the act of punishment is a strange act. "As I live, saith the Lord God, I have no pleasure in the death of the wicked" (Ezekiel 33:11).... Yet He will "by no means clear the guilty." "The Lord is slow to anger, and great in power, and will not at all acquit the wicked" (Exodus 34:6,7; Nahum 1:3). By terrible things in righteousness He will vindicate the authority of His downtrodden law. The severity of the retribution awaiting the transgressor may be judged by the Lord's reluctance to execute justice. The nation with which He bears long, and which He will not smite until it has filled up the measure of its iniquity in God's account, will finally drink the cup of wrath unmixed with mercy.

When Christ ceases His intercession in the sanctuary, the unmingled wrath threatened against those who worship the beast and his image and receive his mark (Revelation 14:9,10), will be poured out. The plagues upon Egypt when God was about to deliver Israel were similar in character to those more terrible and extensive judgments which are to fall upon the world just before the final deliverance of God's people. (*The Great Controversy*, 627)

REFLECTION: *By condemning the innocent, the worshipers of the beast have condemned themselves.*

THE MILLENNIUM

And I saw an angel come down from heaven, having the key of the bottomless pit and a great chain in his hand. And he laid hold on the dragon, that old serpent, which is the Devil, and Satan, and bound him a thousand years.
Revelation 20:1, 2

The revelator foretells the banishment of Satan and the condition of chaos and desolation to which the earth is to be reduced, and he declares that this condition will exist for a thousand years. After presenting the scenes of the Lord's second coming and the destruction of the wicked, the prophecy continues: "I saw an angel come down from heaven, having the key of the bottomless pit." ...

Here is to be the home of Satan with his evil angels for a thousand years. Limited to the earth, he will not have access to other worlds to tempt and annoy those who have never fallen. It is in this sense that he is bound: there are none remaining, upon whom he can exercise his power. He is wholly cut off from the work of deception and ruin which for so many centuries has been his sole delight. ...

For six thousand years, Satan's work of rebellion has "made the earth to tremble." He had "made the world as a wilderness, and destroyed the cities thereof." And he "opened not the house of his prisoners." For six thousand years his prison house has received God's people, and he would have held them captive forever; but Christ had broken his bonds and set the prisoners free. (*The Great Controversy*, 658, 659)

REFLECTION: *There will have been six thousand years of sin, and now Satan must contemplate during the seventh millennium his work of deception.*

WHEN THE MILLENNIUM IS OVER

*And they went up on the breadth of the earth, and compassed
the camp of the saints about, and the beloved city: and fire
came down from God out of heaven, and devoured them.*
Revelation 20:9

He will marshal all the armies of the lost under his banner and through them endeavor to execute his plans. The wicked are Satan's captives. In rejecting Christ they have accepted the rule of the rebel leader. They are ready to receive his suggestions and to do his bidding. Yet, true to his early cunning, he does not acknowledge himself to be Satan. He claims to be the prince who is the rightful owner of the world and whose inheritance has been unlawfully wrested from him. He represents himself to his deluded subjects as a redeemer, assuring them that his power has brought them forth from their graves and that he is about to rescue them from the most cruel tyranny. The presence of Christ having been removed, Satan works wonders to support his claims. He makes the weak strong and inspires all with his own spirit and energy. He proposes to lead them against the camp of the saints and to take possession of the City of God. With fiendish exultation he points to the unnumbered millions who have been raised from the dead and declares that as their leader he is well able to overthrow the city and regain his throne and his kingdom. (*The Great Controversy*, 663)

REFLECTION: *The sentence of guilt is pronounced, and fire comes down from heaven and destroys the rebellion.*

DECEMBER 30

The New Earth

*And I saw a new heaven and a new earth: for the first heaven and
the first earth were passed away; and there was no more sea.*
Revelation 21:1

*T*he fire that consumes the wicked purifies the earth.
Every trace of the curse is swept away. No eternally
burning hell will keep before the ransomed the fearful
consequences of sin.

One reminder alone remains: Our Redeemer will ever bear
the marks of His crucifixion. Upon His wounded head, upon His
side, His hands and feet, are the only traces of the cruel work that
sin has wrought. Says the prophet, beholding Christ in His glory:
"He had bright beams coming out of His side: and there was the
hiding of His power" (Habakkuk 3:4). That pierced side whence
flowed the crimson stream that reconciled man to God—there
is the Saviour's glory, there "the hiding of His power." "Mighty
to save," through the sacrifice of redemption, He was therefore
strong to execute justice upon them that despised God's mercy. And the tokens of His humiliation are His highest honor;
through the eternal ages the wounds of Calvary will show forth
His praise and declare His power. ...

All that was lost by sin has been restored. "Thus saith
the Lord ... that formed the earth and made it; He hath established it, He created it not in vain, He formed it to be inhabited" (Isaiah 45:18). God's original purpose in the creation of the
earth is fulfilled as it is made the eternal abode of the redeemed.
"The righteous shall inherit the land, and dwell therein forever"
(Psalm 37:29). (*The Great Controversy*, 674)

REFLECTION: *In the Earth made new will be the new capital of the universe, the New Jerusalem. The tree of life will be there. May each one
of us be there!*

COME QUICKLY

He which testifieth these things saith, Surely I come
quickly. Amen. Even so, come, Lord Jesus.
Revelation 22:20

The coming of the Lord has been in all ages the hope of His true followers. The Saviour's parting promise upon Olivet, that He would come again, lighted up the future for His disciples, filling their hearts with joy and hope that sorrow could not quench nor trials dim. Amid suffering and persecution, the "appearing of the great God and our Saviour Jesus Christ" was the "blessed hope." When the Thessalonian Christians were filled with grief as they buried their loved ones, who had hoped to live to witness the coming of the Lord, Paul, their teacher, pointed them to the resurrection, to take place at the Saviour's advent. Then the dead in Christ should rise, and together with the living be caught up to meet the Lord in the air. "And so," he said, "shall we ever be with the Lord. Wherefore comfort one another with these words" (1 Thessalonians 4:16–18).

On rocky Patmos the beloved disciple hears the promise, "Surely I come quickly," and his longing response voices the prayer of the church in all her pilgrimage, "Even so, come, Lord Jesus" (Revelation 22:20). (*The Great Controversy*, 302)

REFLECTION: *Down through the ages comes this one great plea, "Come, Lord Jesus." We wait with earnest expectation for the redemption of all things. The most important question is, "Will I be ready?" Today is the day of salvation. Don't put it off!*

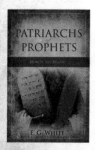 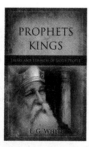  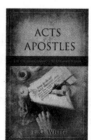 

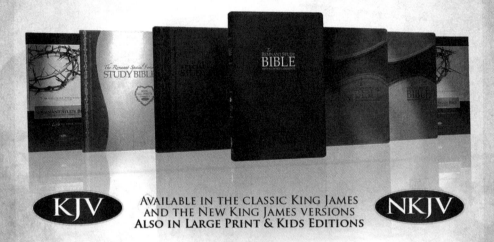